Invocational Media

Invocational Media

Reconceptualising the Computer

Chris Chesher

BLOOMSBURY ACADEMIC
NEW YORK · LONDON · OXFORD · NEW DELHI · SYDNEY

BLOOMSBURY ACADEMIC
Bloomsbury Publishing Inc
1385 Broadway, New York, NY 10018, USA
50 Bedford Square, London, WC1B 3DP, UK
29 Earlsfort Terrace, Dublin 2, Ireland

BLOOMSBURY, BLOOMSBURY ACADEMIC and the Diana logo are trademarks
of Bloomsbury Publishing Plc

First published in the United States of America 2024

Copyright © Chris Chesher, 2024

For legal purposes the Acknowledgements on p. vii constitute an extension of this
copyright page.

Cover image © Yagi Studio / Getty Images

All rights reserved. No part of this publication may be reproduced or transmitted in
any form or by any means, electronic or mechanical, including photocopying, recording,
or any information storage or retrieval system, without prior permission in writing
from the publishers.

Bloomsbury Publishing Inc does not have any control over, or responsibility for, any
third-party websites referred to or in this book. All internet addresses given in this
book were correct at the time of going to press. The author and publisher regret
any inconvenience caused if addresses have changed or sites have ceased to exist,
but can accept no responsibility for any such changes.

A catalog record for this book is available from the Library of Congress.

ISBN: HB: 978-1-5013-6362-7
ePDF: 978-1-5013-6360-3
eBook: 978-1-5013-6361-0

Typeset by Deanta Global Publishing Services, Chennai, India

To find out more about our authors and books visit www.bloomsbury.com
and sign up for our newsletters.

Contents

List of illustrations		vi
Acknowledgements		vii
1	Invocational media	1
2	Invoking concepts	39
3	Invoking histories	83
4	Invocational machines and assemblages	135
5	Invoking users	191
Conclusions		229
References		233
Index		255

Illustrations

Figures

1	The familiar diagram of the first-level invocational components	23
2	The dynamics of second-order invocational assemblages	27

Tables

1	Features of Common Convocations	52
2	Singular Moments in the History of Invocational Media	86
3	Metaphors of Machine Intelligence	95
4	Technical Components and Machines in Invocational Assemblages	136
5	The Three Modes of Operation of Input Devices	148
6	Language Acts Performed by Smart Speakers	205
7	Classification of Voice Assistant Invocationary Acts	206

Acknowledgements

Many people have contributed to the thinking and writing of this book over the long period of its creation, and I cannot name them all here. McKenzie Wark inspired the project' early stages. Lone Bertelsen, Scott Sharpe and Maria Hynes are friendships nurtured in a Deleuze and Guattari reading group. Geert Lovink, Ned Rossiter, Esther Milne, Ingrid Richardson, Lisa Gye, David Teh, Michele Willson, Danny Butt, Anna Munster and Adrian Miles have been members of the brilliant fibreculture collective that gave me confidence and collegiality. Henry Jenkins, Richard Grusin and Zoe Sofoulis gave encouragement and feedback. I have been lucky to have had as colleagues in Media and Communications and Digital Cultures scholars such as Philip Bell, Scott Shaner, Gillian Fuller, Brigid Costello, Alyssa Rothwell, Kate Crawford, Anne Dunn, Steven Maras, Grant Bollmer, Gerard Goggin, John Tonkin, Grant Bollmer, Kathy Cleland, Heather Horst, Justine Humphry, Catharine Lumby, Jonathon Hutchinson, Fiona Martin, Olga Boichak, Mark Johnson, Terry Flew and Jo Gray, among others. I have been inspired by research students I have supervised, many of whom are now friends and peers: Rowan Tulloch, Adam Ho, César Albarrán Torres, Punit Jagasia, Eugenia Lee, Vaibhavi Deshpande, Jorge Valdovinos and Conor Spence. A shout-out goes to students in my classes over the years in units of study such as Cyberworlds, Researching Digital Cultures, Technology and Culture, Digital Research and Publishing, Digital Media and Society and Elements of Digital Cultures, from whom I have learned so much. I want to thank Anne Cranny-Francis, Andrew Murphie and James Bean, who read the manuscript thoroughly, refining it at critical moments in the life of the project. I have valued connections with scholars such as Gil Rodman, Lucy Suchman, Gary Hall, Mark Poster, Lev Manovich, Herbert Hrachovec, Willard McCarty, Adrian Mackenzie, Mark Coeckelbergh, Jean Burgess and Melissa Gregg. I get by with help from friends such as Belinda Barnet, Michael Garbutt, Imogen Craney, Tamira Stevensen, Sophea Lerner, Arabella Lee, Paul McCarthy, Nickolas Vakas and Sam Petty.

I would also like to acknowledge the love and support of my family: Terry Chesher, Sally Chesher, Brendan Dwan, Dylan Chesher, Alice Chesher, Pauline

O'Callaghan, David Browne, Jennifer O'Callaghan, Josephine Browne and William Browne. Also Flash and Cino.

The most special thanks and love go to my wife Cathy O'Callaghan and daughter Jessica Chesher who have supported and loved me unconditionally through thick and thin.

I dedicate this book to the memory of my brother Tony Chesher and father Dr Greg Chesher.

Some sections of the book include edited extracts from previously published work:

Chesher, C. (2003). Layers of code, layers of subjectivity. *CultureMachine, 5*. https://culturemachine.net/the-e-issue/layers-of-code/

Chesher, C. (2019). Trusting intelligent agents: A typology of invocationary acts. Association of Internet Researchers conference, QUT Brisbane, 2–5 October 2019.

Chesher, C. (2022). The evocations that haunt the computer interface. International Association for Media and Communication Research, China (Online), 11–15 July 2022.

Chesher, C. (2023). As evocações que assombram a interface do computador. *Novos Olhares, 11*(2), 205337. https://doi.org/10.11606/issn.2238-7714.no.2022.205337.

1

Invocational media

Hey Siri, call Sam at home.
Alexa, what is the capital of Tanzania?
OK Google, turn on the living room lights.
Cortana, set an alarm for 7 am.

The digital voice assistant responds seemingly magically to a user's voice with a voice of its own, answering questions, telling jokes, turning on lights and playing music. Popularised in the late 2010s, this computerised media device is convenient but surveillant, charming but sometimes stupid, an entertainment technology, a source of fragments of conventional knowledge and a consumer gadget in our most intimate private spaces. In the appearance of this little gadget there is little trace of its ancestors: the massive early computers which wielded military, corporate and state power. This commodified, domesticated everyday technology passes as a friendly and faithful assistant, concealing its advanced artificial intelligence and global networking. It is one of many media assemblages based on technologies usually known as digital computers.

Voice user interface designers refer to what we say to these smart devices as *invocations*. This term seems particularly apt: like classical invocations to gods in antiquity, the quasi-magical calls that we vocalise summon immediate answers, guidance or inspiration from a powerful but unreliable non-human at a moment of need.

However, invocations to computers need not involve a human voice. The term 'invocation' is often used in programming to refer to the act of calling a function, method, library or other resource. Invocation is a common concept in programming languages, and terms related to it are used in various contexts, for example, when calling a function in a program, executing a command in a command-line interface, making requests to remote systems. In some cases, the term 'invocation' may be used more broadly to refer to the act of using or activating any particular feature or capability of a system or software application.

Even for end users, entering a URL, performing a Google search or writing a text prompt for generative AI has the structure and experience of an invocation.

The term 'invocation' has other meanings that are also relevant to understanding how computers mediate everyday relationships. For example, many non-computer invocations occur in situations where authorised speakers claim executive power. Police invoke powers of search and arrest that allow them to use 'reasonable force' that overrides the normal rights of citizens. In court, prosecuting and defence lawyers invoke statutes and common law precedents in arguments to judges and juries. Democratically elected governments invoke the constitution and the popular mandate of voters. Academics use citations to invoke the work of previous authors to reference existing knowledge and clear a space for their own research. Fiat money carries value because it invokes the backing of a government and the judgement of the currency markets.

When these existing practices of invocation were computerised – for example, connecting criminal courts with police to issue warrants more quickly (Cowan, 2014), tracing precedents and legislation in legal databases, accepting and tallying votes with voting machines, handling references with citation managers, detecting plagiarism with software, transferring funds electronically and mining cryptocurrencies – they were not only translated but also transformed. Invocations that had been spoken, imagined or paper-bound became automated, algorithmic and mediated through computing hardware and software. This was often framed in terms of efficiency or progress, but it has brought about widely recognised dramatic changes as individual and social practices have become invocational.

This book reconceptualises computers as invocational media. Whereas the computing concept emphasises the machine's rationality, instrumentalism and capacity for abstract representation, the invocation concept stresses its situated performances as distinctive media forms that have changed how people perceive, think and act in the world. Focusing on invocation emphasises performativity and social embeddedness rather than representation and detached calculation. I aim neither to celebrate nor deprecate invocational media but to raise critical questions to capture their ambivalent place in contemporary life, their participation in social interaction and creativity and their roles in the command and control of people and territories. I aim to defamiliarise the computer by identifying alternative histories, including by recovering the often-disavowed historical legacy of magic in technology – magic that at different times may be enchanting, deceptive, empowering or dangerous.

Invocational Media 3

In developing this concept, I adopt an approach influenced by Deleuze and Guattari (1983) to argue that invocations are events of deterritorialisation and reterritorialisation. An invocation detaches something from one territory and immediately attaches it somewhere else. For example, a web search escapes the search field and reterritorialises on the results page as uniform ranked results. Yet, the results offer connections to wider 'machinic assemblages' – with a multiplicity of concrete and virtual components, including database records, material objects, user personas, language, human thought and feelings and extensive territories. Yet the reterritorialisations of are only relative. Driven by the abstract machine of the invocation, invocational media divide the abstracted world into coded, invocable segments and offer them conditionally to users. In some cases, they belong to state assemblages, such as in government databases that abstract the world for state power. In other cases, they are embedded in capitalist assemblages such as Amazon, Meta and Google, which operate with quasi-universals, privatising social life, trade, labour and advertising. At other times, invocational media can liberate nomadic assemblages directed towards more participatory, open-ended and revolutionary trajectories, such as in art or progressive politics that might achieve moments of absolute territorialisation to produce something creative or liberating (Nail, 2017).

In this chapter, I will discuss the limitations of the computing concept, its association with instrumental reason, the 'computer as human' concept and its history of involvement in relationships of domination. Diverging from this history of computation, I explore a prehistory of invocational media in what I refer to as invocatory devices, such as levers and push buttons, which simplify tasks by allowing users to invoke predetermined outcomes with less physical or mental effort. In the following section, I identify three interwoven levels of invocation: (1) the sociotechnical; (2) the experiential; and (3) wider assemblages and discourses. I conclude by identifying some of the risks and limitations of the invocational concept and provide an outline of the structure of the remainder of the book. However, I will begin by introducing some provocations that establish some impressions of invocational events.

Probing the meanings of invocations

Throughout this book, I develop the concept of invocation more systematically, but in the following section, I will invoke some probes – not concepts – but rapid interventions in thought and perception about invocational media (McLuhan, Carson & Mo Cohen, 2007):

- An invocation is an ancient magical act (alongside incantations, prayers, etc.) calling upon an outside non-human (god) for guidance, support or intervention in a crisis.
- In computing discourse, an invocation is a programmed event that calls to another process or resource (such as a subroutine, software object or peripheral device).
- At the most fundamental level of the fetch-execute cycle, a computer's central processing unit operates with invocations: it retrieves a program instruction from memory (the primary invocation), interprets it and carries out the prescribed action (the secondary invocation).
- Invocations often justify the exercise of power (such as invoking laws, regulations, divine right or a democratic mandate).
- Invocations mediate existing power relationships and protocols.
- Under capitalism, technologically mediated power is not evenly distributed. There is a tendency towards monopolies of invocation (IBM services, Microsoft software and Google search).
- Invocation is associated with creative practices. Ancient heroes, poets, musicians and artists invoke the Muses for the breath of inspiration.
- Generative AI invokes large language models to produce original texts, images, music and moving images in ways mysterious even to their developers.
- Invocation is associated with authorising knowledge claims and exploring intertextual networks. In academic writing, authors invoke the work of others through citation. In electronic writing, hyperlinks allow users to summon related texts, transcending the linearity of conventional texts.
- An invocation usually (but not always) involves a voice and, therefore, some agency, intentionality, persona, style or sense of identity.
- Invocations have their genesis in desire but sometimes also anxiety or fear. Their success can bring pleasure, their failure can bring frustration or even despair.
- An invocation initiates a program of action at a singular moment. Unlike computation, an invocation is never simply repetition.
- Invocations often call entities by name. Names have power. What cannot be named cannot be summoned.

- Stored labour is often made invocable in commodity form. It may have use value or exchange value consumed through acts of invocation.
- Invocations delegate and externalise work. They often ascribe responsibility to something or someone outside – an externality.
- Invocations may be conservative or radical, building on existing structures, networks, givens (data), standards and relationships or calling up something new.
- Making the world invocable requires violence: destroying differences that cannot be digitally encoded and forcing diverse meanings into predetermined templates.
- In an era dominated by the invocation – remembering, transacting, planning, navigating, working and playing – more heterogeneous legacy cultural practices are diminished.
- To speak of invocational media is also ironic, drawing attention to the mythical status often ascribed to high technology in advertising and popular culture.

The problem with computing

Computing discourse colours our imagination and understanding of invocational media, engendering certain habits of thought and ways of talking about and using them. Beyond mathematics and engineering, the early developers of computers began colonising everyday language by adopting a mix of metaphors. For example, many drew from an understanding of the human body, brain and mind to inform the basic model of computers and robots. Von Neumann (1958) refers to components in the computer as 'organs' and divides the machine's operations accordingly and makes a direct comparison between digital machines and the brain. Turing (1950) defers the question of intelligence by proposing an 'imitation game' that posits a potential equivalence between humans and machines.

Before the computer concept took hold, many people referred to these machines as 'giant brains' (Berkeley, 1949), and this analogy with the brain has persisted in computer science and philosophy. Personifying metaphors (Lakoff & Johnson, 1980) were embedded in the apparently anthropomorphic design of a set of components resembling the human body: inputs could 'sense' the world; a central processing unit could 'compute' or 'think' by manipulating symbols; 'memory' could 'recall' information sensed and computed. This narrow anthropomorphism was modelled on a particular conception of humans – as rational actors – emphasising the primacy of reason and logical argumentation as ways to gain knowledge about the world in order to make plans for acting in it. This approach is reflected in formal methods such as mathematical logic, set theory and type theory to describe and analyse computational systems. The prevalence of rationalist epistemologies in early computing reflected the disciplinary training of its developers in mathematics, physics, electrical engineering and other disciplines (Tedre, 2015) and served for a long time to alienate more diverse users.

The 'computer as human' concept took an even more ambitious form in AI, a slippery idea that has fostered much philosophical discussion and a diverse range of technological projects. In their critiques of AI, Dreyfus (1972) and Searle (1980) highlight what they see as the inevitable limitations of symbolic approaches to AI. Dreyfus argues that AI systems lack the ability to truly understand and engage with the world due to their lack of embodied experience or 'being-in-the-world' (Dreyfus, 1972). He contends that AI systems are unable to fully grasp the complexity and nuance of the world. In his famous Chinese Room thought experiment, Searle (1980) also highlights the limitations of representation-based approaches to AI. In this experiment, he argues that even if an AI system can accurately manipulate symbols and perform complex calculations, it still lacks a genuine understanding of the meanings behind those symbols because it lacks consciousness and subjective experience.

Both these critics are convincing in their argument that symbolic AI is unlikely ever to reproduce human intelligence or consciousness. However, these conclusions may not go far enough. Rather than focusing on the failure of AI systems, they might have identified what has been achieved with invoked intelligence. Dreyfus might have observed that invocations are embedded in being-in-the-world. Searle might have noticed that invocations are about not merely symbolic representation but also performative language. Looking beyond Searle and Dreyfus' concern with simulating human intelligence, we might find that invocational media *participate* in thinking (calculating, remembering, mimicking social actors) rather than attempting to duplicate it. AIs are not our opponents but components in our lifeworld (Heim, 1993). They are meaningful only in their situated pragmatic and social contexts. For example, the DALL•E 2 text-to-image generator and the large language model ChatGPT are not autonomous actors but lively participants in invocational relationships with their users.

AI critics also ignored the politics of invocational media, as the 'computer as a human' metaphor reflects social relations of domination implicit in the invocational relationship. The term 'computer' originally referred to human workers – mainly women – who from the mid-nineteenth century performed complex calculations and information gathering within the hierarchical contexts of bureaucracies in the military, government and corporations (Grier, 2005). Computers could follow 'instructions' to perform procedures mechanically and deliver the results to superiors. Therefore, the term 'computer' was already closely associated with situations in which men delegated abstracted logical, mathematical and research tasks to lower-ranked others to perform menial mental labour. When applied to the computer, the analogy gave primacy to the medium's dominant representationalist, rationalist, formalist, masculine and computational dimensions (Golumbia, 2009).

Intelligence is only one of the metaphors invoked in computing discourse, many of which retain traces of colonial and bureaucratic discourses of instrumental rationality. Spatial metaphors proliferate in computing, particularly the illusionary spaces of virtual reality, and the extended, networked spaces of cyberspace, each associated with expansionist imaginaries. Other spatial constructs draw from workplaces, for example, filing systems, electronic mail and desktops. Many other metaphors come from social domains: permissions for accessing resources or friend relationships in social media. The 'server' invokes social relationships of servility (Krajewsky, 2018). The metaphorical concept of the 'interface' suggests a kind of membrane between the user-subject and an otherwise inaccessible object world (van den Boomen, 2014). Again, these concepts are problematic because they retain ideological traces of their institutional origins. Abstractions such as computing, AI and virtual reality are problematic because they are not abstract enough.

Just as problematic as the noun 'computer' is the verb 'to compute', which encompasses only one part of the invocational assemblage's activity. There are many related metaphorical verbs for what computers do in operation, including running and processing (industrial), calculating (anthropomorphic) and executing (interpersonal). Dozens of more specialised terms refer to more specific operations – rendering, compiling, simulating, interacting, sensing, encoding, decoding, downloading and so on – but these don't hold together a unifying image of thought about the invocational assemblage. In fact, with the emergence of a range of diverse platforms and environments – social media, tablets, laptops, games consoles, smartphones, smart home devices, voice assistants and so on – the generic term 'computer' has gradually dropped away from common usage, to refer predominantly to the market niche of the desktop 'PC'.

The most common umbrella term for these devices is the nominalised adjective 'the digital'. The term 'digital' originally referred to fingers and how they allowed people to count discrete values – the origins of the decimal system. In computing, the term distinguished analogue from digital computers. The former are invocatory devices that work with continuous flows of physical quantities such as voltages, currents, hydraulics or sand to perform simulations or calculations. Invocational media, by contrast, operate through the transmission, manipulation and storage of measurable binary differences in a range of material media: electronic, magnetic, optical and so on. Virtually all invocational media since the 1950s have operated digitally (Kempf, 2000; Ceruzzi, 1983). The fact that most use the binary code of 1s and 0s is crucial because it is an enabling feature of digital invocations, with their strict adherence to logical codes, addresses, names, procedures and decision-making. Data and operations in invocational components are digitally encoded and addressed. However, invocational assemblages are only partly digital as they are always psychologically, socially and materially continuous, embodied and situated. They inhabit and intervene in worlds of spaces, sounds, images, bodies and commodities.

Computer programmers in the 1960s borrowed the concept of the invocation as a metaphor for the structured programming technique of invoking or calling subprograms rather than writing new code for every step. Invocation became a core feature of object-oriented programming languages such as Smalltalk and Java, in which processes invoke methods to actuate software objects. More evocatively, programmers introduced the concept of daemons, which would hide from view until the moment they were invoked. McKelvey (2018) describes the internet as a distributed pandemonium in which '[p]acket inspection, queuing, routing, and policy daemons all modulate flow control' (p. 95). De Landa (1991) also uses the term more narrowly for 'demons . . . "invoked" into action by changes in their environment' (p. 120). Contemporary devices often turn *us* into daemons, regularly sending alerts that invoke us to respond.

If we extend the metaphor, we can see most basic computer operations as invocations. Billions of times per second, a modern CPU, sometimes with multiple cores, performs sequences of digital invocations in the 'machine cycle' or 'fetch-decode-execute cycle'. In fact, this invocation is a double event. The control unit mediates primary invocations that call on memory registers for instructions. Then secondary invocations in the arithmetical logic unit decode those instructions and execute them with machine commands. Depending on the instruction, a CPU might write or read to memory, change pixel values on a screen, perform an arithmetical and logical operation, make a network connection or jump to a different code sequence.

Everything invocable is indexed with addresses and names and kept on standby. All these are *invocable domains* – resources prepared and arranged to be invoked. In a modern computer, there are many forms of invocable domain – input devices, output devices, arithmetical and logical circuits, clocks, memory, storage, code, data and remote devices. These components are explored in detail in Chapter 4, but the important point is that they establish arrays of components invocable through software, in limited ways, by users. Invocable domains are often conceptualised as hierarchical layers through which invocations pass, for example, the Open Systems Interconnection (OSI) model, which sets a common spatial standard for networked invocable domains. Bratton's (2015) concept of 'the Stack' proposes a more expansive reconceptualisation of sociotechnical layers associated with contemporary technologies (earth layer, cloud layer, city layer, address layer, interface layer and user layer). It focuses less on the distinctiveness of the medium or the primacy of invocational events among the layers. However, Bratton's approach does suggest that there is always an excess to what is invocable. There is always something lost in the acts of violence that makes things invocable.

Even the most basic invocations depend on a critical feature of invocational media: programmability, or what Chun (2011) refers to as 'sourcery'. Programmers transform the machine, using formal languages, into any number of virtual machines. While users only experience the machine at the interface level, including programmers who write source code, their experience of invocational events is grounded in processes at the largely imperceptible level of software, circuits and other hardware. Users may think they can perform invocations directly, but before invoking anything, users are already called. An operating system addresses input devices and enters modes that allow users to act. To do anything, users must invoke the encoded work of engineers and programmers. All actors, human and non-human, must follow protocols that enable, govern and control the performance of invocations (Galloway, 2004). Software can have great invocational power, but users are unaware of the precise details of their invocations. Even the most basic operation is a mystery (Cox & McLean, 2013). For example, a flashing cursor on the screen prompts users to start typing. This sequence of invocations gives them some power – summoning words on the screen as if by magic. Invocational media have special relationships to time. Invocations occur in the present, drawing on pre-arranged resources from the past and at a distance to produce something algorithmically for the future. The medium's capacity to control programmed invocations and make decisions based on machine states and the sensed environment is the basis of their aesthetic and political power.

In considering the specificity of invocational media, we can observe how they are materially and diagrammatically different from other media. For example, by contrast, print media are grounded in the mechanical imprinting of ink onto surfaces and physically circulating these objects to readers. Broadcast media on the other hand, are based on institutionalised centres of production transmitting flows of sound and images using radio waves on a licensed frequency across a territory to audiences with receivers. In comparison, invocational media operate through sensing, transforming, storing and expressing differences through miniaturised and globally addressable components. Through invocational magic, they are reconfigurable, software-controlled, shape-shifting metamedia.

With the proliferation of invocational media, everyday life is increasingly mediated by digital electronic invocations. The medium offers invoked environments in which actions are metaphorically configured: launching a web browser, entering a search query, going forwards and backwards, playing a game and so on. Invocational media typically invoke material metaphors to establish new media environments. We read text and images from tablets and e-readers as well as from the inked surface of books or newspapers. We invoke movies from streaming services on the smart TV or the phone as well as by tuning in to broadcasts, using physical discs or attending a cinema. We encounter knowledge through search engines more often than by consulting reference books or experts. We invoke the presence of friends on social media or networked games just as easily as through encountering them physically. However, while these are new experiences, they reterritorialise long-standing cultural practices and respond to long-standing desires in the cultural imaginary for invocational powers.

Understanding invocation

So, what is the origin of the invocation, and what does it suggest about invocational media? This question is important to the claim that there is some continuity in media logic and cultural imaginary between ancient practices and contemporary technology. Invocations have been part of magical and religious practices for thousands of years, most notably in ancient Egyptian,

Greek and Roman cultures but also in Christian, Hindu, Buddhist, African, Native American and European pagan traditions. They are ritual speech acts directed towards non-humans for guidance, support, inspiration or recollection at moments of crisis. They externalise knowledge, narrative and authority by attributing new information to something outside themselves. In performing invocations, invoking subjects deferentially attribute guidance and stories to the immortal gods rather than themselves, deflecting potential personal criticism while claiming the authority to speak for that higher being.

Shamans, sorcerers, priests and storytellers developed special relationships with non-human agents to allow them to make invocations. They understood the protocols and had the know-how and knowledge to perform rituals and recite stories. That is, they changed themselves to take up the invocatory role:

> The seer combines the functions of poet, prophet and philosopher: he has the gifts of poetry and of special knowledge, both of which are believed to be the result of divine inspiration. (Murray, 1983, p. 2)

This allowed the privileged invoking subject to claim extraordinary powers that resemble those more recently attributed to information technologies: sensing at a distance, remembering the past and visualising what is possible:

> The divine sources of the poet give access to knowledge extensive in space and time. The poet is able to report on events in all parts of the human world, in the world of the gods on Olympus, and in the world of the dead beneath the earth. He ranges far back in time, and has perfect recall of events long past . . . [and they] enable him to visualise, and describe for the audience, the events narrated in a particularly vivid way. (Hardie, 2019, p. 20)

Among the most commonly invoked ancient mythical figures are the Muses, minor goddesses who inspired poets, artists, scientists and musicians in their creative practice (Schindler, 2019). These highly intelligent personas were assigned to different disciplines of the arts, many of which would ultimately be remediated by invocational media: Calliope for epic poetry, Clio for history, Erato for love poetry, Euterpe for music, Melpomene for tragic drama, Polyhymnia for sacred music, Terpsichore for dance, Thalia for comedy and Urania for astronomy. However, the Muses were 'inferior deities' – they did not have the same kinds of direct power as Uranus (the sky), Cronus (time) or Zeus (king of gods) (Murray, 1954). The fact that the Muses were the daughters of Zeus, the god of command, and Mnemosyne, the goddess of memory, seems to parallel core components of the CPU and RAM in the invocational assemblage.

Like angels in the Christian tradition, the Muses were intermediaries who assisted, channelled and interceded with powers of communication (Serres, 1995). Although their effects were largely immaterial, Muses were powerful cultural catalysts and accelerants. They helped advance 'civilisation' – hence the terms 'museum' (the seat of the Muses) and 'music' (the art of the Muses).

While they lacked claimed spiritual powers of priests and shamans, storytellers' social positions came from claiming divine inspiration for their stories. In auratic performances, they supplicated themselves to these deities. More pragmatic and immediate than prayers, invocations sought assistance at a moment of crisis when the speaker needed guidance or authority. In some accounts, the outcomes of invocations seemed to follow entirely automatically:

> [A] mortal first-person speaker addresses a superior immortal authority in order to voice a request. Unlike the prayer, however, the plea for inspiration is always successful. (Schindler, 2019, p. 491)

Invocations to the Muses were characterised by a particular asymmetrical form of dialogue that involved requesting and providing information. The Muses were information technologies that required users to adhere to protocols to avoid unexpected outcomes. When successful, the Muses' answers were often systematic and strategic – not just stories but also catalogues:

> [T]he invocation is framed as a question in which the poet asks for the material of his poem, often in quantitative terms (who? what? how many?), and what follows has the form of an answer, characteristically supplying the information in the form of a catalogue or *ordered enumeration*. (Minton, 1962, p. 18, italics in the original)

In other cases, invocations were more precarious. There was some mystery – a black hole, a degree of risk, an ontological gap – between invocations and their consequences. The immortal authorities invoked could be indifferent or even malicious. For example, in the *Iliad*, when the minstrel Thamyris challenged the Muses, they took out his eyes and 'robbed him of his divine power of song, and thenceforth he could strike the lyre no more' (Homer, 2009 [800 BCE]).

The parallels between our experience with computers and these figures from ancient myths suggest some vestigial influence in the Western tradition of formalised ritual contact between non-humans and humans. They recall some of the same media logic. However, modern invocations have been desacralised, domesticated, commoditised and delegated to consumer electronics. We invoke advice about the weather and business decisions, knowledge about the world, communication with distant others and so on. We use these invocations to support creativity in media production and the arts. With AI, we even ask them to write for us, create art for us and compose music for us, with little comprehension of how exactly this works. Invocational media on their own lack the direct physical agency of big technologies like dams, jet aeroplanes, hydrogen bombs or rockets. They are guides, governing action, mediating communication, generating simulations and creating illusions. We use invocational media constantly, but they have become so complex that nobody fully understands them. The devices we invoke are capricious and subject to unexpected failures from misconfigurations, incompatibilities, bugs, errors, crashes, corruptions, obsolescence and hacks. We supplicate ourselves to their enigmatic powers despite their being controlled by technocrats, governments and corporations.

The implicit patriarchal power of many invocational media is apparent in the traditional invocations of male heroes to the female Muses. Just as the Muses formed alliances with other forces by invoking Prometheus, who stole fire from the gods, and Hermes, the messenger, invocational media control weapons, manufacturing, global communication and other hardware. This gendered power relation between masculine humans and feminine non-humans resonates in invocational media. For example, Brahnam, Karanikas and Weaver (2011) argue that from the early history of interactive computing, a foundational but hidden metaphor is that 'computer is woman' (p. 402). They argue that representations in advertising and human interface design have systematically configured and asserted dominant gender relations in the feminisation of the machine.

Why invocation now?

This claim that digital media are contemporary translations of a mythical ritual practice may seem romantic, metaphysical or even ridiculous. Clearly, the parallels enumerated earlier are somewhat selective and speculative. However, it is helpful for the purposes of this book to pursue the intuition that invocation has been translated, miniaturised, accelerated, commodified and adopted as a technical diagram, becoming the dominant form of mediation today. The influence of invocational media has been transformative for society, culture and everyday life. They have become metamedia that operate with invocations in an unprecedented diversity of contexts and configurations. Invocation is the medium's essence and key to its radical abstraction and versatility.

If so, why has the instrumental and representational concept of the computer persisted despite its limitations? Deleuze (1986) argues that anything new begins by hiding behind something already existing. In *Cinema 1*, Deleuze describes how it took some time before people became aware of what cinema was and how it worked. Cinema hid its 'essence' for decades:

> We know that things and people are forced to conceal themselves . . . when they begin. What else could they do? They come into being within a set which no longer includes them and, in order not to be rejected, have to project the characteristics which they retain in common with the set. The essence of a thing never appears at the outset, but in the middle, in the course of its development, when its strength is assured. (Deleuze, 1986, pp. 2–3)

The same is true for invocational media. They have hidden in a mix of metaphors at various times as electronic brains, calculators, big brothers, information processors, information appliances, artificial intelligence, digital assistants, virtual realities and media channels (see Chapter 3). These metaphors were not sufficiently abstract to encompass the foundational media logic of this technological lineage or to make the connection between the sociotechnical, experiential and conceptual levels that I explore later. But first, we must reconsider the conventional prehistories of computing with an examination of technologies that transform language-like statements into action.

Invocatory devices

The history of invocational media has a different lineage from that of computing. Their ancestors are technologies that perform in the world so that someone (or something) can act symbolically or physically in the world almost as easily as speaking. Many invocatory devices are familiar objects that offer materialised speaking positions using artefacts pragmatically, such as a door knocker, a piano or a mechanical calculator. Invocatory devices and their associated social arrangements established key invocatory features later exploited with invocational media: chains of command; systems of names and addresses for invoking arranged resources (proto-invocable domains like hierarchies and archives); media that mediate and perform decisions; digital communication at a distance (telegraphy); vocations for media performances (Leni Riefenstahl's Nazi propaganda films; Winston Churchill's wartime radio broadcasts); and techniques of archiving and automated reproducibility. These devices forged alliances with more prominent, power-wielding media such as tools, motors, explosives and transmitters.

In its most disenchanted form, a mechanical invocation is a technological action that simply calls on an external resource to produce a given action, reducing the labour and uncertainty involved in achieving that goal with a human body. It establishes a material grammatical relationship between subject, mediator and object. The lever is an archetypical primitive invocatory device. It reduces the effort required to move one thing with another but ties the action to a fulcrum, an intermediary that opposes input and output. It operates to apply force from a subject to an object through a name and an address. It expresses a decision articulated by a user with an effort that is becoming linguistic. For example, using the door knocker is a form of the lever that expresses an invocatory statement, 'I [person at the door] request entry to this house', replacing a speech act with a gesture. Displacing the voice, the sound is amplified. However, the timbre of the voice in the visitor's call is lost. To compensate, regular visitors may develop their own style in mobilising the affordances and expressive potential of the knocker.

The key, trigger, button and switch are modern refinements of the invocatory lever that allow for the abstraction and deterritorialisation of an event. They are used in conjunction with the hand and fingers, creating a form of speech/writing that allows force to be applied on demand. The gun is an invocatory device. A handgun stands ready for a crucial moment when it can invoke the force of the explosion of gunpowder, as well as the weight and shape of the projectile. As weapons technology improved, invocation became more reliable. The matchlock mechanism, developed in the 1400s, which used a glowing wick to ignite the gunpowder to fire the weapon, was just one of many inventions that made weapon invocations more reliable and powerful. Using a gun also involves the invocation of the resources, both physical and cognitive, of the chemists, designers, blacksmiths and armourers who designed and manufactured it. And other invocations are associated with the use of a gun: the shooter may invoke a legal defence to justify the act of shooting, such as self-defence or a state of war. It is no coincidence that the trigger is a popular feature in video games, as it playfully invokes a series of events that calculate damage, create spectacular effects and evoke in the player senses of agency and injury.

The power of modern invocational media is grounded in the historical mastery of electricity in the eighteenth century when people came to understand the uncontrolled natural invocatory force of lightning. Benjamin Franklin's legendary experiment with a kite during a thunderstorm brought lightning down to earth. He demonstrated the connection between lightning and the less powerful forms of electricity that could be generated by hand (Schiffer, 2003). He performed public shows with electricity which combined education, entertainment and entrepreneurialism – 'the experiment and the amusement were not distinguishable' (Hankins & Silverman, 1995, p. 197). Lightning played a starring role in the imagination of his shows, as did the Leyden jar, a precursor to the modern capacitor in electronics, which could store electricity until its shocking and noisy invocation in front of a stunned crowd.

While we take for granted the everyday act of switching on an electric light, it retains a trace of awe in revealing a world previously in darkness. With less effort than it takes to say, 'Let there be light!', there is light. The light switch performs as a statement: an invocation with material and social effects. The form of command that a light switch performs has many social parallels: using language (asking someone to light a candle), enacting social power (delegating the task to a lower-ranked person), conducting a scientific experiment (the Leyden jar) and performing magic (using secret methods and materials to create an effect).

McLuhan (1964) argues that the electric light is itself a form of media, but the 'content' of electric light includes the activities that it makes possible: night baseball, brain surgery and so on. Without lights, these cultural practices would not happen in the same way. But not only did the presence of lights reveal the world in new ways, the invocatory act of switching also became significant. Think of ceremonially turning on Christmas lights or officially lighting a building or a bridge. Or the magical moment when a spotlight reveals a performer on stage. Or when a flashlight betrays two lovers hiding in the dark. Or peek-a-boo with a child. These instants of revealing have their own special intensity. They are decisive invocatory moments when an invocation transforms the situation.

Here we might recall a grand dedication ceremony that celebrated perhaps the most important innovation in invocatory communication of its time. On 24 May 1844 at the Supreme Court in Washington, DC, Samuel Morse initiated the first official test of the telegraph, sending a message in Morse code to his assistant Alfred Vailes in Baltimore (Sconce, 2000, p. 21). Morse's invocatory code assigned letters of the alphabet to patterns of invocatory switching – the digital dots and dashes that are the ancestors of the zeros and ones of digital circuitry – allowing senders and receivers to invoke other people over large distances at the speed of light, far exceeding the fastest horse messenger. His dispatch 'What hath God wrought?' invoked a deity in an expression of awed surprise at the almost supernatural feat of communicating instantly across such a distance. According to Marvin (1988), the telegraph was the key precursor to the computer: 'In a historical sense, the computer is no more than an instantaneous telegraph with a prodigious memory, and all the communications inventions in between have simply been elaborations on the telegraph's original work' (p. 3).

Many invocatory devices required some people to dedicate themselves to a fully fledged vocation – telegraph and telephone operators, for example. Others became known as typewriters, requiring them to internalise the positions of the keys and to master high-speed invocation of documents (Kittler, 1999). Another invocatory technology popular in the nineteenth century was the piano, whose players practised for hours to aspire to the vocation of piano virtuoso or at least to the avocation of the amateur musician in the bourgeois home. The keys on the piano are invocatory devices arranged in a manually invocable domain of eighty-eight keys tuned to the Western chromatic scale. This design imposed the hegemonic standard of the Western musical system on all adopters of this instrument, making it impossible to work with other scales and systems of tuning. Further, each properly tuned key is a component in a larger assemblage of heterogeneous elements and practices, including piano lessons, piano manufacturers, retailers, sheet music, composers, musical genres, ways of listening and sites of performance.

Around the turn of the twentieth century, automated player pianos took performance out of the human piano player's hands and into the cogs and wheels of an automated invocatory device. The player piano stored machine-readable instructions, recorded as holes in a fragile roll of paper, that served as its memory (Suisman, 2009). The player piano did not invoke a sound recording, like its competitor the phonograph, but rather algorithmic information that it used to reproduce the physical labour of performance. The approach of piano-roll producers anticipated aesthetic strategies of invocational media (Wendte, 2016). For example, some recordings accentuated the mechanical regularity of a non-human invocatory performance. Others sought to invoke the feel and virtuosity of a masterful human performance, using more sophisticated 'reproducing player pianos' driven by electric motors to control dynamics, tempo and pedalling. Others created works for the player piano that were so complex that they could never have been performed with human hands (Wente, 2016). Science-fiction author Kurt Vonnegut (2000 [1952]) used the player piano metonymically in the novel *Player Piano* to critique automation's displacement of human creative labour.

Controversies about the lack of soul in automated music arose in the mid-twentieth century with the advent of electronic music. Once again, some critics accused music-generating machines of being 'lacking in subjectivity, creativity or human sentiment' (Roosth, 2017, p. 99). Musicians such as Kraftwerk, Gary Numan and Tangerine Dream embraced and accentuated the machine aesthetic, celebrating the delegation of performance and even composition to invocatory devices and, later, to invocational media. Performers like Laurie Anderson exploited an uncanny digital effect in the song 'O Superman' (1982) by repeatedly invoking a breathy sound bite – 'Ha' – on the Eventide H910 Harmonizer. Designers of sampling synthesisers, beginning with the Fairlight CMI in 1979, followed the high-fidelity route, using digital electronics to sample real instruments. But musicians like Kate Bush and Peter Gabriel used it to incorporate in their performances and recordings samples of everyday sounds rather than musical notes (Harkins, 2015). The MIDI standard, released in 1981, allowed musicians to sequence and control multiple digital instruments. Like the player piano, it stored and transmitted information that invoked synthesisers to perform music, rather than recording sound.

Another medium that emerged in the nineteenth century and worked with decisive and invocatory moments was the photographic shutter. It instantly invoked light, a scene, optics, mechanics and photochemical reactions to capture images. The ritual practices that followed in the temple of the darkroom revealed the photograph and its evocative powers. In the 1860s, spiritualist movements claimed that this emerging medium could detect the presence of dead people, even if this was based on simple tricks like double exposure or darkroom effects (Natale, 2012). While this belief in spirit photographs was widely debunked, photography's association with death and the mystical imagination around photography recurred. In capturing images at a singular moment, cameras would sometimes create what Barthes (1982) refers to as the 'punctum' – a 'sting, speck, cut, little hole – and also a cast of the dice' (p. 27) that appeared in only select images. He argues that 'the [p]hotograph's punctum is that accident that pricks me (but also bruises me – is poignant to me)' (p. 27). The punctum is the evidence of that decisive moment of invocation, which exceeds the photographer's intentions and captures particularly evocative meanings. The trace of that invocatory moment gathers meaning as time passes to allow specific images to establish evocative affectivity, particularly when it draws attention to human mortality.

The telephone also began as an invocatory technology, with Alexander Graham Bell observing an auditory excess produced when circuits switched on and off. His inspiration for telephony came from the observation that an electromagnet generated sound when connected and disconnected:

> It has long been known that an electromagnet gives forth a decided sound when it is suddenly magnetised or demagnetised. When the circuit upon which it is placed is rapidly made and broken, a succession of explosive noises proceeds from the magnet. These sounds produce upon the ear the effect of a musical note. (Bell, 1876, p. 1)

Bell's famous 1876 telephony patent relied on a 'liquid transmitter', a rudimentary microphone that used magnets within a container of diluted acid to convert sound vibrations into undulating changes in electrical resistance, which caused a reed at the end of a wire to reproduce sound. This double articulation – the sender's articulation in forming speech and the articulation from vibrations in the air to electrical undulations and back again – translated and extended the voice in analogue form.

Along with the challenge of transmitting the voice clearly, telephone engineers faced the problem of invoking the right person: the problem of addressing. The telegraph had already adopted short, registered cable addresses in the first global invocable domain: unique codenames sent at the beginning of a message that needed to be looked up by personnel at each telegraph office to forward the message to somewhere closer. However, the problem with telephone exchanges involved developing a system for connecting callers directly: speaking rather than writing. Millions of switchboard operators, predominantly women, performed the labour of manually invoking connections. The companies trained these staff to be compliant and transparent intermediaries, but in popular culture, the figure of the telephone operator who performed this invocatory work took on a character somewhat like a Muse: 'ingenious, independent, and subversive – a maverick who flouts the rules and blithely transgresses social boundaries' (Middeljans, 2010, p. 38). Gradually this invocatory work was delegated to automated switches in systems of relays, valves, transistors and, ultimately, invocational media.

20   *Invocational Media*

Just over a century after the 1844 ceremony that debuted Morse's invocatory communication assemblage, another ceremony heralded the emergence of invocational media. On 15 February 1946, at the Moore School in Pennsylvania, Major General Barnes pressed a button to turn on the Electronic Numerical Integrator and Computer (ENIAC), credited as being the first large-scale electronic digital general-purpose computer (Goldstine, 1993).

Early histories of computing

The origin stories of many histories of computers centre on inventions made by reputedly brilliant mathematicians and engineers (De Mol & Bullync, 2018). The first histories of computers were written by the protagonists, institutions and corporations themselves and tended to concentrate on the technological advances in logic, mathematics and engineering that brought about the computer. For example, Goldstine's *The Computer from Pascal to von Neumann* (1993) framed a narrative of breakthrough innovations by mathematically gifted individuals such as Charles Babbage, Vannevar Bush and John von Neumann. These dominant narratives regularly distinguished male geniuses from those who merely followed in the path of their breakthroughs. 'Policing the distinction between origination and execution could protect the creative potential of the creator and isolate originators from mere executors' (Jones, 2016). It was typical in the early days of computing that men would design the hardware, while women such as Grace Hopper would be the operators and programmers, roles that demanded a high degree of innovation, often unacknowledged.

Similar myths of human geniuses and intelligent machines appear in Randell's (1973) collection of primary sources from computing history, which includes the voices almost entirely of men, including Babbage, Zuse, Aiken, Bell Labs and others whom Randell considered had made key contributions to modern computing (Grace Hopper is the notable exception). Slater's (1987) *Portraits in Silicon* also contains the voices of only men, except for Hopper. The erasure of women's agency in accounts of the development of computing partly reflected the hierarchical and gendered division of labour in the military and institutional contexts of early electronic computing (Light, 1999). There is a similar pattern in another genre of computing history that positioned computers within the history of technology, and particularly electrical engineering, computer science and software engineering, such as Mahoney's *The Histories of Computing* (2011).

These dominant approaches to computing history overlooked women's active role in computer development (Gürer, 2002), and this invisibility of women in the industry continues to affect women's choices to avoid technical areas of computing today (Vitores & Gil-Juárez, 2016). Despite recent high-profile efforts to address the low proportion of women in programming and engineering, these trends have continued. The association of computers with masculinity seems ingrained. Of course, there are many women excelling in using and developing invocational media.

In the 2000s, the computer tended to fade from the centre of discourse as some scholars framed cultural and technological arrangements as 'new media'. This conceptualisation moved the frame from computing to media but relied on a weak periodisation that simply split the old from the new. Bringing in humanities concepts, Manovich (2002) placed new media within the histories of both cinema and computing. The important distinctive features of new media he identified – numerical representation, modularity, automation, variability and transcoding – are notable for the absence of a salient verb. Bolter and Grusin (1999) also framed new media culturally and historically, seeing it as an emergent example of remediation. Their useful distinction between media that give a sense of immersive immediacy and those that offer the hypermediacy of a panoply of media elements stays predominantly at the level of visual culture. Remediation is clearly related to invocation, but is not a theory of medium specificity and they do not account for the performativity of sociotechnical, experiential and conceptual events. From the mid 2000s, other humanities and social science-based theorists of computer-based technologies as distinct media forms chose to focus on particular computer-based sociotechnical forms: the internet (Tsatsou, 2014); mobile media (Goggin, 2006); games (Aarseth, 2001); social media; and, later, TikTok (Stokel-Walker, 2021). Other theorists moved their focus from computers and software to address digital cultural practices. For example, Bollmer (2018) identifies 'networks, participation, remix, bricolage and glitch' as distinctive elements of digital cultures. Clearly, each of these digital cultural practices is invocational, in that:

- networks are extensive invocable domains;
- calls for participation draw users into action (avocations);
- both remix and bricolage invoke digitised cultural records, transforming and recontextualising them; and
- artists' uses of glitches exploit the aesthetics of invocational breakdowns.

However, emphases on new media and digital cultures leave open questions about how the two are connected. How did so many cultural forms adopt the same fundamental way of mediating events and the same diagrammatic relation between components? What are the pasts and futures of the medium if they are not about computation? What defines new media apart from them being new?

At this point, we need to get beyond computer histories focused on mathematics, logic and tabulation, beyond the theories of new media and beyond the research into particular invocational media forms. We have already proposed that the prehistory of invocational media can be found in invocatory devices – ritually used material actors that mediate events as easily as speech or writing. However, invocational media are significantly different from invocatory devices. Where an invocatory device invokes a limited set of preconfigured effects (lifting the door knocker to knock on the door, winding and releasing clockwork, using a switch to turn on a light, hitting a key to play a note, etc.), invocational media are programmable mediators of flows of invocational events through an array of specialised components. The next step is to analyse how invocations are not only technical events but also psychological, social and conceptual.

Levels of invocation

The power of invocational media lies in their capacity to perform seamless, if precarious, articulations between technical events, lived experiences and broader cultural and social milieux. For example, using a search engine involves: (1) a technical performance of a database query through search terms, software, networks, hardware and databases; (2) a user's experience of desires, thought processes, pleasure or frustration; and (3) invocations of a mix of metaphors and codes ('searching' for 'results' through an 'engine' using the English language, for example, and program code) and the institutions and social worlds of its production.

When programmers instruct computers to invoke logical and mathematical operations, these are performed at the lowest imperceptible levels of technical invocation. The technical operations do not fully account for either their consequent qualitative user experience or their social impacts. For example, video game code may calculate how gravity acts on a falling body, but this tells us little about how a game player feels when their avatar's body falls limply to earth (Carter, Gibbs & Wadley, 2013). Even for programmers, software is experienced only through second-level expression. Finally, invocational assemblages must be judged by their third-level invocations. A programmer may code a big data system using elegant first-level technical code and engaging user experience, but its implementations in surveillance applications for the National Security Agency or a criminal syndicate must be critiqued in terms of the mediatisation of power (Lyon, 2014).

These three interwoven levels of invocation – sociotechnical, phenomenological and metacultural – can be discerned in all operations of invocational media, so I will address them later in the text.

First-level invocations: Sociotechnical

While first-level invocations performed through electronic, optical, mechanical and software components may seem purely technical, they are already culturally loaded and bring this legacy into their operations. All these components reflect many negotiations and decisions over specifications, production practices, cost and functionality. As the components participate in invocational events in the material universes of the CPU and invocable domains – such as sensing, recording, transforming or expressing data and code – they consistently exceed the technical event in mediating physical, mental, ideological, economic and social universes.

The first-level hardware components in the invocational assemblage represented in Figure 1 are based on a mixed metaphor. In one sense it is a diagram of a body with senses, a brain, limbs and a voice. In another sense it is a machine with a user, inputs for raw materials that are processed and outputs. And in another sense, it is a node in a network of social or technical connections. In Chapter 4 I explore in more detail the cultural heritage of these components in machines of surveillance, spectacle, calculation, expression and connection. For the moment, though, this diagram is quite literal in mapping

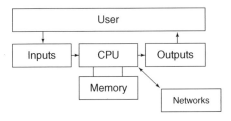

Figure 1 The familiar diagram of the first-level invocational components (Author).

the physical body of the computer. The components such as inputs (keyboard, mouse), outputs (speakers, screen), memory (RAM and hard drive) and central processing units (CPUs) can be identified easily, and they are clearly connected with buses, circuits and wires. However, this reveals little about its operation. First, the dynamics of invocational assemblages cannot be understood without powering them, booting them up and invoking software and user environments. Much of the work in producing these artefacts, and the work that they perform, is, of course, in software in a running machine. Second, the diagram gives little away about the experience of generating inputs that can be 'understood' by the processor or about making use of the outputs.

Few programmers today address the lowest-level invocable domains directly in machine code. Instead, they enrol operating systems, programming languages, middleware and other environments that establish their invocational syntax and semantics for creating executable applications. Since the 1950s, different programming languages have been appropriate for specific communities and people and, in turn, produced communities and subjects for those who learned to master these languages. To begin with, programming languages are usually based on a natural base language and therefore 'tie into the long legacy of linguistic imperialism' (Marino, 2020). Then there are different foci for languages – invocational dialects – most notably the classic pair of FORTRAN and COBOL. Scientific and engineering communities often used FORTRAN (for FORmula TRANslation) for practices such as data analysis and simulations. By contrast, COBOL (COmmon Business Oriented Language) was known for its simple and structured syntax and was widely used in business for financial systems and recordkeeping. By contrast, structured programming code in languages like ALGOL broke up code into invocable modules. The object-oriented programming approach of the language C++ structures coding further to introduce invocable objects modelled on real-life entities, each with its own methods. This was a way of organising programmers in a large project as well as a way of organising code (Chun, 2011). Java is a pastiche of previous languages, borrowing heavily from C++ and others. Its logic centres on establishing a highly structured environment for invocability. 'Java programs are structured around invocations of existing pieces of code (objects) organised in a class hierarchy descending from a single generic class at the top called "Object"' (Mackenzie, 2006, p. 105).

To understand the first level of invocation at a technical level, we might recall Kittler's (1997) provocative argument that because everything computers do involves digital switching in hardware circuits, there is no software. To this, we can confirm that invocations are always manifest as first-level discrete events of voltage variations, optical signals, magnetic variations and so on. However, we must then look to Manovich's (2013) intervention in 'software studies', where he responds to Kittler by saying that there 'is only software' (p. 147). He claims it is software that defines what is new about new media or metamedia: 'The new ways of media access, distribution, analysis, generation, and manipulation all come from software' (p. 148). Of course, despite the formal and material differences between hardware and software, functional systems are defined not so much by their components but by the external relations between components so that invocations circulate between hardware, software, people and environments as invocational assemblages.

While first-level invocations are technical and logical, they also often mediate social actions expressed as second- and third-level events. As I discuss in detail in Chapter 2, invocations often perform speech acts that allow users to make truth claims, requests, commands, promises or even expressions of emotion (Searle, 1969). For invocationary speech acts to be fulfilled, though, they must be articulated through all three levels: the technical level, the second level of performance in everyday spaces and the third level of social institutional meanings and power (Bourdieu, 1991). Lessig (2006) makes the connection between code and law, to which we can add that events are often invoked simultaneously at these three levels – electronics, experience and discourse. In many situations, coded invocations invoke symbolic power, automatically registering commitments and even making judgements with legal effect. When I make a bid on my eBay app in Australia, I am (whether I know it or not) invoking Australia's Electronic Transactions Regulations 2000, the eBay user agreement and a range of common law rights and obligations. By encoding many of the relevant legal, financial and social conditions into the invocations, eBay reduces or eliminates any deviance from the proper procedures. I use the app to make offers and promises that I am obliged to respect. However, it is not only users that create invocations. Many are performed by automatic decision-making processes, in which the person in authority is obscured. If I reach my credit card limit, 'the bank' refuses to fulfil my invocation to purchase the eBay item. The invocational event performs simultaneously technical, user experience and socio-legal operations that actualise coded abstractions.

Stereotypes about people working close to first level of invocation suggest that while they are masters of the dark arts of programming, they become disconnected from interpersonal and social relationships. According to Feenberg (2002), these professions have come to inhabit a world apart:

> It is a rationalistic world that bears little or no connection to everyday experience, in which thinking consists in linear operations on unambiguous representations of artificial, decontextualized, and well-defined objects; problems are clear-cut and solutions definitively testable. (p. 98)

Ullman (1997) tells the story of her experience as a developer getting some harsh feedback from users on a system she was working on. She found it hard to identify with peoples' reactions. 'The system pre-existed the people. Screens were prototyped. Data elements were defined. The machine events already had more reality, had been with me longer, than the human beings' (Ullman, 1997, p. 12). However, while she realised that she was accountable to these people at the second level of invocation – the system 'had no life without the user' (p. 13) – she felt closest to mastery at the first level: 'I'd like to claim a sudden sense of real-world responsibility. But that would be lying. What I really thought was this: I must save the system' (p. 13).

This stereotype is perhaps a generalisation. Narratives from programmers suggest that many are aware of the creative challenges of integrating first-, second- and third-level invocations. Software development is often reported to be a creative problem-solving process of working within the constraints of cost, speed and capabilities of available invocable domains to draw the three levels together. In *Racing the Beam*, Montford and Bogost (2009) analyse how game designers worked around the limits of the 1977 Atari VCS games platform, such as limited memory, graphics and audio hardware. For example, in preparing the soundtrack for the 1982 game *Star Wars: The Empire Strikes Back*, programmers found the VCS's in-built repertoire of sounds did not map onto the Western chromatic scale. They needed to ask a musical composer to develop effective musical sequences within the systems' hardware limitations (p. 131). It is only through working within the constraints in the first level of invocation that the second level of experience – sensation and affect – and the third level of cultural meaning-making, social relations and economic feasibility could be evoked effectively.

Second-level invocations: Experience

The second level of invocation encompasses the everyday lived experience of working and playing with invocations: the time people are involved with

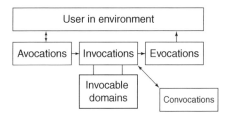

Figure 2 The dynamics of second-order invocational assemblages (Author).

perceptual, cognitive and affective interactions with interfaces and the look and feel of calling things up. For users, invocational devices are black boxes – characterised only by their inputs and outputs. Users can perceive only indirect evidence of first-level invocations. In events of the second level, inputs and outputs take on semiotic and performative meanings, mediating cognitive events and generating affective intensities through phenomena of avocation and evocation. Therefore, we need to adapt the diagram of hardware components (Figure 1) to address the dynamics of second-level invocational assemblages (Figure 2). Unlike the input and output devices, which are very concrete, avocations and evocations encompass the complex perceptual and affective forces in the relations between users and devices in invocational assemblages. Unlike the implied stable, rational user in Figure 1, users in this diagram bring their individual identity to the machine and experience it in processes of continuous modulation: desiring, problem-solving, learning, producing, being influenced and so on. While users, avocations and evocations can be highly contingent and emergent, the events of invocation and the structures of invocable domains are relatively simple and stable.

In the experience of using invocational media, the unlimited forces that influence a user's invocations are *avocations*. These include advertising, training, friendships, documentation and interface elements. The user's experience of perceptible and meaningful outputs of invocations produces *evocations*. These are the highly variable cognitive and affective events emerging from exposure to output images, sounds, vibrations, printouts and so on.

Early computers were not particularly evocative media in comparison with painting, cinema or music. However, even digits on a screen can evoke strong emotions in the context of a gambling machine or a dramatic change in stock prices. Traditional media are usually defined as passive in comparison with computer interactive media, but this underplays how active gallery visitors, movie viewers and music audiences can be in their experience of these media.

All media consumption involves work. What is different in invocational media assemblages is the intercession of the invocational events. In the flow of user experience, many evocations serve as avocations that invite the users to perform the next action, even something as simple as a dialogue box presenting a button to prompt the user's next invocation. For the uninitiated, this can already be quite confronting: 'What do I do now?' For other users, playing a first-person shooter, for example, might produce more intense invocationary action when the game world is full of frighteningly evocative opponents and challenging environments, and the player has avocations for moving and shooting that produce further evocations such as kills or damage to the player. While avocations and evocations are intricately connected, I will introduce them separately here. I address them in more detail in Chapter 5.

Avocations

Avocations encourage users to perform effective invocations by guiding, educating and enculturating them into the repertoire of techniques, protocols, concepts and desires associated with the practice of adopting and using invocational assemblages. Avocations are a minor form of vocation. Where vocations are lifelong callings to an identity, avocations are diversions from the ways in which users would otherwise perform a task (Weber, 1946). Avocations attract, seduce, inform, guide or coerce possible users to take up that role. They may entail formal organisational requirements or appear as entertainment. Either way, they serve to enhance the digital capital people accumulate as part of their everyday experiences with invocational media (Park, 2017). However, in this process, they gradually foster habits and constitute the part-subjectivity of users, such as Excel experts or advanced Fortnite players. Many avocations are material, exploiting embodied knowledge and competencies of users: the configuration of typewriter keys, the layout of books, the relation between hand, mouse and on-screen pointer and so on. Avocations also take the form of interpersonal relations: early adopters proselytise, and teachers develop pedagogical strategies to support others in becoming proficient users. Designing avocations is an industry, as designers, marketers, writers and educators adopt strategies to educate, assist and nudge users to buy, adopt and become experts in systems.

The past seventy years have seen several avocational paradigms and invocational dialects. In the early days of computing, from Colossus and ENIAC onwards, operators and programmers apprenticed peers in the dark material arts of building, maintaining, programming and using these machines (Haigh, Priestley, Rope, Aspray & Misa, 2016). Their interpersonal avocations became formalised in an emerging vocation of computer science that developed in the late 1950s. Several universities created computer science departments in the early 1960s, fostering vocations distinct from electrical engineering and mathematics (Dasgupta, 2014). From this moment, learning about invocational media became more institutionalised, and manuals and textbooks provided the avocations that schooled specialists in performing invocations in various systems and languages. By the mid-1980s, with a much broader uptake of invocational media, the graphical user interface paradigm provided designed avocational guidance within the software itself, using memory aids, direct manipulation and metaphors such as windows, icons, menus and pointing devices (Shneiderman, 1986). As computers became consumer commodities, the range of users expanded dramatically in both offices and homes. In the 1990s, in the CD-ROM multimedia era, many 'interactives' and games incorporated cryptic, playful avocations that mediated interactions with 'media content'.

Unlike computer science, which works predominantly on the first level, the human–computer interaction (HCI) tradition that emerged in the early 1980s was an 'inter-discipline' (Blackwell, 2015) that designed and evaluated interactions with invocational media. The HCI community emerged partly in reaction to the human factors tradition in engineering that treated humans as components in the system, analysing human vision, hands and so on. By the 1990s, HCI attracted people in a broader range of disciplines in the human sciences, the arts, humanities and design, as well as domain specialists (e.g. in medicine or biology). In the early 1990s, Don Norman (2013 [1988]) popularised an even broader conception of user experience design (UXD), and later user experience research (UXR), that moved focus from interfaces and artefacts to the overall experience of technology within everyday lifeworlds. UXD makes avocations. In the mid-2000s, the smartphone era invited users to touch and gesture with a large selection of apps, each with its own set of avocations, invocations and evocations that afforded 'embodied interaction . . . in a world of physical and social reality' (Dourish, 2004, p. 3). By the 2010s, designers of a range of AI applications and robots designed devices that were not intended to be *used*, so much as to perform as autonomous invocationary actors capable of independently planning and initiating actions, making judgements and responding to other physical and social actors.

30 *Invocational Media*

For the most part, though, avocations foster in the user a desire to form invocations. When they are summoned, they reflect the persona of an implied user who is doubled and ventriloquised. They draw on the third level of cultural imaginaries and social environments, which we will come to presently. Users take up personas embedded in software – programmers, authors, email correspondents, social media friends, citizens, customers and so on. In everyday use, depending on these roles, they must show faith in much of what they call up; all activities involve precomposed avocations, invocations and programs. Even for programmers working at the first level, invocation works with given resources and avocations, with no way of knowing the full details of their implementation.

Outputs and evocations

The products of invocations are expressed as evocations – perceptible, cognitive and affective events that impact on subjects' sensations, affects and thoughts in everyday experience. Evocations can be produced through visibilities: numerical readouts, printed texts, photographic or graphical images and simulations. They can be auditory: voice, music and sounds. They can be physical events such as vibrations or a robot's movements. More than simply outputting data, evocations produce situated meanings that invoke semiotic codes, such as written or spoken language, cinematic framing and editing, musical melody and rhythm, interpersonal presence and gesture in a robot or other cultural codes. Digital data are finite, but evocations are potentially infinite, offering meanings and feelings that are experienced differently by each user each time. Even the output of numerical values can affect users' thoughts and feelings differently within various social situations and physical places.

Many evocations immediately feed back cybernetically as avocations. The evocations from one invocation can constitute new avocations that make possible further invocationary action. A search engine offers a search field and then, after a moment, returns an evocative page of results that features a list of hyperlink avocations. Evocation is inherently temporal and situated: the duration between invocation and evocation affects the user experience. The situation affects the event: the office, home or Google map on a smartphone. A critical invocational aesthetic emerges at the point when avocations, invocations and evocations are bound together in real-time invocationary action, such as the physical mouse movement repeated as a pointer within the screen space or a 3D engine rendering a scene in real time. I explore invocational experience in more depth in Chapter 5.

Third-level invocations: Assemblages and discourses

Beyond their changing technical and experiential dimensions, innovations in invocational media have emerged through third-level invocations, whereby previous practices, concepts and metaphors are translated to inform the design and promotion of invocational environments. In a process usually referred to too uniformly as 'computerisation', enthusiasts, programmers, engineers and institutions extracted and adapted existing cultural resources to design and popularise invocational media applications for specific milieux. This is better considered as a process of invocational mediatisation, whereby invocational assemblages, with their own metamedia logic, are able, through extensions to its software and hardware, to invoke and transform the media logics of previously existing technologies, identities and practices.

For example, email invokes, remediates and displaces the practice of writing memos or letters, the persona of the correspondent and techniques of addressing and transporting communications. It invokes familiar metaphors of messages, mailboxes, addresses and so on, only to transform and make obsolete the existing objects and practices. These metaphors inform the design of first-level invocations – text editing, database, network connections and servers – and the development of standards (such as SMTP, POP and IMAP). Third-level invocations influence the second-level avocations in their use of interactive icons, buttons, message lists, editors and so on. The whole assemblage invokes the long-standing practices of correspondence on paper, while at the same time, cultural practices have changed to suit the new spatial and temporal affordances of the medium. Third-level invocations help to constitute the genres, identities, metaphors and operations of invocational applications. They hold together the operative avocations and evocations, securing the integrity of technical operations and the efficacy of the pragmatic and legal events.

To interrogate this process, we can explore third-level invocations at different moments in the history of invocational media, as we do in Chapter 3. In the 1940s, they mediatised computational practices for code-breaking, nuclear physics, astronomy and engineering and in the process reimagined and re-engineered human and non-human intelligence. In the 1950s, they began mediatising business and government practices. However, in resistance to these third-level invocations, computers took on another set of meanings, associated with dehumanisation, surveillance and corporate and government power. The history of invocational media has been characterised by struggles over the meanings and mediations of invocational assemblages and efforts to harmonise all three levels of invocation.

The hazards of the concept of invocational media

Writing a book developing the concept of invocational media presents certain risks. Not only does it move outside sociological, historical or textual methodological boundaries, but even within the domains of cultural studies or media studies it could easily be read as suspect and problematic. As my focus is on invocational technologies that perform as media shaping social actions, a predictable accusation would be that this is a technologically determinist approach (Williams, 1990). A claim that the theory of invocational media is technologically determinist would miss the point of my undertaking. An artefact is always meaningless outside of the attachments it creates with other actors to participate in assemblages, which are always in processes of reconfiguration. It is invocational media's capacity to make so many, varied attachments that gives it cultural and social prominence. Invocations are part of many assemblages, across cultural contexts and social situations – from police stations to game arcades, weapons systems to online voting, from TikTok videos to higher mathematics. These domains seem to share little in common except that they have come to be mediated by invocational media. By exploring the diversity of assemblages in which humans and non-humans collaboratively perform at the three levels of invocation, I will avoid simplistically attributing cultural phenomena to technological causes.

Some critics might contend that the metaphor of the invoking voice repeats a metaphysical error in seeing data and computing as essentially ephemeral and magical. Various forms of new materialism were reactions to excessive belief in the immateriality of digital media phenomena (Casemajor, 2015). These critics may argue that I will neglect the roles of other modes of communication – data, writing, bodies, images and sound – in the operations of computing. In fact, I will be exploring how each of these elements is remediated in its translation into invocational form. Each is sensed, encoded, stored, transformed, generated, decoded and expressed invocationally. This remediation has implications for each of these modes of communication. For example, in popular music and art, invocability favours digital bricolage, where creators transform, remix and layer pre-existing elements (Borschke, 2017). Hip-hop, photomontage, copy and paste, using programming libraries and so on are practices that exploit these forms of invocation. The multiple forms of encoding and decoding employed for different data types (e.g. how sound can either be sampled or modelled) influence aesthetic styles based on the available creative repertoire in invocational musical assemblages.

Perhaps even more problematically, invocation might seem to privilege an invoking subject as the active agent. Here I must stress that most invocations are not initiated by a user but are programmed events with no immediate human intention. While these could theoretically be attributed ultimately to a programmer, or to an error-prone 'user', this attribution is tenuous. In fact, most invocations live largely non-human lives, and it is only with significant extra effort that human accountability can be securely attached to them. User invocations only take place when software allows them, and when it does accept inputs, it places strong constraints on the modes of invocation available. As I will explore in Chapter 5, users are products of the medium as much as its masters.

Another danger in using the term 'invocation' is that readers might believe I am claiming that computers are literally religious or magical. This is not my goal, even if there is no doubt that technology has long had associations in culture with religion and magic. Noble (1997, para. 6) makes the historical argument that 'modern technology and religion have evolved together and that, as a result, the technological enterprise has been and remains suffused with religious belief'. In some cases, I will identify such continuities, but they are only a small part of the argument.

In magic, a distinction is often made between magic that makes metaphysical claims and magic that is presented as stage illusion. For example, cultural groups such as technopagans and extropians claim that computer technologies are intrinsically spiritually or politically liberating (Aupers, 2011). Erik Davis's *Techgnosis* (Davis, 1998) is a classic that thoroughly explores these links between technology, religion and the occult. On the other hand, information technologies can be productively compared with stage magic. Many invocational media create marvellous illusions that exceed our rational understanding (Coeckelbergh, 2019). At a more everyday level, it is appropriate to call out companies using metaphors of technological magic to sell more computers. Stahl (1999) is critical of powerful organisations and capitalists making mystifying quasi-religious ideological assertions: 'Some have claimed we are going through a transformation comparable to the industrial revolution which will usher in a qualitatively different kind of society based on information technology' (p. 7). He notes that over ten years from 1979, '36 percent of the 175 articles on computers in *Time* magazine used explicitly magical or religious language to refer to computers or to those who make, program, or use them' (p. 80).

More recently, Bogost (2015) rails against the tendency to reify and worship algorithms:

> Algorithms aren't gods. We need not believe that they rule the world in order to admit that they influence it, sometimes profoundly. Let's bring algorithms down to earth again. Let's keep the computer around without fetishizing it, without bowing down to it or shrugging away its inevitable power over us, without melting everything down into it as a new name for fate. (para. 36)

Another, more conservative, argument is that computers are displacing religion to become a dehumanising faith of their own:

> Man, redefined by a man-made idol, must always be diminished. In the last few years we have built idols of silicon, and our increasing belief in them makes us all more inhuman, for the silicon idol is not human. (Shallis, 1984, p. 169)

These arguments are interesting to a point, but they are not related to the case I am making for the concept of invocational media. I must admit to some deliberate irony in using the term 'invocational media', irony that evokes the hubris of many of the dreams of invocational power. Computing discourse is replete with exaggerated claims about the power of computing. Magical thinking is apparent in many supposedly rational domains. For example, the late 1990s internet bubble, the 2008 financial crisis and the 2020s cryptocurrency fever had invocationally mediatised thinking that can only be described as magical. The archetype for such magical thinking in market bubbles is Holland's 'tulip mania' of the 1600s, when a collective obsession for tulips – the biotech and media technologies of their day – created a huge financial bubble for future flowers. The bubble burst in February 1637 (Schama, 1997). Similar bubbles occurred around railways in Britain in the 1840s and radio in the United States in the 1920s. Economists traditionally invoke 'animal spirits' – bulls and bears – to explain the dynamics of the market (Mangee, 2021). However, the invocational mediatisation of markets has served to support what proved to be irrational beliefs in the future profitability of technology companies, subprime mortgage products, the Theranos scam and cryptocurrencies. In addition, invocational media have allowed markets to operate at higher speeds, making its 'sentiment' visible in infographics, accelerating and automating transactions beyond the temporal threshold of human capabilities. As with the sorcerer's apprentice, invocational media can have unintended consequences out of proportion to the actions of any one user.

In writing about invocation, I don't want to deprecate writers who genuinely address the mystical or magical imaginary in contemporary or historical cultures. I will not be pursuing mysticism beyond its relationship to the technological imaginary: that's other peoples' work. And I'm not stealing the word 'invocation' forever, I'm just borrowing it to create a new concept.

Structure of the book

Each chapter in the book serves to develop the concept of invocational media. Creating a concept requires first clearing a space and making connections with other concepts. Chapter 2 explains the practice of reconceptualisation, answering several questions on invocational media by drawing on conceptual resources from the social sciences and humanities. In Deleuze and Guattari's sense, this chapter charts planes of immanence that allow me to establish the concept of invocational media. Through these third-level invocations, it assembles and refines a toolkit to build a more usable and robust concept of invocational media. Among the productive connections in this chapter are references to media ecology; the speech act in linguistics and sociology; Heidegger's 'standing-reserve'; the critiques of capitalism and vectoralism in the post-Marxist tradition; Althusser's ideological call of the 'interpellation'; the psychodynamics of invocation; and Deleuze and Guattari's 'abstract machine' and 'order-word'.

Chapter 3 presents an impressionistic history of invocational media by invoking the structures of feeling in moments at which computers reflected the social, economic, political and cultural milieux in which they were developed and used – the third-level invocations that drew invocational media deeper into society and culture. Invocational machines have been abstract enough to mediatise all manner of cultural practices even as they have been accelerated by dramatic advances in speed and invocable domains. Invocational media embody the prevailing environments and their distinctive resources, meanings, values, needs, desires, anxieties and hopes. This is apparent from the metaphors that applied at different times, such as when proponents imagined they were creating brains, imposing social order, mastering the battlefield, selling consumer delights, exploring spaces, mapping the world or keeping connected. These metaphors are not so much mimetic as invocational in that they summon resources to call up something familiar yet new. The rich mimetic capacities of invocational media emerged through the invocation, the genetic event of the medium, which is fundamentally abstract and layered. These discursive moves served to help integrate invocational media into institutions and everyday life. If invocation is an event mediated by what Turing referred to as the universal machine, third-order invocational assemblages have served to make this technology increasingly universal.

Chapter 4 analyses the distinctive machines in invocational assemblages: command (inputs); archiving (memory and storage); code (software); time (clocks); calculation and decision (CPU); force and evocations (outputs); and connections and convocations (networking). Where command technologies use speed to compress distance, archival technologies extend duration of traces over time – a distinction Harold Innis (1951) refers to as space-binding and time-binding media. Computers enhance both command and memory by seamlessly blending the two functions within the same dynamic assemblage, while also automating events of decision. Networked convocations – digitised spaces for sociality and communication support a diversity of media/cultures – databases, discussion groups, electronic mail, social media, online gaming and workflow software, each with its own ways of presenting personas, organising social connections, managing information, communication and so on.

In the final chapter, we come to the ways in which invocational assemblages use personas to create spaces for subjects, constituting new vocations and new forms of user subjectivity. Although they offer power, it is always conditional and asks users for much in return. Chapter 5 explores how these powers and constraints generate user subjects and part-subjects. Users bend to fit and resist the system. 'User design' is best understood literally as designing *users*, which comes with designing machines for users. Invocational media incorporate spaces for users at four levels: hardware, avocations, user modes and avatars. At each of these levels, new forms of identity are mediated through a media form that simultaneously empowers and constrains its users.

As I have suggested, the project of concept generation is something of a philosophical experiment, but it is an approach appropriate to cultural studies, media studies and studies of digital cultures. Each chapter does this work in a different manner. This approach allows me to address a range of empirical and intellectual territories while remaining tightly focused on the task of creating the concept. The concept of invocational media not only offers a new name for computers but also challenges the dominant practices and discourses about them in social sciences, humanities and computer science.

2

Invoking concepts

Reconceptualising computers as invocational media entails developing integrated concepts that give us the potential to reimagine digital media's design, practice, policy and critique. This does not mean working from raw cloth; it is a generative task based on invocations of intellectual traditions. I begin this chapter by exploring what it means to mobilise, produce and refine concepts and then move on to mine the humanities canon for resources to refine the concept of invocation.

This chapter asks a series of questions and calls on an interdisciplinary array of resources in the humanities and social sciences to answer them. To begin, the media studies tradition helps understand how invocational media produced environments that deviated from previous media assemblages such as print, cinema and broadcasting. Compared with these media, invocational mediation recalls the dynamism and liveness of oral communication in mediascapes with non-human and human interactants. Where Ong saw phenomena such as television newsreaders as secondary orality, and Meyrowitz saw electronic media as producing social situations, I argue that invocational media produce many orality-like forms that I call convocations, which call people and things together in various ways. From here, I address the performativity of language and consider invocations as mediatised speech acts, or what I will refer to as invocationary acts. However, the efficacy of invocationary acts is contingent upon social arrangements of symbolic and material resources that are addressed as digitised automation, memories or connections. This arrangement resonates with Heidegger's more philosophical concept of 'standing-reserve', the tendency of modern technology to store up resources to make them available on call. Even where invocation is more convenient and efficient than prior techniques of creativity of communication, it can be at the cost of destroying traditional practices closer to the human scale and more heterogeneous in character. But Heidegger's approach lacks an account of social and economic relations of domination under capitalism. Contemporary invocation is a product of capitalist commoditisation and mass customisation. At the same time, using Althusser, I argue that users are themselves called or interpellated through processes I refer to as avocation – all the resources that attract and guide people to become users. I then examine the psychology of invocation and its association with magical thinking, desire and pleasure. However, rather than following Freud's pleasure principle, I draw again on Deleuze and Guattari, concluding that invocational media are 'desiring machines' that accelerate the production of subjectivity in connection with other machines: psychological, social, semiotic, material and technological.

What does it mean to reconceptualise computers?

I use the term 'concept' in a precise sense developed by Deleuze and Guattari in *What Is Philosophy?* (1994). The last book they wrote together, it looks back on their previous work to explain their overall project. They conclude that their approach to philosophical work has always been to create concepts. Their concept of the concept disavows claims that philosophy contemplates a priori ideas or searches for universals. Instead, they argue it is a distinctive creative activity that produces historically particular concepts that circulate and intervene in becomings of thought. Concepts are created with their own planes of immanence – 'the reservoir or reserve of purely conceptual events' (p. 36). To say that philosophy creates concepts might seem obvious, but it is important because of what it is not. It does not see language as simply referring to, representing or describing things. Language is a productive performance rather than a distant reflection. It is creative and powerful, enacting a variety of linguistic events, expressing sensory experience and emotions, creating concepts and imposing order. To build the concept of invocation, I critique the rationalist concept of the computer and question its dominant discourses and institutions. In their place, I build and mobilise a creative toolkit in a productive project of reconceptualisation of the invocational assemblage.

In this chapter, I experiment with a panoply of concepts, some of which would usually be considered incompatible. All concepts are built with invocations to what Deleuze and Guattari refer to as planes of immanence: 'Concepts are events, but the plane is the horizon of events, the reservoir or reserve of purely conceptual events' (p. 36). When reinvoked concepts are repeated, they are also transformed

Invoking Concepts 41

and reterritorialised. When philosophers cite the work of another, they reiterate and transmute concepts for a new context. In many scholarly communities, the plane of immanence is highly policed and its invocations are regulated, leading to a relatively stable consensus over the constitution of the field:

> Over a long period philosophers can create new concepts while remaining on the same plane and presupposing the same image as an earlier philosopher whom they invoke as their master: Plato and the neo-Platonists, Kant and the neo-Kantians. (Deleuze & Guattari, 1994, p. 57)

This is not my approach, however, as in this chapter, I aim not to remain on a single plane but to draw on heterogeneous concepts across different planes, invoking various traditions and disciplines. This is not far from Deleuze and Guattari's insistence that a concept is never simple: 'Every concept has its components and is defined by them. It therefore has a combination . . . It is a multiplicity' (Deleuze & Guattari, 1994, p. 15). In creating new texts, invocations call on resources available at that moment to generate something else. This means more than adhering to intellectual property law and conventions of academic honesty, which insist authors must never repeat an existing work. An invocation is never simply the recurrence of a previous event. In Deleuze and Guattari's (1987, p. 300) terms, it is a 'refrain' in that invocations are somehow musical. The task of this book is not to recount the history of computing but to invoke and transform concepts and planes of immanence to reconceptualise it.

For Deleuze and Guattari (1994), philosophy, science and art are distinct practices that create different things. Philosophy creates concepts. Science, by contrast, is a totally different creative activity. It attempts to create accurate representations of a world or truth outside by creating functions or propositions that themselves intervene in the world. It works by laying down grids and working with *functives* on systems of reference. This is much (but not all) of the creative work of programmers and mathematicians. Computer science is constantly laying down grids, working with invocable domains – planes of reference including memory addresses, software objects and inputs. However, computing has often been conceptually limited by the associated rationalist ontology I contest.

Computers also always had an artistic or aesthetic dimension. For Deleuze and Guattari (1994), art does something different again: it works with blocs of sensation, or *percepts* and *affects*. Unlike perceptions and affections, which are actual, percepts and affects are virtual and exceed the lived experiences of those who encounter them. They exist in themselves. Notably, Deleuze and Guattari (1994) draw from examples in the high arts of literature, sculpture and painting, where an artwork 'must stand up on its own' (p. 164). If art often works with resemblances, they say, it is with methods, materials and techniques associated with the medium. For example, in a portrait 'the smile is made solely with colours, lines, shadow and light' (p. 166). Artworks have a plane of the material and a plane of composition. The plane of the material refers to the physical components of the work, such as the colours, lines, shadow and light in a painting. The plane of composition refers to how these materials are combined and organised to create meaning and expression.

However, invocational art practices allowed artists to keep the materiality and composition of the work in flux. For example, media production software allowed creators to organise their content without being spatially or temporally fixed. Media objects became manipulable in layers, tracks, channels and timelines. By the late twentieth century, invocational media's expressive capabilities facilitated their colonisation of whole universes of art, design, play and performance. While even the most instrumental interfaces generated sensations and affections, many applications of invocational media transformed creative practices of illustration, design, photography and video and film production. Previously heterogeneous practices become increasingly integrated into a common invocational environment – writing, typography, drawing, photography and beyond. Unlike the materiality of paint or theatrical performance, deterritorialised invocable elements have different potentials: they can be called up, transformed and expressed indefinitely. At one moment, they may appear on a screen the size of a human palm, at another they may be projected onto the side of a building or wrapped onto the surface of a virtual three-dimensional object. Even more radically, creative work can be automated, complicating the intentionality and persona of an artist. For example, game spaces can be generated procedurally, or images can be created with the invocation of AI diffusion models. While these texts are constructed using scientific methods of simulation or image diffusion, games and image generators can produce evocative images at the speed of invocationary action.

While Deleuze and Guattari distinguish between science, art and philosophy as different kinds of creative intellectual work, irreconcilably different from one another, these fields are always combined. Work in these practices connects with the others: actual art has concepts and functions. Philosophy has percepts, affects and scientific functions. Science has concepts, percepts and affects. Therefore, invocational media events necessarily have scientific, artistic and philosophical dimensions. These relate to the levels of invocation identified in the previous chapter – first level (technical, scientific), second level (experiential, artistic) and third level (cultural, conceptual).

At the first level of invocation, the computer plots everything on invocable domains, or what Deleuze and Guattari call planes of reference (memory addresses, registers, network nodes, etc.). These work with discrete events rather than continuous variations. While first-level invocations operate at incredible speed, they are, in fact, 'a fantastic slowing down' (p. 118) because, in a scientific spirit, they define a limit and scale by reducing continuous changes to numerical values. For example, with a recording of someone speaking, a sampling process digitises a sound signal at a certain depth and speed to preserve a 'bloc of sensation' that captures not only what is said but also the timbre of the voice and the ambience of the room. This recording is later reterritorialised and experienced at the level of sensation, expressing meanings, emotions, references and concepts in the contexts of their invocation. At the third level of cultural form, the recording may become invocable in the genre of a podcast or as a private diary, impacting an audience. At any moment, the data may be subject again to first-level logical events to transform or transcode them to generate new events. When I invoke a voice assistant, for example, patterns in my voice are transcoded through speech-to-text algorithms, automatically interpreting my words and responding to me with its own somewhat evocative speech.

The invocation is not a universal. Invocations are always historically, technically and materially situated events. My approach throughout the book is grounded in cultural and media studies, so I often reference human, geographic and historical objects, events and phenomena in developing theory. This is not so far from Deleuze and Guattari's philosophy of events, which builds concepts with references to history, anthropology, linguistics, geology and biology. Concepts, affects and functives are not truths for all time but historical and contingent events of different character and duration. As the concept of invocational media is tied to constantly changing material technologies, I will dedicate significant space to description, narrative and analysis of the material and embodied histories of the medium.

This chapter performs third-level invocations to concepts, planes of immanence and conceptual personae from multiple traditions, including media ecology, speech act theory, philosophy, sociology and psychology. In some cases, the results are more like McLuhan's probes, which are unpackaged insights designed to create a disturbance (McLuhan, as cited in Marchand, 1989). This will extend beyond philosophy, science and art, as invocational media negotiate complex mediatised technical, aesthetic, linguistic, economic and political assemblages. The material in the book necessarily calls up concepts from many spaces that do not necessarily share the same planes of immanence, reference, materiality or composition: sociologies, histories, cinema, science fiction, blogs, games, technical documentation and everyday conversations. The central point is to develop the concept of invocational media.

What are invocational media? (Invoking media ecology)

While the assumption that computers are a form of media is uncontroversial today, this was long a minority view, with only figures such as Vannevar Bush, J. C. R. Licklider, Marshall McLuhan and Alan Kay prominently proposing social and communicative uses of computing. As I will explore in Chapter 3, the struggles over the conceptualisations of computers saw their meanings and institutionalisations change dramatically over the history of this technology. 'Computer as medium' concepts developed in the 1980s in research in the computer-supported cooperative work (CSCW) and the human–computer interaction (HCI) traditions. By the 1980s, this concept was commoditised as companies sought to expand into consumer markets with games consoles and interactive multimedia. Meanwhile, creative evolution in the invocational technological phylum found designers and artists developing and taking up new affordances and functionalities such as HyperCard, CD-ROM, electronic arts, colour screens and soundcards to establish new aesthetic forms. The popularisation of the internet in the 1990s saw computers become a vehicle for publishing and for interpersonal and group communication.

With a derivation in the Latin *medius* – something in the middle – media have in many contexts been reduced to sources of distortion and bias. In Shannon's (1948) mathematical information theory, for example, the medium is a source of noise in the channel between transmitter and receiver – an engineering problem central to the project of communication. He aimed to improve communication between an information source and a destination by making it as noiseless as possible. In this, he favoured discrete noiseless systems such as teletype and telegraphy instead of continuously variable systems such as analogue broadcasts. He acknowledged that he was ignoring the meanings and social

Invoking Concepts   45

significance of the technological concepts he examined: '[the] semantic aspects of communication are irrelevant to the engineering problem' (p. 1). Shannon's mathematical approach was a powerful influence in computer science, with the 1948 article anticipating file compression and error correction in digital communication. However, it also fostered an assumption that the problem for media was noise and that this could be overcome with mathematical analysis and technological fixes.

In the mediasphere of analogue invocatory devices that prevailed through the twentieth century, including printing, the phonograph, photography, typewriter, telegraph, cinema, radio and television, each medium had its own materials, genres, spaces, practices, professions and institutions. All these media could be judged in engineering terms as conduits for communication evaluated according to their fidelity and noise. For media ecologists, though, the way these changed the cultural environment was more significant than any of the communicative acts performed through them. In the same way, the individual requests performed through invocations are not as significant as the ongoing practices of living with invocationally mediated environments.

The media studies tradition that emerged in the 1950s began to contest the neutrality of media, although it was not until 1968 that the term 'media ecology' was popularised by Neil Postman (Anton, 2016). This discovery of the importance of media was not just a coming to awareness of the features of media technologies but also a recognition that media rendered communication always partial, diversely organised, noisy and dangerous (Guillory, 2010). Writers such as Innis (1951), Havelock (1963), Ong (1982) and McLuhan (1962, 1964) observed that historical changes in media technologies seemed to be associated with transformations in people's experiences, psyches, cultures and societies. Just as nineteenth-century archaeologists traced human cultural evolution through the predominant materials – the Stone Age, Bronze Age and Iron Age – the medium theorists identified media epochs, most typically following a narrative through oral–aural culture, writing, print and electric media.

They argued that oral practices were qualitatively different from those associated with writing and print. Print media in particular were characterised by objectivity, fixity, visuality and abstraction. Innis (1951) observes that 'the spoken word was in its origins a half-way house between singing and speech, an outlet for intense feelings rather than intelligible expression' (p. 20). According to McLuhan (1962), oral cultures inhabit a 'magical resonating world' (p. 158) in which people are surrounded by sound and involved in a way that is lost with

46   *Invocational Media*

the printing press when the eye provides only a single point of view. McLuhan sometimes presents the emergence of scribal and later print cultures as a tragedy for orality. As Towns (2022) observes, though, unlike Innis, McLuhan's (1964) romanticising references to tribalism are symptomatic of an unstated influence of social Darwinism that casts non-white people as more primitive without acknowledging the history of colonialism and slavery.

Ong (1982), once supervised by McLuhan for his MA, takes a slightly different approach, moving away from McLuhan's aphoristic style, hyperbole and emphasis on media to start by analysing what he refers to as the psychodynamics of orality. He says this 'primary' orality was bound to its immediate lifeworld and its spatial and social context. As it relied on sound, it was always performed in the ephemeral present. He argues that 'names give human beings power over what they name' (p. 33). Unlike the private and silent reading of decontextualised texts, he argues, spoken performances in oral cultures had a 'magical potency' (p. 32) and were dynamic and immediately embedded in social relationships.

Innis, McLuhan and Ong see the emergence of scriptural and print cultures as bringing a significant cultural disruption. Innis views writing as bound up with the centralisation of power and control over resources and empire:

> Writing enormously enhanced a capacity for abstract thinking . . . Man's activities and powers were roughly extended in proportion to the increased use and perfection of written records. The old magic was transformed into a new and more potent record of the written word. (Innis, 1951, p. 24)

By contrast, McLuhan emphasises changes in sensory experience, arguing that the phonetic alphabet detribalised society, imposing rationality and a 'neutral visual world' for the 'literate man'. Print-based society became regimented and homogenised, linearised and rationalised. Knowledge became specialised, accumulative and based on credentials:

> The invention of the alphabet, like the invention of the wheel, was the translation or reduction of a complex, organic interplay of spaces into a single space. The phonetic alphabet reduced the use of all the senses at once, which is oral speech, to a merely visual code. (McLuhan, 1962, p. 168)

For Ong, the emergence of literacy saw a shift from sound and memory to sight and writing, with profound implications for human experience and thought. Ong sees writing as a useful but unnatural and externalised technology that readers internalised, producing literate people who could never recover the pristine state of orality. When exposed to writing, those embedded in a primarily oral culture could not trust its autonomous discourse and context-free language, as the text could not be questioned or verified by a speaker's presence and voice. Ong argues that in the transition from orality to literacy, writing faced many of the same criticisms people were now making about computers:

> Writing, Plato has Socrates say in the *Phaedrus*, is inhuman, pretending to establish outside the mind what in reality can be only in the mind. It is a thing, a manufactured product. The same of course is said of computers. (p. 78)

Ong observes that ancient critics of writing claimed that when people could write things down, they would lose the discipline of memorisation. He points out that critics of pocket calculators in the 1980s made similar arguments about how these devices would undermine peoples' capacities for mental arithmetic. Another criticism of both writing and computers Ong identifies is that both are dead and unresponsive. They cannot answer back: 'you get nothing except the same, often stupid, words which called for your question in the first place' (p. 78). Both writing and computers, he argued, were 'passive, out of it, in an unreal unnatural world' (p. 78). But Ong may have underestimated the liveliness of invocational media. In developments since the 1980s, the expansion of invocational powers of technologies like targeted advertising, the voice assistant and ChatGPT have seen these perform a range of invocationary actions.

Considering these developments, where computing is the apotheosis of the rationalism, of order and of calculative logics associated with writing, invocational media represent a return to oral cultural forms. In the 1960s, McLuhan suggested that print culture was being challenged by a new media environment powered by electricity and electronics. He proposed that they were returning us to 'new shapes and structures of human interdependence and of expression which are "oral" in form' (McLuhan, 1962, p. 3). McLuhan sees 'electric' media as a return to mental and mythological features of ancient or primitive oral–aural media:

> Electric circuitry confers a mythic dimension on our ordinary individual and group actions . . . Myth means putting on the audience, putting on one's environment . . . putting on a whole vesture, a whole time, a Zeit. (McLuhan, 1967, p. 114)

He argues that where specialist technologies like writing tend to 'detribalise' people, culture and society (1964, p. 24), the more generalist technologies, like television, retribalise them.

Ong develops a more rigorous but more modest concept of secondary orality, using the example of the television news anchor to analyse the re-emergence of orality. He argues that the telephone, radio, television and tape recording all recall patterns of thought and ritual lost in the transition to writing:

> This new orality has striking resemblances to the old in its participatory mystique, its fostering of a communal sense, its concentration on the present moment, and even its use of formulas. (Ong, 1982, p. 133)

Ong might have extended secondary orality to invocational media. Despite substantial differences, they certainly share some dynamics: participation, community, present-centredness and use of algorithms. Unlike the relative fixity of printed books, interactions such as text messages and social media posts are situated in the immediate flow of the everyday lifeworld, generating spaces for social interaction and even invoking non-human interactants. As in oral cultures, language in invocable domains has a magical potency – variables, usernames, search queries and hashtags – that summons things from the past or from a distance.

Here we might compare interactions with invocational assemblages to ancient invocations to Muses. Homer presented his epic poems as invocations, reinforcing one of the most enduring conventions in the genre. McLuhan describes Homer's work as the 'cultural encyclopedia of pre-literate Greece' (McLuhan, 1967, p. 113). Still, it was a spoken encyclopaedia, personified in the Muses, sustained by memories and voices over generations. The Muses featured as key imaginary personae in the memorised narratives, rituals and songs that oral cultures relied on to preserve cultural memories over time. Homer's *Odyssey* begins with an invocation to the Muse Calliope:

> Tell me, O Muse, of that ingenious hero who travelled far and wide after he had sacked the famous town of Troy. (Homer, 2009 [800 BCE])

In making this request, storytellers rhetorically invoked Muses to stir their recollections and set the scene for retelling a story that was already familiar to many of those present. Its recitation fostered cultural continuity while allowing for variation, adaptation and style changes. Claiming access to a Muse gave storytellers authority to speak within their social circle.

Pursuing this example, we find connections between epic narration and everyday electronic invocations. In the twenty-first century, a child interested in the classics might ask their smart voice assistant, 'What is the story of the *Odyssey*?' and immediately hear a quick summary of the plot. If they are keen, they could invoke a search engine to discover the full text of the *Odyssey* in the Internet Classics Archive. They could play the Spartan mercenary Alexios or Kassandra in the branching narrative open-world game *Assassin's Creed: Odyssey* (Ubisoft, 2018). They could even invoke an AI agent like ChatGPT to write original pieces of text resembling an answer to their questions. In forming these queries, though, they must already know that the *Odyssey* exists and have the desire to know more. The invocation is key.

Further parallels exist between ancient and modern invocations in their relationships to time, collective authorship and fluidity of meanings. Just as epics conventionally begin *in media res* ('in the middle of things'), internet search results appear in the middle of things – ranked not by alphabetical position or physical location but by their relevance according to secret algorithms. We might also recall that many have argued that Homeric stories were not the work of any individual author but collectively held invocable knowledge of a community passed from person to person over a long time (Ong, 1982). In a new way, search results or AI-generated answers are collectively authored rather than the product of individuals. They offer a provisional assortment of fragments created by many people that can be called up at any random moment. Search results tell a different story depending on the phrasing of the search, the user's profile and location and the changing body of data. ChatGPT composes original responses in conversational style when prompted by complex questions. These invocationary acts cannot be entirely anticipated, as they emerge through an assemblage – comprising content creators, the query's author, algorithms and an element of randomness – that is constantly in flux.

Where Google and Wikipedia dominate control how populations discover knowledge, Meta owns most of the US-based platforms for social connection including Facebook, Instagram and WhatsApp, and it has the aspiration to control the metaverse. These invocationally constituted places have architectures that support technical, experiential and social space.

This intersection between medium and place is a primary focus in Meyrowitz's *No Sense of Place* (1985), which considers how electronic media such as telephones, television, radio and computers complicate social space. He combines McLuhan's media determinism with Goffman's analysis of social situations to observe that electronic media complicate peoples' relationships to their physical and social places:

> [E]lectronic media affect social behaviour – not through the power of their messages but by reorganizing the social settings in which people interact and by weakening the once strong relationship between physical place and social 'place'. (Meyrowitz, 1985, p. ix)

Meyrowitz draws on Goffman's analysis of formal social situations and physical spaces, which often determine their participants' social roles. He argues that space was divided up in a society dominated by print media, so people knew their place. For example, the church constitutes both the conventional roles and spaces for churchgoers and the role and places of the priest. Many institutions restrict physical access and visibility to assert differences in social roles. With electronic media, Meyrowitz argues, people get connected to places they could previously not access, undermining social and psychological distinctions, enabling them to question norms about their place. In an anecdote about his childhood, he writes, 'I responded to television as if it was a "secret revelation machine" that exposed aspects of the adult world to me that would have otherwise remained hidden' (p. x). Access to information plays a central role: 'To have information from an environment is to be partially "in" that environment. Information access opens the door to physical access' (p. 181).

Public bulletin boards and the early public internet were characterised by information spaces that radically dissociated physical space from social place, consistent with Meyrowitz's argument about electronic media. However, this was not inherent in the invocational medium, as military, government and corporate networks had long protected their information spaces. While advocates of the early Web 2.0 in the 2000s stressed the way in which APIs allowed open ad hoc connections between different services, most of these sites required users to register, which established distinctions between different classes of user, defining offstage and onstage spaces and distinguishing levels of user.

These phenomena are convocations – they call together and assemble participants into a shared space and time mediatised by invocational media. However, public convocations are the exception. Convocations mostly establish permissions, roles and powers associated with institutional roles that define the social place of participants. While owners may have the greatest privileges, the administrators or superusers typically have permissions of trusted henchmen. Other users are granted privileges appropriate to their station. This is evident in role-playing games that divide players into classes or races. For example, players in the invoked magical convocation of *Destiny 2* adopt a role in one of three core mythological classes – Titans, Warlocks and Hunters. Each has distinctive powers and moves. In multiplayer mode, players join squads and face enemies in player-versus-player conflicts. As well as assigning particular weapons to players in each class, the game is engineered with tightly defined social relations and situations that provide a strong sense of social place within the game universe.

A social media site such as Meta's Facebook invokes a convocation tailored for social interaction by providing an environment for performing identity and acting socially within an egocentric convocation of flattened friendship relations. Friendships are consensually constituted and may be broken by either party. Facebook attempts to stabilise users' authentic identities within its walled garden. It also invokes a range of everyday conventional social practices, such as creating and joining groups, scheduling calendar events and sending messages. Translated into convocational software, each of these features constitutes social situations with appropriate avocations and algorithms. Creating a group turns on a setting that exposes the user to posts within that group and makes its members visible and addressable. It requires owners to specify a name and a cover image to define it as a purposive space and can require users to be invited or approved. Establishing an event, which can be private or public, users are offered the avocation of the RSVP. In different sociotechnical situations, users can perform carefully regulated speech acts, each of which acts within the social world.

However, the biggest sociotechnical divisions on the Facebook convocation are between managers, employees, advertisers and billions of users, as we will explore later in this chapter. Every action on the Facebook convocation also performs involuntary invocations for these users. Simply using the site builds the user's profile in the interest of selling targeted advertising. Users perform free labour: generating texts, enrolling friends, profiling themselves, consuming advertising and informing the system's predictions of their actions (Zuboff, 2019).

Where Ong argued that electronic media engender a secondary orality, and Meyrowitz argued that they break down social distinctions, convocations are more particular to each implementation, invoking any number of mediatised communicative situations, each with distinctive roles, psychodynamics, textuality, visuality, spatiality and temporality. Each convocation invokes an imaginative, experiential, cultural and mediatised assemblage with its own

Table 1 Features of Common Convocations

Type of Convocation	Features of Convocations	Examples
Intranet	Private network services within an organisation	Microsoft SharePoint, Yammer
Publication	Readable, downloadable or streamable content segments (sometimes with feedback or discussion)	Blogs, YouTube, Wikipedia
Textual chat/ group chat	Communication with distant others using text	SMS, Messenger, Reddit, WhatsApp, WeChat, Discord
Audiovisual livecasting	One-to-many casting of video streams (sometimes with audience feedback)	Twitch, Facebook, YouTube
Audio/visual group chat	Many-to-many video connections	Zoom, FaceTime
Spatial mediators	Situated visualisation and guidance through physical locations with mobile devices	Smartphone apps: Google Maps, Find My, Snap Map
Spatial simulators	Navigable, playable or virtual space	Games: GTA V, Destiny 2; Game engine: Unity, Unreal
Social spatial simulators	Invoking of navigable virtual spaces for embodied social interaction	Second Life, VRChat

conventions (see Table 1). While many convocations have some of the liveness and situatedness of oral communication, and the social spatiality discussed by Meyrowitz, many add constraints and controls. Each convocation has a signature 'media logic' with 'technical, aesthetic and institutional dimensions' (Hjarvard, 2018, p. 72).

Some convocations bring people together within proprietary real-time invoked codespaces (Kitchin & Dodge, 2011). Asynchronous convocational spaces such as discussion boards, social media groups and Reddit allow many people to send and read messages asynchronously. Wikipedia is a reference work like *Encyclopedia Britannica*, but its ongoing authorship is distributed and produced through its wiki convocation. It is ordered invocationally rather than alphabetically.

Although most of these convocations use the first-level TCP/IP protocol and internet infrastructure, each has quite different textual, technical and social protocols and structures. Social media convocations are strategically tailored to target advertising based on machine invocations of users' previous invocations. Social media corporations construct each convocational platform with its own strategic sociotechnical and economic configurations and its own repertoire of invocationary acts that extract what Zuboff (2019) refers to as 'behavioural surplus' through involuntary invocations.

Each convocation has its way of mediating voices expressed in different modalities (numbers, text strings, sounds, images, videos, etc.) and positioned in specific relation to a set of implied and actual speakers and listeners. Many have only one active participant, for example, the word processor, which invokes a space for an author's voice. Others have many participants, such as a database that awakens and reterritorialises stored-up voices with every invocation. Real-time chat in convocations resembles spoken language between participants rather than the text of printed books. Some convocations are characterised by heated conversations – 'flame wars' (Dery, 1994) – while others confine invocations to an in-group – 'filter bubbles' (Pariser, 2011). Convocations tend to be constantly emerging products of designers, moderators and participants.

While invocational media perform with the liveness of quasi-speech, they hide their interiorities, which are based on writing. Here we may turn to Derrida (1997), who argues that speech has been unfairly privileged over writing since Socrates. Living thoughts and speech were primary, while writing was after and outside that primary event. Derrida argues that this metaphysics of presence has continued through Western history. He argues against this privileging of speech by arguing that 'the supplementary menace of writing is older than what some think to exalt by the name of "speech"' (p. 167). We might also say that invocatory devices – physical objects that serve to communicate or amplify action – also preceded speech. Of course, we can't forget that programming is a form of writing that is foundational in invocational media. The spoken words of the voice assistant are automatically written before the device speaks them, with text-to-speech algorithms. Ultimately, speech, writing and electronic traces are radically intertwined. However, the next section addresses the ways in which invocationally mediated language in all these modes has come to perform invocationary actions.

What are invocationary acts? (Invoking speech act theory)

While I have argued that invocations are a special kind of magical spoken performance, for the tradition of speech act theory, the invocation is only a particular case, where the speech act is quite explicit. However, from the perspective of some speech act theorists, all language is active and even magical. In Chapter 1, I discussed how the dominant conception of what computers do is to represent or simulate states in the world. For example, a database record in a library catalogue stands for the book on the shelves. When the book is borrowed, the book's status in the database changes from being available in the library to being on loan to a particular borrower. To give another example, if a businessperson creates a spreadsheet to communicate sales figures, they may populate the spreadsheet with current data and calculate results, perhaps motivating changes in marketing strategy. Or another: a robot uses sensors to create a map of its surroundings and plan its future actions based on this map.

In each of these cases, the computer holds a representation in memory that stands for the state of the world, and in each example, the data could be tested: is the book on the shelf? Did actual sales confirm sales goals? Is the robot hitting a wall? But this attention to truth conditions risks missing the pragmatics of the wider situation.

Looked at in a more invocational manner, using a database to lend out a book doesn't merely represent the state of the book; it performs the act of lending, which implicitly includes a formalised promise from the borrower that they will return it before the due date. The salesperson may invoke the spreadsheet to strengthen a claim to convince the superiors of the wisdom of the sales strategy. An accurate map and the right permissions may allow the robot to navigate successfully through a space. In each case, the borrower, the salesperson and the robot make a commitment for which they can be held accountable. In each case, we can assess not only the truth of the data but also the performativity of the invocationary act. Here it is appropriate to recall Austin's introduction of the concept of language acts and the writers since that have used these concepts in relation to computers.

In *How to Do Things with Words* (1975 [1962]), philosopher of language J. L. Austin first introduces a theory of speech acts (also known as language acts or performatives). He starts by distinguishing the most common understanding of what language does: it makes constative statements. That is, statements make propositions that might be verified as logically consistent and judged as empirically true or false (p. 3). However, Austin argues that language does more than report or describe events. In addition, it produces events. Making a promise by saying 'I promise such and such' is not reporting the act of promising but making the promise in saying the words. Based on this premise, he distinguishes three components of the speech act: the locutionary, the illocutionary and perlocutionary.

The locutionary component of a speech act is the event of uttering sounds (in the case of speech) or making marks in the case of written language acts. If I make a promise, the series of sounds in the utterance 'I'll meet you on the Town Hall steps at one o'clock' are the locutionary act. If I leave you a note on paper with the same statement, then that document performs a locutionary act in a different medium, but creates a similar effect, or illocutionary act. The illocutionary act is the abstract promise itself. It takes the form of a proposition (meeting on the Town Halls steps at 1 pm), backed up with a force (I am committed to doing this). The perlocutionary act is what comes about because of that act. Promising might have the immediate perlocutionary effect of informing the friend and the longer-term effect of physically meeting the friend at the Town Hall. Speech acts are like technology, since they are ways of trying to control the future course of events. Speakers and listeners negotiate with exchanges of speech acts to create interpersonal commitments that try to predetermine a particular result.

Critics of speech act theory have argued that the efficacy of many speech acts most often relies on pre-existing relations of social power. This may even apply when meeting a friend, but it takes on more gravity with speech acts in relationships with institutions. Pierre Bourdieu argues that the efficacy of speech acts has less to do with linguistic competence and more to do with the power between the speakers and the 'social magic' associated with its performance (Bourdieu, 1991). The words someone says are effective only if the charismatic force of those negotiating the commitments is believed and if they are backed up with the possibility of other forms of coercion:

> Austin's account of performative utterances cannot be restricted to the sphere of linguistics. The magical efficacy of these acts of institution is inseparable from the existence of an institution defining the conditions (regarding the agent, the time, the place, etc.) which have to be fulfilled for the magic words to operate. (Bourdieu, 1991, p. 73)

So, perhaps the primary operations of language are not about meaning but force. Deleuze and Guattari argue that all uses of language are acts of power: '[t]he elementary unit of language – the statement – is the order-word . . . language is made not to be believed but to be obeyed' (Deleuze & Guattari, 1987, p. 76). Every statement implicitly sets things in order. This reverses the order in which Austin presents speech acts. For Deleuze and Guattari, the order-word *begins* with systems of implicit and presupposed social obligations. The virtual dimension of every statement, the conditions for the mysterious 'perlocutionary' act, precedes the performance of the locutionary act. So, before I make any request, the circumstances that make its execution possible are already in place, even if there is no certainty the request will be supported. When the order-word is articulated it performs 'incorporeal transformations' (p. 80) which instantly make some change in those relationships that it presupposes. My request attempts to impose some obligation on the person I am addressing. However, this intervention happens in relation to power relations that establish the force and likely efficacy of the incorporeal transformation.

Different collective assemblages have their own order-words, allowing particular speakers to perform specific incorporeal transformations. The economy has the loan, which creates creditors and debtors; health has the diagnosis, which separates the well from the sick; the police have the charge, which creates the suspect; the courts have the verdict, which separates the guilty from the innocent. The limits of these roles are sometimes challenged: for example, trials by media and vigilantes contest the legitimacy of official order-words and substitute their own.

Winograd and Flores (1986) apply the speech act theory approach to designing computer systems by focusing on what commitments, requests and other speech acts users should be able to perform with their information systems. They advocate that information systems designers start by analysing the typical ongoing conversations and commitments within the relevant work domain. They propose that software should be designed to transmit, track and record common language acts.

However, Suchman (1994) argues that applying speech act theory in system design would lose the flexibility and contingency of speech acts in natural language. More problematically, it would impose 'an agenda of discipline and control over organisation members' actions' (p. 178). She usefully argues that the approach Winograd and Flores advocate is to build a 'tool for the reproduction of a social order' (p. 186). She says that a workplace system Winograd and Flores developed called 'The Coordinator' is likely to produce an inflexible system that fails to support the openness of everyday language use. She argues that rather than seeing conversation as the exchange of pre-established speech acts, we should pay attention to the more contingent, interactive practices of talk. She observes that the way in which users within organisations use systems does not necessarily adhere to the pathways designers anticipated. They tend to

Invoking Concepts

work out their own solutions, accepting some features while ignoring others. However, her argument vacillates between advocating the more liberal talk-like heterogeneous interactions of situated users and recognising that organisations want to constrain and track the language acts that their workers perform:

> The machine thus becomes the instructor, the monitor of one's actions, keeping track of temporal relations and warning of potential breakdowns. It provides as well, of course, a record that can subsequently be invoked by organisation members in calling each others' actions to account. (p. 181)

Since Suchman (1994) wrote her defence of talk in information systems, many practices in everyday life have gradually incorporated the strategic management of language acts. For the most part, we have accepted this in the name of convenience and even pleasure. We willingly use websites and apps to facilitate the performance of invocationary acts to share pictures of ourselves, buy things, do our banking, send messages and so on. Meanwhile, institutions have surreptitiously gained greater control, efficiency and imposition of accountability. AI systems in loan approvals, medical diagnostics, predictive policing and court outcome prediction automatically generate order-words that intervene in the flow of events.

If we add invocational media to my arrangements to meet at the Town Hall I described earlier, we can see that the three components in Austin's schema – locutions, illocutions and perlocutions – operate in a different manner, as each is mediated through invocationary acts. If I want to get to the Town Hall, I could use the Uber app to call for a ride instead of taking the train. The app allows me to form the locutionary act by opening it, establishing the proposition by specifying my destination and allowing the GPS to speak for me by automatically adding my location. I execute the speech act of requesting the ride with the confirm button. This locutionary act is immediately received by the driver as an evocation on the Uber Driver app that the driver confirms, leading to the perlocutionary act of the driver changing course and picking me up. As the app continues to track our progress, there is ongoing invocationary action as the system continues to invoke our location on the map until we reach the destination.

So, the relationship between rider and driver is based not on negotiation or conversation but on the invocationary exchange of prepared order-words, even if both believe they are consenting. I make the request for a ride, but I also create my own obligation to pay the fare. It is the platform, with little human intervention, that mediates and regulates the invocationary acts that passengers and drivers perform. Unlike workplaces in which employees can negotiate industrial rights, Uber positions drivers as contractors who provide their own vehicle and lack access to sick leave or holidays. At the same time, they have their performance monitored even more than a typical employee does. Both passenger and driver are manipulated with gamified avocations that appear playful but impose an automated Taylorist monitoring in the cause of efficiency but with the consequence of coercion. The passenger is fascinated by the animated cars and upsold to take rides that are more luxurious. The driver is given incentives such as quests to complete a set number of trips within a particular time. Uber manages both driver and passenger with an ongoing regime of mutual surveillance as each is asked to rate the other; so even the practice of everyday small talk is incentivised.

Here we can see how invocationary acts are also articulations. The term 'articulation' is used by Stuart Hall (as cited in Grossberg, 1996) to address the problem of determination and contingency. It retains the meaning of speaking but more importantly has the sense of joining things together (as in an articulated lorry). The invocational articulation joins together language, technology, perception and action. In doing so, it offers speaking positions, avocations, algorithms and invocable domains. So, Uber structures the performance of trips and the ideology of precarious labour under capitalism but does not need to control the course of the conversation, the driver's tiredness or the holiday's excitement.

Many other invocationary infrastructures seek to articulate invocations to accelerate the completion of the perlocutionary act, such as Amazon's strategy of integrating its logistics (Geraci, 2020). It aims to articulate everything from user profiling to anticipating the desires of consumers through the avocation of one-click ordering, which minimises effort and reflection time. The invocation also accelerates the dispatch of goods, for example, by using robots to move the goods to human packers instead of having the packers move to the shelves. At the same time, workers' performances are automatically planned, monitored and controlled not through interpersonal relationships but through apps that can even fire employees for poor performance (Geraci, 2020). In this way, this articulation is highly structured, and its deliverable is to maximise sales and speed of delivery.

This is the cost of securing the universal possibility of invocationary acts – the world must be pre-prepared in ways that make it invocable. The expansion of invocable resources – data, knowledge, action, production and consumption –

required massive containerisation of the world. Everything seemed to become addressable, and what was not addressable dropped from awareness. To develop this further I will turn briefly to Heidegger and the concepts of standing-reserve and 'Enframing' (Heidegger 1977a p. 20), which help develop the central concept of invocable domains.

What are invocable domains? (Invoking Heidegger)

> Everywhere everything is ordered to stand by, to be immediately at hand, indeed to stand there just so that it may be on call for a further ordering. Whatever is ordered about in this way has its own standing. We call it the standing-reserve. (Heidegger, 1977a, p. 17)

In the previous section, I showed how the concept of language as representation was complicated by speech act theory. In this section, I turn to the phenomenology and existentialism of Heidegger, which challenges the conceptual foundations of computing. Winograd and Flores (1986) draw on Heidegger in their critique of the dominant ontologies of computing. They mobilise Heidegger's earlier work and the concept of 'being-in-the-world'. This concept rejects the scientific aspiration to become an objective observer, arguing rather that we are thrown into the world. We lack perfect knowledge and must act, whether or not we are prepared. In designing computers, they argue, developers should account for this experiential and situated dimension of computer use.

In this section, though, I turn to the later Heidegger (1977a, 1977b) where he is more critical of technology than in his earlier work. While he writes little about computers, I will argue that his critique of the dam and the airport runway can be shrunk down to the level of microelectronics. His approach to large-scale technologies is to critique a modern imperative to rearrange the world in the interests of making things available on demand. The flexible and natural spaces of fields and rivers are destroyed for the sake of making hydroelectricity or flight available on call. The environment is not available for its diversity of lived and poetic experiences but only as standing-reserve. In this section, I will evaluate the extent to which the design of computer components is driven by the same modern imperative and seek to identify what is lost in the process.

Heidegger develops this concept in the essay 'The Question Concerning Technology' (1977a) as part of a reconceptualisation of the essence of technology. He argues that the essence of technology is not primarily in the artefacts themselves, the processes of their production or their intended end uses. So, although it is *correct* that computers are a means to an end (processing and storing information), this does not capture their distinctive ontological implications. Rather, Heidegger argues, instrumental devices create a new technological relationship to Being-in-the-world. If Heidegger is right, we should be able to see how invocational media change humankind's whole world.

We might see from this Heideggerian perspective that the essence of invocation is related to *poiesis:* a Greek word for 'bringing forth' [*Her-vor-bringen*] (1977a, p. 10) or 'revealing' [*das Entbergen*] of truth (pp. 11–12). Technology's essence is in the process by which something is revealed. When raw materials undergo a process that arranges them in a particular way, an envisioned final product is brought into 'presencing' [*Anwesen*] (p. 11) – revealed in a tangible and particular form. A windmill reveals the energy in the wind, brings it into presencing. What was previously not in our presence is brought forth. The technological encompasses not only the means to particular ends but a whole set of relationships in the world. We can see that invocational media perform the presencing of images, calculations, sounds and other data.

For Heidegger, modern technology is a forceful and invasive kind of revealing that dramatically changes people's relationship with the world: it makes the real available as 'standing-reserve' [*Bestand*] (p. 17). More than *poiesis* (revealing), it is a 'challenging' [*Herausfordern*] of nature to reveal itself on demand (p. 14). Modern technology 'unlocks and exposes' nature (p. 15). Coal is mined and 'challenged' to reveal the energy stored in it; it is stockpiled so that the energy is on call to produce heat in furnaces. Heidegger uses the landscape – the Rhine River – as another example. The river is dammed to store up energy and make it available as hydroelectric power. In fact, the river is put on call not only for energy but also for tourism: the vacation industry puts it on call as a beautiful river in the landscape. Once revealed in this way, the river itself and tourist experiences are stored, switched about, transformed and distributed. For Heidegger, once the world is converted into standing-reserve, a deeper potential for truth is lost.

In the case of invocational media, data from heterogeneous spatial locations are prepared and sorted for reduction into symbolic forms for invocable domains of inputs, outputs, networks and memory. They are forced into information architectures to create a 'standing-reserve of bits' (Barney, 2000, p. 192). For example, when a user's typing was stored in the now-outmoded 8-bit American Standard Code for Information Interchange (ASCII) standard, any markings that did not belong within the 256 characters in the code could not be recorded. With Unicode, which has 1,114,112 possible characters, the invocable domain becomes much larger but is still finite. Anything that cannot be assimilated disappears from those invocable domains.

Revisiting the invocational assemblage, we can see how all components function as invocable domains:

- Random-access memory (RAM) and storage devices store information in indexed arrays of memory addresses, making data or instructions invocable. Every program, every number and every piece of text is indexed and stored in memory, ready to be invoked. These are the invocable memory domains: the digitally mapped resources for each invocation.
- Input devices such as the keyboard, mouse and camera are invocable domains called by the operating system to sense environmental changes through switching and sampling.
- Output devices are invocable domains that affect the environment. For example, computer monitors form images typically through video RAM (VRAM) invoking each pixel to display a specified colour value. This means there is a large but finite number of possible images, as determined by the number of pixels and the amount of information per pixel.
- The control units in CPUs are the mediators for most invocations, addressing all the other components, including the algorithmic logic unit (ALU), registers, input/output circuits, memory and storage. They call circuits in ALU to invoke arithmetical and logical operations.
- Software operations address hardware, invoked entities in memory such as variables, arrays and objects. This is where much of the invocational magic is performed and provides the instructions that the device follows to address all the invocable domains in hardware.

Heidegger might have argued that this standard arrangement of hardware and software in the invocational assemblage offers the whole world as standing-reserves, reducing all events and data to invocations at the cost of other modes of revealing.

So, what are the ethical and aesthetic implications of translating almost all forms of discourse, calculation and creativity into invocational form? Heidegger (1977b) emphasises that modern technology and science are characterised by a practice of 'Enframing' [*Gestell*] (p. 19). Invocations are structured and substantially predestined by avocations and algorithms. They are enframed and revealed on screens. This means more than just images appearing in a screen's frame. If you perform a Google search, no matter what you search for, you will discover only *search results* ordered by Google's algorithmically determined measure of relevance. When you follow a link, you still end up with a world shrunk to the size and location of your screen. All images are materialised on screen or paper according to the material and symbolic limits of the technology. However apparently convenient and abundant, the datafied events are flattened and homogenised and differ radically from the heterogeneous knowledge and experience encountered in conversations, libraries, archives, experiences and places. Google's corporate mission 'to organize the world's information and make it universally accessible and useful' necessarily omits an infinity of phenomena that are uninvocable.

The computer seems to be the apotheosis of Heidegger's world picture. A computer invokes only what has been digitised. It models data according to algorithms that create maps that stand in for parts of the world. They represent the world in order 'to set out before oneself and to set forth in relation to oneself' (p. 132). The Covid-19 pandemic lockdowns served to emphasise this impoverishment of experience. Invocation gives users a unified way to relate to the world. The physical world is arranged to suit invocations, and everything begins to resemble invocable domains. Products are tagged with bar codes or RFID tags. Goods are enclosed in identically sized shipping containers. People identify themselves with debit cards, credit cards, mobile phones and even their bodies and faces, to mark themselves as users, workers, customers or citizens. Sensors such as cameras and motion detectors make physical spaces into invocable domains.

Heidegger's critique of modern technology seems to extend the concept of invocation beyond it being simply a transparent, convenient instrumental question, making it into an ontological one. Invocational media are a particular mode of revealing. However, Heidegger's analysis has a certain essentialism with a totalising image of the modern world. When he warns of the 'danger' that 'Enframing' blocks 'a more original revealing' and 'more primal truth' (1977a, p. 28), the argument becomes circular; his argument that technology blinds us to some more primeval truth – a mystical, idealised 'nature' or spiritual knowledge – romanticises a past that preceded modern technology. He rejects all contemporary technology in one stroke. When he does address specific technological and social formations, he sees them as mere instances of a wider monolithic process undermining older modes of Being. His allusion to the possibility of a 'saving power', which is 'also where the danger is' (p. 28), is intriguing but ill defined.

Invocational media tend towards crises of referentiality when the digital ontological realm loses synchronisation with the physical world. The connections between data and their referents are fragile and can easily snap apart because of the difference in the nature of an *address* in space (noun) and invocational *address* (verb). Actions in invocable domains start taking on their own logic. The stock market crash of 1987 (Wark, 1994) and the global financial crisis of 2008 occurred in the virtual geographies of the invocable domains of digitised markets. While objects in invocable domains become more readily accessible than those in the physical world, physical objects can become misaligned with the databases that attempt to order them. The logical solution to this instability is logistics: organise the world in ways that make it more reliable and quickly invocable. The example of Amazon applies again, as objects in warehouses are arranged spatially as standing-reserve to maximise efficient invocability. However, with the introduction of robotics into warehouses, the goods become moving reserves in a constant flow of invocationary action that lubricates the supply chain, from sourcing to dispatch and delivery.

Critics have argued that Heidegger's distinction between non-modern and modern technologies is too simplistic, and his account of the social world is impoverished. Don Ihde (1993) identifies a tendency for Heidegger to privilege 'good' technologies such as the stone bridge over 'bad' ones like the steel highway bridge. He argues that Heidegger tends to be nostalgic for technologies that give an embodied relation to the world. For example, he rejects the typewriter in favour of handwriting. Ihde says Heidegger's nostalgia avoids the politics of artefacts, a politics that writers such as Langdon Winner (1977) later explore. If applied to the Nazi regime, in which Heidegger was notoriously implicated, his analysis could make no distinction between a highway bridge and a death camp, as both are in his terms, modern forms of standing-reserve. Tom Rockmore is even more damning, saying 'there is no indication . . . Heidegger . . . has a real comprehension of the nature of society' (1995, p. 141).

Heidegger's distinction between modern and premodern technologies has also been questioned by actor–network theorists. Bruno Latour (1993) argues against Heidegger that attributing all the modern ontological and technological changes to Descartes's thought is premature. He points out a big gap between the philosophical agendas of modernity and how these ideas played out. He argues that in fact we have never been modern, undermining Heidegger's distinction.

He accuses Heidegger of losing touch with empirical beings by believing too strongly in the ambitions articulated in the 'modern Constitution' (pp. 65–7). Latour refuses to accept Heidegger's claim that a condition of modernity was ever achieved. His own ethnographic work on science as an activity showed that, in practice, there never *was* any pure scientific knowledge, never were any pure economic markets or never was any purely instrumental technology (Latour & Woolgar, 1979; Latour, 1987). While announced, pure science and rational politics were never (and could never be) actualised. If, according to Latour, this program of making the world into a picture was never fully implemented, what effects did the modernist strategies achieve? Actor–network theory shows how social and material processes were always partial and inconsistent and always mixed up with hybrids of humans and non-humans. The questions that remain emerge from the singular dynamics of invocational events, which tend to play out within hybrid assemblages that consistently exceed the event of invocation.

While Heidegger's concepts of the world picture and standing-reserve are initially fruitful, they lack attention to the historical struggles over the constitution of particular standing-reserves. There is no single world picture. There are different possibilities with different implementations of invocational media. In attributing an intrinsic metaphysical bias to technology, Heidegger leaves open political questions, such as the identity of invocational voices. Who is silenced? Who is commanded? What alliances do they form? What codes do they use? Who writes the spells and whose interests do they serve? Who owns and controls the invocable domains? If technology brings new forms of power, what are the possibilities for turning those forms to progressive, or even revolutionary, ends?

Who controls the means of invocation? (Invoking post-Marxisms)

Beyond their early uses in government, science and the military, invocational media quickly proved particularly amenable to capitalism but never without a struggle. With socioeconomic relations already highly abstracted, the capacity to accelerate and automate social actions and transactions afforded further centralisation of corporate power and control. From the 1950s, many business practices were translated and transformed into invocationary events. Therefore, control over the means of invocation became critical to maintaining control over the means of production. At the same time, there has been disagreement among critics of capitalism over how to negotiate invocational power.

In his 1980 book *Architect or Bee?*, Mike Cooley critiques the use of technology in the workplace, arguing that it is often used by managers to reduce workers' control and power. He cites a quote from *Engineer* magazine, 'People are trouble, but machines obey' (p. 96), to summarise this idea. Cooley is also concerned that the use of computers in the workplace can lead to a loss of creativity among workers, as diverse work practices in many fields are converted into forms of computerised production. He asserts that machines extract skills from workers, stating that 'the worker has conferred life on the machine' (p. 9). Cooley's perspective is that technology serves the interests of those who control capital rather than those who work for access to it. He views the development of technology not simply as a pursuit of optimal design but as an ongoing struggle for power.

In the late twentieth century, the place of information technology became more complex as computers became domestic commodities and work tools. Feenberg (2002) observes workers' ambivalence about computers. On the one hand, technology can encode and reproduce relations of domination, alienating workers from their labour. On the other hand, they can be turned to creative and even transgressive uses. In this way, he identifies two conflicting principles applying to computerisation: the 'principle of the conservation of hierarchy' and the 'principle of democratic rationalisation' (p. 92).

When invocational media offered people more autonomy to manage their immediate productive, communicative and organisational practices using the same technology for work, leisure and communication, we might recall Marx's occasional optimism about contradictions in capitalism that allowed technology to be turned to revolutionary ends:

> Modern bourgeois society, with its relations of production, of exchange and of property, a society that has conjured up such gigantic means of production and of exchange, is like the sorcerer who is no longer able to control the powers of the nether world whom he has called up by his spells . . . The productive forces at the disposal of society . . . bring disorder into the whole of bourgeois society, endanger the existence of bourgeois property. (Marx & Engels, 1848)

The early Marx was influenced by the father of French socialism, Saint-Simon, celebrating technological advancement and the command over nature that capitalism was creating (Mitcham, 1994, p. 79). For Marx, the problem with modern machine technology is not in the *forces of production* but the social *relations of production* (Marx, 1867). In this view, capitalists are driven to develop more and more efficient technologies by the need constantly to increase profits. Although technology alienates workers, Marx proposes in the *Grundrisse* (1973) that the powers of capitalist technologies could be turned to bringing the system down and could be redesigned under socialism (Wendling, 2009). Capitalism could build a resource of collective intelligence that he called the 'general intellect', which was embedded in technology and intellectual capital and could dramatically reduce the required working time. There are echoes of this belief in the bourgeois discourses of the microcomputer revolution in the 1970s and the internet in the 1990s, with claims that technology was 'revolutionary' and could produce productivity gains.

In the 1990s, Manuel Castells (1996) claims that computer networks were playing a progressive role for social movements. He argues that the decentralised and horizontal nature of network technologies allows for the emergence of 'networked social movements', characterised by their ability to rapidly mobilise large numbers of people, often around a specific issue or cause. These movements are able to challenge traditional power structures and bring about social change through the use of tactics such as boycotts, protests and other forms of civil disobedience.

Another example of 21st century anti-capitalism is the autonomists, who proposed that the proletariat could use invocational media to organise and communicate independently of corporations and government (Katsiaficas, 2006). Invocationary action could foster new forms of social organisation and resistance. In each of these examples, activists did not see information technologies as inherently capitalistic.

Another turn of the century example of anticapitalism is Barbrook's (2000) proposal for cybercommunism. He suggests that cyber technologies are intrinsically democratic and progressive and are capable of counteracting hierarchies and transforming society. He proposes that the internet fosters a gift economy that resists the 'Californian ideology' associated with the development of cyberculture. Unlike markets, he argues, participants in gift economies receive far more than they contribute. When they do contribute, such as academics publishing research in an open access journal, software writers distributing free software or artists sharing their work, their contributions are rewarded with recognition and career advancement. In a deliberately provocative and speculative text, Barbrook argues that cybercommunism will ultimately prevail, especially in intellectual property domains, because the 'scarcity of copyright cannot compete against the abundance of gifts' (p. 21). He casts the vested interests protecting copyrighted commodities as new Stalinists:

> Across the industrialised world, this conservative appropriation of Stalinism now dominates discussions about the Net. Every guru celebrates the emergence of the new technocracy: the digerati. Every pundit claims that these pioneers of the Net are building a new utopia: the information society. (Barbrook, 2000, p. 15)

Technological-social optimism persists in the 2020s in the peer-to-peer (P2P) movement and in Web3, with some advocating digital media's capacity to transcend capitalism. Michel Bauwens, Vasilis Kostakis and Alex Pazaitis (2019) propose a commons-based future based on P2P arrangements, which they claim can usher in new modes of production. Drawing from examples such as Wikipedia and the freeware software web server Apache, they extrapolate the possibility of revolutionary social change mediated by technology. They claim that with unfettered capacity to connect with others and with shared resources, digital media can foster new forms of property and a new economy. Technical P2P techniques such as file or resource sharing can be transferred into P2P social relations.

However, despite all utopian efforts, progressive uses of invocational media remain marginal. From the lowest level of the invocational assemblage, in the double invocation in the fetch-execute cycle, ideological mechanisms are at work. The user is ideologically fetched and executed before they can even begin resisting. The user always encounters the machine with avocations that address them and prompt them to respond with invocations in terms that reinforce the dominant ideology.

By the mid-2010s, Geert Lovink (2016) argues that everyday social media have reformatted sociality to the point where they are not only ideological but they are themselves ideology:

> Without noticing, we have arrived at a new, yet unnamed, stage: the hegemonic era of social media platforms as ideology . . . The social, political, and economic promise of the internet as a decentralized network of networks lies in tatters. (Lovink, 2016, p. 4)

For Lovink, purely economic critique is no longer sufficient. He turns to Althusser in proposing an ideological process of 'becoming user'. He outlines how a social media initiate completes their profile, chooses a username and password, creates an account and then enters the gateway to the everyday subjectifying processes of participating in social media. Here I will directly invoke Althusser:

> I shall then suggest that ideology 'acts' or 'functions' in such a way that it 'recruits' subjects among the individuals (it recruits them all), or 'transforms' the individuals into subjects (it transforms them all) by that very precise operation which I have called interpellation or hailing, and which can be imagined along the lines of the most commonplace everyday police (or other) hailing: 'Hey, you there!' (Althusser, 1971, p. 18)

Earlier in the book, I argued that invocational media invoke users before users invoke them. I will further pursue this by analysing how the user is called to capitalist ideology. Althusser's concept of interpellation refers to the ideological processes that ameliorate capitalism's contradictions, which would otherwise bring the system down. When applied to invocational media, this suggests that while users are offered invocational power, they are also hailed as subjects by the ideologies implicit in the architectures and operation of these media. Following Althusser, we might see that invocational media serve ideological functions above the machinery of economics and labour. Althusser sees capitalism reproducing itself through a combination of repressive state apparatuses (RSAs) and ideological state apparatuses (ISAs). Undoubtedly, invocational media facilitate the operations of RSAs such as the police, the courts and the military in the mobilisation of surveillance technologies, data analysis and weapons systems. But Althusser would also see invocational media as resources for ISAs in line with other educational, communicational and cultural ISAs. Each of these 'teaches "know-how", but in forms which ensure subjection to the ruling ideology or the mastery of its "practice"' (p. 133).

Following Althusser's logic, using invocational media requires forms of know-how that are ideologically embedded, such as using spreadsheets, e-commerce, and large language models social media. In the process, users are hailed into dominant ideological formations. Acquiring powers of invocation involves knowledge and skills already inflected with ideology, such as running financial data, trading goods or celebrating social media influencers' consumption of prestige brands. These practices offer convenience and entertainment while constituting users as capitalist subjects. There is a paradox, then, in the agency that software offers user subjects:

> If the subject is to some extent constituted in language and code, then to think that someone saying and doing something is a straightforward demonstration of

Invoking Concepts

agency misses the point; language and code constituted them in the first place, and as such the formation of the human subject is always an unfinished project. Interpellation seems to be bound up in contradiction in this respect, poised between the subject that speaks and the subject that is constituted through speech. (Cox & McLean, 2013, p. 5)

Althusser's use of Christianity as the model for interpellation resonates with the religious and magical associations of the invocation. God (or His equivalent) is the ultimate authority in interpellations (pp. 165–8). He exists outside the social field, functioning literally as the last word. He addresses by name individuals who are 'always already interpellated as subjects with a personal identity' (p. 166). Religious intermediaries like Moses, the commandments, rituals of baptism, confirmation and communion mediate His call. But it is the 'Unique, Absolute, Other Subject' (p. 166) who is always ultimately the hailer. His subjects recognise themselves in a 'duplicate mirror structure' (p. 180) of collective recognition through these mutual interpellations. In this sense, there is also a psychological dimension to the interpellated, invoked subject that we will explore in a moment.

The concept of the avocation that I proposed in Chapter 1 owes a particular debt to Althusser's concept of interpellation. At the human–computer interface, interpellation is a precondition for users' invocations in the provision of menus, icons and commands. With these affordances, users are called to constitute themselves as subjects by generating invocations at all levels: precisely technically articulated, experienced fluidly at the second level and embraced discursively and ideologically at the third level. If we accept Althusser's argument, each level – code, interface and conceptual/social relations – is ideological. As I will discuss in Chapter 5, invocational assemblages are producers of subjectivities even more complex, pragmatic and embodied than Althusser's image of subjects submitting to ideology.

However, some argue that changes in the past century have been more than ideological and superstructural but represent changes in actual class structures. McKenzie Wark (2004) would consider the P2P movement as a product of a new class, which she dubs 'the hackers':

We are the hackers of abstraction. We produce new concepts, new perceptions, new sensations, hacked out of raw data. Whatever code we hack, be it programming language, poetic language, math or music, curves or colourings, we are the abstracters of new worlds. (Wark, 2004, paragraph 002)

Wark defines the hacker class by its role in creating new abstractions, such as new intellectual properties, designs, software, stories, images, rituals, techniques, ideas and so on. Like Bauwens et al. (2019), she argues that 'the hacker class can realise . . . that the means are at hand to decommodify information [because] information is the gift that may be shared without diminishing anything but its scarcity' (paragraph 253). However, Wark situates this hope within a more pessimistic analysis of class conflict. She argues that hackers emerged alongside the establishment of a new dominating class called the vectoralists: tech companies, film studios, media oligarchs, drug companies and other corporations that capture and monopolise the hacks – intellectual properties and control vectors of communication such as telecommunications infrastructures, online services and social media. Hackers and vectoralists are mutually dependent but vigorously opposed to one another. Like the capitalist and the worker, they are unequal in power. Vectoralists own the means of communication but depend on the hacker class to create content, innovative ideas and algorithms. Vectoralists commoditise and exploit the hackers' creative work.

While hackers are the conjurors developing invocational and invocable hacks, many work for corporations, alienated from both the capitalists' means of production and the vectoralists' means of communication. Allowing ruling classes to capture and commodify these hacks as property for sale or rent, hackers lack the power to exploit the avocations, invocations and evocations of their design. Vectoralists monopolise access to hackers' work, seeking legal protections of patents and copyrights, exploiting market intelligence and subjecting users to surveillance by using the work of hackers. On the other hand, they secure cash flow by renting access to invocational vectors to markets through advertising, access fees, software licences and subscriptions. Despite the meritocratic myths of capitalism, only a tiny minority of hackers attract venture capital and become vectoralists. Wark's hopes for the hacker class are different from the P2P utopians or the revolutionaries mentioned earlier, relating to hackers' quotidian capacities for expression. An expressive politics is quite abstract: 'It seeks to permeate existing states with a new state of existence. It spreads the seeds of an alternative practice of everyday life' (paragraph 257).

Therefore there is a realpolitik in struggles over who controls invocations. Like the crafty ancient storytellers who sought favour from the powerful through their command over ritual supplications to Muses, programmers script the rituals that generate and protect wealth. While some argue that the internet democratises knowledge, its means of invocation have never been so centralised and hegemonic. Big tech companies control access to the most powerful invocable domains. Over 90 per cent of internet searches invoke Google, while Meta owns three of the top four social platforms: Facebook, WhatsApp and Instagram.

Where Barbrook, the autonomists and Wark see prospects for turning technology to progressive uses, Crary (2022) sees the 'internet complex' as irredeemable. For Crary, despite people's widespread use of the internet at work and play, it is associated with total alienation and the domination of billionaires:

> For the majority of the earth's population on whom it has been imposed, the internet complex is the implacable engine of addiction, loneliness, false hopes, cruelty, psychosis, indebtedness, squandered life, the corrosion of memory, and social disintegration. (Crary, 2022, chapter 1, paragraph 2)

Crary effectively advocates that instead of reforming the invocation, we should move to prioritise smaller-scale face-to-face relationships and interpersonal political organisation:

> [T]he direct encounter between human beings is something other than and incomparable with the exchange or transmission of words, images, or information. It is always suffused with nonlinguistic and non-visual elements . . . It is an immersion, an inhabiting of an atmospherics, affecting every sense, whether consciously or not. This kind of meeting, this proximity, is literally a con-spiracy, a breathing together. (Crary, 2022, chapter 3, paragraph 10)

While this seems to recall Heidegger's preference for traditional technologies and poetic modes of Being, Crary's post-Marxist progressive political project is not a philosophical questioning of technology but rather a form of 'pamphleteering' to challenge the assumption that the internet is inevitably here to stay. He claims there is no place for digital invocations in a post-capitalist world.

Whether it is false consciousness or an authentic desire for self-actualisation through technology, it may be the psychology of the invocation that is the intractable barrier to a rejection of the sociotechnical mode of invocation and its impacts on people and the environment.

What is the psychology of invocations? (Invoking psychoanalysis)

If invocations are media, linguistic, philosophical, ideological and economic events, they are undoubtedly also psychological events. The pursuit of pleasurable invocations is an underacknowledged driving force in the take-up of invocational media, despite its dangers, frustrations and disappointments. In this sense, it invokes not only Freud's pleasure principle but also his death drive: a willingness to take risks repeatedly. For other writers in the broad psychoanalytic tradition, the intangibility of information technology presents psychological challenges. Barglow argues that they affect users' sense of vocation, while Žižek sees them as traumatic in disempowering the repressive but somehow reassuring figure of the Big Other.

After examining these psychoanalytic approaches, I will argue that Deleuze and Guattari's concept of desiring machines that work in concert with economic, material, linguistic, biological and technical machines is more productive in understanding invocational assemblages. Their political and ethical critique of state forms and capitalism exposes how these rationalised hierarchical formations restrict more heterogeneous and productive modes of becoming.

Using invocational media is subject to some particular psychological dynamics. We can start with an idealised sketch of the psychodynamics of second-level invocationary acts. Within an everyday situation of using invocational media, a subject's invocational desire may form as an inspiration, impulse or habit that forms a will to act. The possible action will be informed by the available avocations – the material and software affordances and their relation to the user's cultural and digital capital – that make invocation an attractive option. Composing and initiating the invocation can be a rational act of articulating invocational desires with precision and force, but it could also be habitual or reactive. At this moment of decision, the user performs the material invocationary act with some degree of confidence or hope. After a period from as short as milliseconds to hours or days later, the invocation produces outputs as evidence of some of the invoked events at the first level. In the lifeworld of the user, outputs are perceived events that evoke sensations, meanings and, sometimes, feelings of pleasure. It would be an oversimplification to reduce the affective dimensions in the lead-up to invocation to the action of adrenaline, and the moments of evocation to dopamine, but there is undoubtedly a biological aspect to many invocational experiences.

The everyday experience of actual invocations rarely follows this script, as it is in the medium's character that invocationary acts are highly variable. Most invocationary action is not a series of discrete events but an ongoing flow of invocations, occasionally punctuated by breakthroughs or breakdowns. Human

Invoking Concepts 73

attention in invocationary action is often fragmented, distracted, disenchanted and attracted again, unlike the ideal experience of immersion in a narrative. Developers of invocational texts write for these psychic dynamics, developing the disreputable techniques of clickbait and malware. But even everyday advertisers have become experts in creating texts that are both persuasive and avocational.

Many forms of invocational pleasure have been deplored or pathologised – online gambling, video game playing, porn, social media and trading – because they can be risky and obsessive. Beyond providing moralistic or political economy critiques, we can treat these phenomena psychoanalytically. For Freud (Freud & Gay, 1995a [1920]), the human psyche is driven by two conflicting instincts: *Eros*, which strives for pleasure and the continuation of life, and *Thanatos*, which seeks to return to a state of inorganic matter through aggression and destruction. In this view, the psychology of everyday repetitions of invocations can be associated with this tension.

Even before microcomputers when computing time was exclusive and expensive, many early personal accounts report the pleasures of building and using computers (Abbate, 2010). In the environments of the designers of earlier computers there was space for camaraderie and exploration (Galliers, 2022). Even when data was prepared offline and data processing was performed with gaps of hours between invocations and evocations, computers retained a certain aura. The first computer game, *Spacewar!*, was created when interactive systems like the Digital Equipment Corporation (DEC) PDP-1 became available at MIT. It drew inspiration from science fiction, space exploration and the Cold War and included gameplay that simulated gravity physics (Hong, 2021). In the 1960s art using only ASCII text characters emerged. The early chatbot program ELIZA, which simulated a psychotherapist, was remarkable for the emotional reactions of its users (Natale, 2019). Early internet users formed fan communities on newsgroups such as *rec.arts.startrek* (Jindra, 1994). These playful activities indicate motivations outside work. In Deleuze and Guattari's terms, invocational media are alive with desiring machines.

If computing is stereotypically associated with detached rationalism, invocations are rarely purely instrumental. Drawing on the psychoanalytic tradition, invocations can be seen as connected with the subconscious. Two of Freud's arguments are pertinent: (1) the scientific imagination is informed by the suppressed belief that thoughts can control the world; and (2) even if modern technology addresses the long-standing desire for magical control over the world, it still does not satisfy the psyche.

74 *Invocational Media*

We can relate the psychic roots of invocational media to the disavowed practice of magical thinking. In *Totem and Taboo*, Freud (1950 [1913]) discusses the history of the belief that thoughts change the world – what he refers to as the omnipotence of thought – in animism, religion and science. In animism, he says, people believe in a direct relationship between thought and world. Through sorcery and magic, they directly seek practical ends such as defending themselves or causing injury to their enemies. In the religious stage, people 'transfer it to the gods, but do not seriously abandon it themselves' (p. 103). Freud says they continue to believe in the efficacy of prayer to exert some control over the world. In the scientific stage, though, the belief in the power of thought does not entirely disappear:

> The scientific view of the universe no longer affords any room for human omnipotence; men have acknowledged their smallness and submitted resignedly to death and to the other necessities of nature. None the less some of the primitive belief in omnipotence still survives in men's faith in the power of the human mind, taking account, as it does, of the laws of reality. (Freud, 1950 [1913], p. 103)

This sense of faith in the powers of the mind in the scientific worldview suggests there would be some residual association of invocational media with magical beliefs, considering a sense that invocational media are extensions of the mind. In psychological terms, invocational media offer a means of articulating a desire to control the world and provide a means for some form of immediate satisfaction, following Freud's (1995a [1920]) concept of the pleasure principle. Or if they don't give satisfaction, they continue to promise the possibility of future satisfaction with further invocations – the reality principle.

Freud's (Freud & Gay, 1995b [1930]) later work in *Civilisation and Its Discontents* reasserts the argument that the psychic drives behind modern technology fit within the history of magical thought. He says that in modern life technological innovations fulfil the same long-standing desire previously performed by religion and magic. Science and technology are more effective in fulfilling these desires, to the point where the technologically enhanced man almost becomes a god:

> These things that, by his science and technology, man has brought about on this earth . . . are an actual fulfilment of every – or of almost every fairytale wish . . . Long ago he formed an ideal conception of omniscience and omnipotence

Invoking Concepts

which he embodied in his gods. To these gods he attributed everything that seemed unattainable to his wishes, or that was forbidden to him . . . Today he has come very close to the attainment of this ideal, he has almost become a god himself. (Freud & Gay, 1995b [1930], pp. 737–8)

Freud argues that despite technology's godlike powers, it is never entirely satisfying. People are not entirely happy with becoming a 'prosthetic god' (Freud & Gay, 1995b, p. 738). Technologies give them trouble. As civilisation developed, it systematically repressed individual freedom in the interests of broader values of beauty, cleanliness and order. These social constraints represent a certain 'cultural frustration' of natural instincts, which, Freud (Freud & Gay, 1995) argues, is intrinsic to 'civilisation', but this feeling is responsible for many forms of modern disorder (p. 742).

Frustration is certainly a part of invocational media. Its magic is two steps removed from pure forms of omnipotent thought. First, instead of capturing a thought, it captures only a voice. In technology, that 'voice' is recognised only through input devices (even with neural interfaces). The omnipotence of thought becomes the omnipotence of the voice. Second, this omnipotence is no longer direct and immediate but delegated to something outside (the CPU and its invocable domains) and expressed by an external force (the output devices). The desire for the direct power of magical thought is answered only by gadgetry.

Several writers in psychoanalytic traditions in the early days of the internet saw information technology as presenting something of a crisis for the psyche (Barglow, 1994; Žižek, 1998). Barglow argues that computer systems change the masculine sense of vocation. Before computers, he says, industrial-age machinery maintained a clear separation between a driver and their vehicle. However, for Barglow, the rise in software and decline in hardware has had disturbing psychic implications. When the phallic car is replaced by the computer, he claims there is a psychoanalytic paradigm shift. The psychic relationship with computers is more complex, permeating the boundaries of the self. The computer–user relation fuses and confuses the driver and the car, creating a crisis of authority:

The automobile is an exemplary Oedipal object, especially for men. It fulfils the classical male fantasy of penetration without entrapment: one hurtles through space to one's destination, but one can stop and exit at any time one wants. Conversely, the rage experienced when one's trajectory is impeded expresses a kind of castration. The computer, on the other hand, tends to operate in the unconscious at a more fundamental level, as the pre-Oedipal object related to its user as a mother is bonded to its child before its own boundaries and personal identity have been consolidated. (Barglow, 1994, p. 14)

Barglow illustrates this crisis by comparing two military recruiting advertisements. The first features an image of a man driving a tank. It reads: '18 years old and you're driving 52 tons of steel' (p. 23). In this case, the technology remains a separate entity which 'you' control. The machine remains safely on the other side of the steering wheel.

By contrast, a US Air Force ad that Barglow analyses features a man with a computer. The soldier sits face to face with the mirror-like screen of the computer. The caption reads: 'Technology which lets you program your own destiny' (p. 24). No longer are you just driving a tank, you're shaping your future through programming. The self and machine become interpenetrated. The user and his or her avatar reflect one another, their voices mingling. This new psychic relationship with technology has radical implications for the notion of vocation, he argues: 'the Calvinist notion of calling, to which an individual is predestined, has been replaced here by another, that of self-destination: one is fully responsible for establishing one's identity' (p. 25). Although Barglow doesn't call it this, vocation has become *in*vocation. Users must take responsibility for their own decisions. This is apparent simply in the flashing cursor in the command-line interface that leaves the user to compose the next command. However, prospects for action are increasingly provided as affordances, avocations and auto-invocations – autoplay in YouTube, autocomplete in Google and notifications and alerts, which anticipate, nudge, push or even perform invocations on the user's behalf. Barglow shows that there are not only physical but also psychological shifts when human–technology relationships shift from industrial devices to invocational media.

Slavoj Žižek (1998) argues that the computer-mediated subject in the context of the emerging internet must deal with a loss of the authority of the 'Big Other' – the symbolic father from the original Oedipal myth. Largely because of technological change, says Žižek, the authority of the father figure in contemporary experience is increasingly diminished:

> What occurs in cyberspace is the passage from the structure of symbolic castration (the intervention of the Third Agency that prohibits or disturbs the subject's entry into the symbolic order), to some new post-Oedipal libidinal economy. (Žižek, 1998, p. 484)

But this newfound independence from the father does not bring joy for the subject, says Žižek. The Oedipal relationship endures but in a new form. In cyberspace, where there are fewer rules, a subject still can't get satisfaction. Because cyberspace is only a simulation of the self, it is not as satisfying as direct experience. The subtle interplays of face-to-face encounters are lost (p. 487). The split subject can no longer be sure of who he is or who the person he's engaging with is. This is all made worse by the realisation that even without the constraints coming from the Big Other, the superego is compelled even more strongly to seek pleasure that it is still denied (pp. 488–91). The displacement of the Big Other of newspaper editorials and authoritative newscasters from internet newsgroups and discussions manifests this crisis in pleasure-seeking.

Žižek's (1998) analysis does capture some sense of how subjectivity shifted with the introduction of the internet. For example, when computers were used mainly by large institutions, they generated fears of the Big Other, Big Brother (see Chapter 3). When the invocational assemblage was domesticated, microcomputers seemed to promise so much. However, psychological and affective relationships with invocational systems vary widely. As desirable consumer goods, invocational gadgets can achieve a particular fetish value. But invocational media often generate ambivalence and frustration as part of daily life. Their attraction relates partly to the tension between these feelings.

But Žižek's analysis based on lack, loss and Oedipal families leaves many questions about the precise nature of new forms of subjectivity. His conclusions are inconsistent. At one point, he diagnoses a new condition of 'perversion' (pp. 502–4) that emerges as masochists try to impose new rules on themselves. Later, though, he claims it might bring the 'most radical experience imaginable: the encounter with our "noumenal Self"' (p. 510). Žižek's strict adherence to Lacanian categorisations seems to encourage a conservatism that refuses to see things that might belong outside the schema.

In another of Žižek's (2007 [1997]) articles around that time, he disputes cyberfeminist claims about the multiplicity of new subjectivities in new media. Andermatt Conley (1999) saw his defence of a set of supposedly stable and natural meanings as of form of patriarchal reaction:

> Žižek ... bemoans the loss of Being, but from his own longing for closure – that is, for universal schemas, based on mastery, castration, canonical masterpieces, traditional world-views and stable meaning, freed from processual cyberfeminist experimentations. (Conley, 1999, p. 136)

A similar criticism might be made of Žižek's (1998) article on cyberspace. He ultimately bemoans the loss of the central figure, the Big Other, contending that this loss leads to perversion and deviance. He gives the reader two alternatives: subjecting yourself to a dominating father or sinking into masochistic perversion. Hardly appealing choices!

However, rather than assuming that invocation is based on lack or loss, we can see how invocational desire emerges in other ways. Bataille (2018) rejects Freud's pleasure principle in favour of play. This makes sense when we look at the more complex psychodynamics of digital art, computer games, memes, TikTok, gambling and other creative practice, which thrive on experiences of the playful and the unexpected. Bataille argues that where work seeks 'a useful and probable outcome' (p. 242), play seeks the natural and the improbable. He associates play with 'poetry, the sacred, eroticism, laughter, witticism' (p. 238), which operate before and outside most invocational mediation. They are associated with myths and rituals often in play in games (Hong, 2015). Bataille argues that '[t]he habit of play has entered into human societies through the door of the unconscious' (p. 239), claiming that play cannot be fully understood through science, presumably also suggesting that click-through metrics are no indication of the quality of the psychic experience an online product offers. While science can have some understanding of the biology of pleasure, and the probability of pleasure, says Bataille, the experience of pleasure cannot be reduced to such equations. They cannot be generated except through play's openness to the unconscious and the unexpected.

Alternatively, can we think of invocation as a desiring machine? Deleuze and Guattari's (1983, 1987) concept of the psyche is of heterogeneous productive processes that operate like a panoply of machines connected to one other to produce and channel flows of desire. Desiring machines move across a diversity of fields and pathways and form connections with other machines. In comparison, Freudian Oedipal relation and Lacan's Big Other are arbitrary and limiting diagrams that miss the heterogeneity of the productive forces in the subconscious. According to Deleuze, Freudianism merely offers:

> a theatrical mise-en-scene that substitutes merely representative tokens for the true productive forces of the subconscious. So desire's machines become more and more like stage machinery: the superego, the death instinct, become a deus ex machina . . . machines for creating illusions, special effects. All desiring production is crippled. (Deleuze, 1990a, p. 16)

While psychoanalysis opened up thought about the unconscious, Deleuze argues, it immediately imposed a new order based on family relations (p. 17). This idealism reduced psychic forces to a theatre of the mythical Oedipal family.

The implication is that with the desiring machine, invocations are not addressed to some father figure but to any number of hyperconnected machines.

Deleuze and Guattari argue that 'desiring machines' are immanent to 'great social machines' (1990a, p. 18). In this sense, 'machines' are not only technical apparatuses but also social, linguistic, biological and technical machines that work together and across each other in assemblages (Deleuze & Guattari, 1983). Desiring machines operate within the very logics of capitalism and inside the transformation from disciplinary societies to control societies (Deleuze, 1990B). This conception relates to Barglow and Lacan's analyses of contemporary computer culture but without invoking the Big Other. While there may be play machines, Bataille's opposition between work and play misses the possibility that machines may cross this divide among others.

Therefore, invocational desiring machines mediate high-speed flows and transformations of psychological, social and cultural machines. This energetic but abstract mediator of desiring machines has driven the emergence and proliferation of invocational assemblages, even when these are captured by capitalism or state forms. The psychological dimensions of these assemblages perform invocationary, symbolic and physical actions in the operations of language, media, social power and other machines. The invocational machine can therefore be considered as connected with desiring machines, enjoyment machines, frustration machines and other psychological intensities:

> A machine may be defined as a system of interruptions or breaks (*coupures*). These breaks should in no way be considered as a separation from reality; rather, they operate along lines that vary according to whatever aspect of them we are considering. Every machine, in the first place, is related to a continual material flow (*hylè*) that it cuts into . . . Far from being the opposite of continuity, the break or interruption conditions this continuity: it presupposes or defines what it cuts into as an ideal continuity. This is because, as we have seen, every machine is a machine of a machine. The machine produces an interruption of the flow only insofar as it is connected to another machine that supposedly produces this flow. And doubtless this second machine in turn is really an interruption or break, too. But it is such only in relationship to a third machine. (Deleuze & Guattari, 1983 [1968], p. 36)

The concept of the machine, then, relates not only to the psychic dimensions of the invocational assemblage but also to the heterogenetic histories and practices of media, speech, becoming and class.

How do invocational media operate as machines?
(Invoking Deleuze and Guattari)

> [Deleuze and Guattari] steal from other authors with glee, but they are more than happy to return the favour. Deleuze's own image for the concept is not a brick, but a 'tool box.' He calls his kind of philosophy 'pragmatics' because its goal is the invention of concepts that do not add up to a system of belief or an architecture or propositions that you either enter or you don't, but instead pack a potential in the way a crowbar in a willing hand envelops the energy of prying. (Massumi, as cited in Deleuze & Guattari, 1987, p. xv)

I have already suggested that my approach in this chapter, after Deleuze and Guattari, is to draw on other concepts to situate invocation on its plane of immanence. I have touched on their concepts along the way. However, my selection of concepts is quite different from Deleuze and Guattari's. I have interrogated and extracted concepts from media ecology, speech act theory, Heidegger, Marx and post-Marxists and Freud and others in psychoanalysis. Some of these, such as speech act theory and psychoanalysis, are familiar to Deleuze and Guattari, as are McLuhan and Heidegger more parenthetically. While Deleuze and Guattari perform searing critiques of some work, more often they invoke and reterritorialise it, turning concepts in new directions. Among the most potent of their concepts is the machine.

Where machines are conventionally considered to be mechanisms that repeatedly produce the same thing, Guattari's ontology of production and becoming looks at them as also generating difference and differentiation. Guattari's machine offers a generative resource in creating the concept of invocational media. He develops a broadened (or inverted) concept of the machine throughout much of his work, alone and in collaboration with Deleuze. The concept appears as the 'desiring machine' in *Anti-Oedipus* (1994b [1972]), as the 'machinic assemblage' and 'abstract machine' in *A Thousand Plateaus* (1987 [1980]) and as 'machinic heterogenesis' in Guattari's essay collection *Chaosmosis* (1995a).

For Guattari, the machine is an inclusive concept that encompasses an ultimately infinite multiplicity of productive forces implicated in forming subjects, societies, technical objects and, in fact, anything that comes out of chaos. Against a background of chaotic complexity, some forces have enough regularity to be identifiable as 'machines'. The machine is more than a mechanical entity or technical object; it is:

Invoking Concepts

a material and semiotic assemblage . . . traversing, not only time and space, but also extremely diverse levels of existence concerning as much brain as biology, sentiments, collective investments. (Guattari, 1996, p. 126)

Where Althusser's ideology relies on binary distinctions between imaginary and real relations and class oppositions, Guattari's machines resist totalisation and encompass a far wider range of forces and relationships, addressed in ethico-aesthetic terms. For Guattari, machines are not just cultural and should not be opposed to 'nature'. Geomorphic or astronomical events can be machinic, as much as events that involve instrumental technologies. Talking about machines also avoids privileging structures. Where structures aim to be permanent, machines tend towards their own destruction. Their ontology entails relations with other machines, all of which are constantly undergoing change.

Guattari (1995a) argues that machines are made up of heterogeneous parts – political, technological, semiotic, psychological and economic. The relations of forces between these parts contribute to ongoing processes that produce not only similar things but also different things. Machines incorporate signifying systems such as language but begin with more abstract asignifying systems – the analogue domains of noises and scribblings. Spoken language has subrepresentational components in common with ritual and dance. In the same way, computers are humming, glowing, tactile objects before they are signifying systems. Machines are proto-subjectivities specific to their time and place (Guattari, 1995b).

These regularities are extracted from an overall virtual image of the practice that Guattari (1995a) calls the 'abstract machine'. We can consider the invocation as an abstract machine. It appears in ancient Greece as a mythical relationship between humans and gods, recurs in neoclassical poetry and appears again in the form of the technical assemblage commonly called the interactive digital computer.

To see the practice of invocation return as modern technology does not mean that it is the same as its ancient progenitor. It is not a repetition but a refrain of an abstract set of relationships: a caller, a code, a call, a medium, a non-human other and a summoned effect. The computer gives the abstract machine of invocation an electronic mediatisation. As Deleuze and Guattari (1987, p. 141) observe, the abstract machine is 'the aspect or moment at which nothing but matters and functions remain'.

The matter of invocational media is the givens, or data – which are materialised in computers as invisible binary states of sets of digital switches.

Invocable domains are materials that work with measurable differences in voltage, magnetism, reflectivity or other media that deterritorialise differences of any kind. The functions in this abstract machine are invocations – circuits and software organised into layers of virtualised machines and algorithms that transform states of the data and convert data into perceptible expression. The combination of data as matter and invocations as functions distinguishes the invocational abstract machine.

Reviewing the theoretical literature on culture and technology has provided the basis for constructing a plane of immanence upon which the concept of invocational media could appear. I have drawn from some primary material in the historical and technical literature relating to computers and other technologies. I have extracted several valuable related concepts from this survey of modern theoretical approaches – standing-reserve, world picture, interpellation, magical thought and the order-word machine.

I have used these concepts in developing new concepts relating to invocational media. Invocation itself has become a machine for writing the book. Some writers within media ecology, phenomenology, psychoanalysis, Marxism, psychoanalysis, philosophy and so on offer overarching theoretical programs, but I have added them to the machinic construction of invocational media. If this book has internal consistency, clarity and cohesion, it is appropriate to perform invocations to heterogeneous sets of references, even if some seem incompatible as complete systems.

If this chapter has addressed questions about the invocational media concept by gathering intellectual resources, I now need to explore some narratives of invocational media by drawing on historical sources to recall their changing meanings and mythologies. In the next chapter, I concentrate on third-level invocations – how discourses, metaphors and institutionalisations have informed the identities, representations, production, consumption and regulation of invocational media.

3

Invoking histories

While their basic design has persisted since their emergence in the 1950s, invocational media have continually adopted new metaphors, capabilities and meanings. They have changed dramatically, not only in their technical performance (first-level invocations) and in how they have been experienced as cultural objects and media (second level) but also in how they have been discursively framed and institutionalised (third level). This practice of invoking new functions, experiences and metaphors characterises a medium that has regularly generated new media environments.

This chapter explores associations between the development of invocational assemblages and their historical contexts. It is a partial and impressionistic history of third-level invocations associated with moments and places in computing history. I will show how the association between technologies and their cultural milieux has inflected the dominant narratives of invocational media which can be seen both to reflect and inform the popular culture of the day. These developments have been associated with feelings of exuberance and anxiety, utopian and dystopian narratives and experiences of audiovisual and material cultures.

This chapter tells the stories of particular invocational assemblages, developed between the 1950s and 2020s, and the places, meanings, concerns and situations with which they were associated. These are not always the most technically significant computers, but they are resonant with historical changes in the social and technical milieux at points of change. This is, therefore, a partial, selective and impressionistic account of third-level invocations associated with singular moments in computing history.

In Raymond Williams's (1965) terms, invocational media emerge in relation to the structures of feeling of their day – the prevailing atmosphere, dominant emotions, ways of life, ideologies and moods of places and times:

a particular sense of life, a particular community of experience hardly needing expression, through which the characteristics of our way of life that an external analyst could describe are in some way passed, giving them a particular and characteristic colour. (Williams, 1965, p. 64)

Invocational media emerged during periods of broader cultural and media change. In the examples in each section in this chapter, the popular culture of the day reveals something of the meanings and values in circulation and the dominant cultural and media forms. For example, the literature and cinema of the 1940s used different discourses from 1950s cold war propaganda and different again from print and TV advertising in the 1960s and 1970s. As invocational media increasingly became media in their own right, from the 1980s, these media forms created complex relationships with traditional media.

However, the focus is not purely on the culture of the times, as the cultural histories are closely associated with the conditions that allowed the development of particular invocational media systems. Large-scale technological innovation requires that its advocates tell good stories about a proposed technology as much as proving its technical viability. These stories must be relevant and compelling in the contemporary structure of feeling. Often the stories have been backed up with demos: a type of performance or material rhetoric that stimulates the imagination of those with the power to give the go-ahead for a project.

Technical inventions are created in relation to what already exists. In Simondon's (2017) terms, the process of individualisation emerges in relation to an 'associated milieu' (p. 59). This process is more than the activity of design and manufacture. The viability of an emerging technology depends on what already exists for it to connect to. This includes the built environment, existing artefacts and the natural world. Individualisation and associated milieu are co-emergent:

This individualisation is made possible by the recurrence of causality within a milieu that the technical object creates around itself and that conditions it, just as it is conditioned by it. This simultaneously technical and natural milieu can be called an associated milieu. It is that through which the technical object conditions itself in its functioning. This milieu is not fabricated [*fabriqué*], or at least not fabricated in its totality; it is a certain regime of natural elements surrounding the technical being, linked to a certain regime of elements that constitute the technical being. The associated milieu mediates the relation between technical, fabricated elements and natural elements, at the heart of which the technical being functions. (Simondon, 2017 [1958], p. 59)

So, this will be a history of structures of feeling and associated milieux. This means more than saying technology is socially shaped (Williams & Edge, 1996). Certainly, technology production is a social process of work practices in organisations. More than this, the values, affects and narratives particular to a place and time inform the design and marketing of machines and provide the conditions for consumption. The industries, institutions, technological systems and collective knowledges are significant because they establish the associated milieux that determine the viability of the new technology.

Others have observed that technologies are socially constructed by their consumers. Pinch and Bijker (2012) argue that technology only exists once social groups find uses for it. They argue that technologies change when relevant groups identify problems and negotiate their needs, influencing the future evolution of the artefact. However, Latour (2005) argues that groups are not stable or given; they are always in formation. As discussed previously, invoking subjects themselves are constantly being produced and reproduced as they internalise invocation practices. Invocational media after the 1980s accelerated the production of associated milieux with easily modified and invoked software and affordable consumer hardware. They also accelerated the acceleration process through networks that distributed such software and supported group formation and communication.

As I will discuss later, the evolution of computers can be read conventionally as a history of innovators, institutions and innovations. A history of invocational media, though, focuses on what can be called up: metaphors, discourses and collective imaginaries that inform the thinking and stories told about the technologies: the structures of feeling. It is also a history of an ongoing process of exploitation and construction of associated milieu: the material and conceptual resources called up with invocations. In Table 2, I outline singular historical moments at which particular tropes and meanings emerged with a technological assemblage within an associated milieu, which I explore for the remainder of this chapter.

Overview of this chapter

Before I embark on a longer-form examination of the pivotal moments in this history of invocational media identified in Table 2, I will give a quick overview of the case studies I am going to explore.

86 *Invocational Media*

Table 2 Singular Moments in the History of Invocational Media

Year	Trope	Meaning	Technology	Associated Milieu
1943	Giant brains	Intelligence	Colossus	Code and Cypher School, Bletchley Park
1948	Big Brother	Control	IBM SSEC	New York City
1952	Cold War	Command	SAGE Defence Network	Massachusetts
1965	Minicomputer	Tool	Digital PDP-8	Massachusetts
1984	Information appliance	Commodity	Apple Macintosh	Silicon Valley, California
1993	Virtual space	Immersion	*Doom, Myst* and NCSA Mosaic	Texas, Washington State, Illinois
2000	Networks	Connection	Web 2.0	California
2007	Mapping Katrina	World view	Google Maps, Facebook	Louisiana
2020	Streaming	Ubiquity	Zoom	Global
2022	AI image and text models	Mimicry	Midjourney, ChatGPT	

1943: Colossus, the codebreakers and the individuation of the invocational assemblage

The first story I will tell in this chapter goes back to the earliest days of the invocational assemblage. Identifying a moment and place when invocational media first emerged is notoriously tricky. I could have chosen Babbage's workshop in nineteenth century London or Konrad Zeus's pre-Second World War facilities in Germany, where the Z3 was built. However, I start by examining the narratives of the first invocational machine used in an institutional context: the Colossus, built at Bletchley Park in Buckinghamshire for breaking codes and cyphers (Schmidhuber, 2006). Alan Turing was among the mathematicians and engineers who were recruited based on their reputed intelligence. They were brought to this secret location to help the military collect intelligence. The Colossus would prove it was possible to build a machine that could do complex work that would previously have been considered intelligent. This environment seems to have produced an 'associated milieu that is the condition for the existence for the invented technical object' (Simondon, 2017, p. 59). The experience of those at Bletchley Park raised the possibility that the computer might someday replicate or even exceed human intelligence. In the 1950s, the press dubbed computers 'giant brains', and to this day the question of computer intelligence remains controversial.

1948: Computers become visible but menacing

From 1948, computing machines first became visible to the public, so this section tells the story of the early impressions of these machines. One of the earliest visible computers was the IBM Selective Sequence Electronic Calculator (SSEC), housed in a room with a window that allowed passers-by to see the massive machine through a window on Madison Avenue in New York City. This was a partly electromechanical computer with some degree of programmability that was obsolete almost as soon as it was commissioned. However, the publicity around it established in the public mind the marvellous but intimidating image of large-scale institutional computing. Consequently, a counternarrative emerged that saw these machines threatening peoples' jobs and turning their non-human intelligence to control people through taxation, insurance, policing, banking, warfare and more. The computer was increasingly seen in the dystopian popular imagination as a mysterious, alienating, even totalitarian machine.

1952: SAGE, the Cold War and networked active defence

In the climate of the Cold War, the US Air Force approved the development of a nationwide defence system called Semi-Automatic Ground Environment (SAGE) in 1952. It was controversial whether this 'shield of faith' would ever have achieved its military objectives. Still, it served as a massive form of corporate welfare, helping secure IBM's status as the industry leader and fostering a suite of inventions and a nationwide community of developers. The associated milieux that allowed the development of these invocational infrastructures included the external threat, cold war mobilisation, existing computers like the Whirlwind, and conditions of national prosperity. For decades, SAGE seeded the development of real-time computing, networking and the internet. So, to what extent do ideological traces of their military origins remain embedded in contemporary invocational assemblages?

1965: PDP-8 minicomputer is almost a consumer product

By 1965 when DEC released the PDP-8 minicomputer, structures of feeling had changed in the United States: forms of authority were now being more actively questioned. This machine was enabled by an associated milieu of cheap and accessible componentry and programmers, engineers and hobbyists familiar with electronics and curious about computing. The minicomputer offered a relatively affordable and luggable commodity device that, while not yet personal, allowed small companies and research groups to tinker on their own time rather than time-sharing on large-scale institutional computers. The magic of computing was available 'in the wild' for the first time, soon followed by microcomputers of the 1970s and 1980s like the Altair, TRS-80, Apple II, Commodore Amiga and BBC Micro. These became platforms for hackers and popular electronics enthusiasts more than corporations or the state, allowing them to invoke attachments to other assemblages and even popular culture. Some were recruited into what Deleuze and Guattari referred to as 'war machines' operating outside state or corporate control, forging new lines of flight beyond established territories (deterritorialisation):

> The assemblage that draws lines of flight is on the same level as they are, and is of the war machine type. Mutations spring from this machine, *which in no way has war as its object*, but rather the emission of quanta of deterritorialisation, the passage of mutant flows (in this sense, every creation is brought about by a war machine). (Deleuze & Guattari, 1987, pp. 229–30)

You might recognise the war machine in Wark's concept of the hacker. With the take-up of microcomputers suddenly millions of people experienced the intriguing power of invocation. However, this precarious subjectivity does not escape forces of domination, even with innovations sold as liberating, like the Macintosh.

1984: Macintosh is sold as the computer for the rest of us

When Apple introduced the Macintosh in 1984, it explicitly distanced itself from IBM's computing paradigm and positioned the Mac as being for 'the rest of us'. The graphical user interface (GUI), which is now ubiquitous, established computers as cohesive media production environments for writing, drawing, painting, calculating, playing and hypermedia. Meanwhile, the IBM PC and its compatibles running Microsoft's DOS became the best-selling computers, only confirmed when Microsoft created its own GUI called Windows. Into the 1990s, CD-ROM drives made Macs and PCs media consumption and entertainment platforms. Everyday experiences with what was presented as 'user-friendly', invocational media were becoming integral components in everyday spatial and lifestyle assemblages.

1993: Mosaic, *Myst* and *Doom* create new spatial experiences

In 1993, personal computers reached threshold points in networking, graphics and processing for software that invoked compelling new experiences of virtual space that marked new structures of feeling. NSCA Mosaic, an early web browser, could invoke an information space of internet pages worldwide. Players of the game *Myst* explored a mysterious island rendered in 3D computer-generated images through space and time. *Doom* was the breakthrough first-person shooter which sent its users into demon-infested military bases on the moons of Mars and in hell itself. These engaging spatialised experiences threw users into second-level invocationary action, recalling the cyberspace envisioned by William Gibson and colonisers of virtual reality.

2000: Networks forge connections rather than space

Where the imaginary of invoked spaces fostered alternative spatial experiences, the network concept that became prominent in the 2000s proposed a new ontology based on connections, not space. As Castells (1996) observed, the space of places was being displaced by a space of network flows. Network theorists like Barabási (2002) and Watts (2003) used network data to generate mathematical graphs of network nodes and the edges that connect them, making this new ontology tangible. Informed by data captured from invocational networks like the internet, they extrapolated these data to visualise sociality and social power as patterns of connections rather than as spatial arrangements. Many in the Web 2.0 movement in the mid-2000s embraced an ethos of open networking by opening their sites up to connections from others. However, the experience of the social networking sites that became more popular proved network theorists' 'power law' principle. Over time, the most connected nodes become exponentially more powerful.

2007: Google Earth juxtaposes invoked and lived space

The early colour photographs of earth from space taken in 1968 and 1972 transformed the collective geographic imagination, displacing hand-drawn maps with the tangible witnessing of a photograph (Cosgrove, 1994). The meaning of these images was ambiguous. Cosgrove (1994) argues that for some, these were images of *One World* (p. 271), a territorial claim of the globe in the spirit of American missionary ideology. While this recalled aspirations for empire,

Cosgrove argues that it was something different: 'The globe was newly – and subtly – interpreted as a sign of spatial and social incorporation rather than of direct imperial domination' (p. 281).

It is hard not to notice the similarity between the famous 1972 image of earth from space and the evocative opening screen of Google Earth, first released in 2005. The globe appears against a starry black background and spins until the virtual camera settles over the user's position. The earth pauses until the user enters the name of a location, sending the camera plunging into earth's atmosphere towards the invoked place. This seamless model of the earth offers users endless possibilities to explore a unified and inclusive borderless world brought to you by Google and its advertisers. This navigable image of *One World* reflects the Western worldview that sees the world as a single, integrated system, dominated by global economic and political processes. Everything is supposedly unified and interconnected and can be understood and controlled through the application of scientific and technological knowledge.

In this story, I look at what went wrong in 2007 when images on Google Earth no longer aligned with the lived experience of people on the ground. With smartphones and apps like Google Earth, people were becoming adapted to everyday juxtapositions of invocations against the phenomenal world: maps, social media, control panels, smart homes and so on. In this structure of feeling, invocational powers reassuringly accompany users wherever they go. This is all fine until errors, incompatibilities, power outages or other failures interrupt the flow of invocationary experience. These first-level failures intrude on user experience as glitches, crashes or complete shutdowns that undermine faith in invocation.

2020: Streaming media were embraced during the pandemic

With shutdowns of cities and countries in the early stages of the Covid-19 pandemic, the infrastructure of invocational media supported an adaptation to the new conditions of home isolation. People adapted their everyday routines to the new conditions, in which with Zoom and other software, homes became primary workplaces or classrooms. At the time, access to the internet was no longer confined to computers, with peoples' smart TVs, smartphones, smart homes and the internet of things already becoming invocational. Entertainment and social connection applications such as Instagram, TikTok, Twitter, Netflix and Facebook were eating into the time of other media and everyday practices. The home was increasingly a codespace (Kitchin and Dodge, 2011), with many everyday practices reliant on invocational systems. As we emerged from the pandemic with vaccines and antivirals, our relationship with invocational media had shifted, and the habits formed under lockdown persisted in many ways.

2022: Midjourney, DALL•E 2 and ChatGPT mimic human creativity

The story of AI has famously been marked by periods of great optimism and growth and periods of disillusionment when funding dried up and projects were abandoned: AI springs and winters. This dynamic was accentuated by regular failures in the quixotic quest for 'strong AI' – a device that matches or exceeds human-level intelligence. This has been a distraction for philosophers and AI scientists who have taken the intelligence metaphor too literally, rather than seeing the AI industry as making various attempts at invoking intelligence. Actual AI research has not followed a linear path towards strong AI. Rather it has pursued a diversity of approaches, each with its own conceptual paradigm, strategy and metaphors. Their actual results were mixed. During the 2010s, equipped with much more powerful computers, AI developers got promising results using neural net and deep learning techniques with real-world applications in personalised advertising, music recommendation, face recognition, fraud detection, voice assistants and autonomous driving.

But 2022 was something of a breakthrough year with the widespread popular uptake of AIs such as DALL•E 2 and Midjourney, which could generate images from a text prompt, and ChatGPT, which could write original texts that passed as human-like writing. These produced both exuberance and alarm as they seemed either to empower everyone to make art, or threatened to decimate the human creative industries.

The remainder of this chapter explores in more detail these singular moments in the history of invocational media to tell stories about significant invocational assemblages and the structures of feeling, associated milieux, institutions and conceptual paradigms with which they were associated.

1943: Giant brains

A collie emerges from the dark waters of a freezing river, shakes herself dry and continues her courageous journey. The dog has a look of tired determination. She must navigate hundreds of miles across the Scottish and English countryside to find the family that sold her because they were too poor to keep her. In the classic 'family' film *Lassie Come Home*, released in 1943, this dog embodied humanistic virtues of courage, loyalty and intelligence.

In the Lassie narrative, the dog passed as a hero on an epic adventure, a role conventionally played by humans. But that's not all. The movie production took place in the United States because England was at war. The scenes of English countryside were shot in Washington state. The Pacific Northwest was passing as Yorkshire. What's more, the female dog who was to play Lassie was unreliable and started losing her hair, so the filmmakers switched her with her stunt double, Pal. So, Lassie was a male dog passing as female. Everything about the Lassie story seemed to be masking a world of shifting identities: things becoming something else.

If a real Lassie had got very lost in 1943, she might have come across an unassuming collection of buildings at Bletchley Park, north of London. The Special Operations Executive had called these grounds the Government Code and Cypher School, but it was also known as Station X. Inside the buildings were a number of early computers, including the mechanical 'bombes' used for breaking German codes from 1940, and soon, the Colossus, the first large-scale electronic computer to go into service (Copeland 2006). This was a special-purpose code-cracking machine used to decrypt messages sent by the German command using a cipher that the British codenamed 'Tunny' (Proudfoot & Copeland, 2019). The Colossus took its name from one of the wonders of the ancient world: the Colossus at Rhodes – a huge bronze statue built in the second century BCE to honour the sun god, Helios. This modern allusion to an ancient engineering feat reflected the classics educations of the researchers who created it. It hinted, indeed with some irony intended, that the designers were aware that making a thinking machine was to invoke the gods.

Like Lassie, Colossus was becoming an intelligent non-human. Colossus automatically performed cryptographic analysis that was otherwise performed by *human* computers. For the engineers and mathematicians who built it, intelligence was highly prized. In one sense, their work was to collect intelligence by cracking cryptography to reveal the enemy's plans. In another sense, the codebreakers were war heroes respected for their superior human intelligence. The complexity of the problems they were solving and the sophistication of the machine itself became a testament to their superior intellect. It seemed only natural for Turing, the most renowned team member at Bletchley Park, to perform a thought experiment less than a decade later positing that computers

Invoking Histories

93

might supersede their creators in the hierarchy of intelligence. However, unlike box-office hit *Lassie Come Home,* all this early work on invocation at in Bletchley Park remained a state secret for generations.

But less than a year after the war ended, the US developers of the world's first programmable, electronic general-purpose digital computer decided to go public. On 15 February 1946, the press was invited to the dedication of a computer called ENIAC at the Moore School of Electrical Engineering at the University of Pennsylvania. Mathematician Arthur Burks demonstrated how ENIAC could perform in seconds a calculation that would take humans days to complete. Newspapers worldwide reported the event, using anthropomorphic metaphors in describing ENIAC variously as an 'electronic brain, magic brain, wonder brain, wizard, and man-made robot brain' (Martin, 1995). A few months later in the UK, the world press covered a speech given to the British Institution of Radio Engineers on 31 October. The speaker was Rear Admiral Louis Mountbatten, who announced, 'It is now considered possible to evolve an electronic brain which will perform functions analogous to those at present undertaken by the semi-automatic portion of the human brain' (Proudfoot & Copeland, 2019, p. 26). Mountbatten's speech is full of third-level metaphoric invocations: evolution, the human brain and machine functions that are analogous to biological semi-automation. Despite the efforts of people like the renowned mathematician D. R. Hartree insisting in a newspaper headline 'The "Electronic Brain": A Misleading Term; No Substitute for Thought' (Martin, 1995, p. 6), this misleading metaphor persisted.

As discussed in Chapter 1, in the following years, even those familiar with these machines began using brain or intelligence metaphors in public. Von Neumann's (1958) *The Computer and the Brain,* a book aimed at popularising the new technology, directly invokes the brain and nervous system. He doesn't mention 'thinking' or 'intelligence' but rather 'operations' (p. 67), 'electrical pulses' (p. 66) and 'memory organs' (p. 96). His analogies, such as 'nerve impulses' (p. 108) and the 'unknown memory subassembly in the nervous system' (p. 139), are early examples of bio-inspiration. Von Neumann does not make a special claim about AI but implies that computers and brains can be likened to each other and may ultimately converge.

The more speculative 'artificial intelligence' project was famously articulated by John McCarthy, Marvin Minsky, Nathaniel Rochester and Claude Shannon (2006 [1955]) as a provocation for a 1956 summer research meeting at Dartmouth College in New Hampshire. The program of the meeting was ambitious, making the 'conjecture that every aspect of learning or any other feature of intelligence can in principle be so precisely described that a machine can be made to simulate it . . . [to] use language, form abstractions and concepts, solve kinds of problems now reserved for humans, and improve themselves' (McCarthy et al., 2006, p. 12). They identified themes, some of which persisted, such as automatic computation, programming, neural nets, self-improvement, abstraction, randomness and creativity.

Turing's (1950) essay 'Computing Machinery and Intelligence' takes up the philosophical question about intelligence directly, sharing his belief that there was no reason it would not be possible to create machine intelligence. His proposed manner of determining intelligence is his famous 'imitation game' that asked participants to judge whether they were interacting with a machine or a human. For Turing this was the preferred way to evaluate whether a machine could pass as a human. The imitation game was never really treated as a scientifically disprovable proposition. It served as a rhetorical intervention in the public imagination, a gamified provocation about the future invocation of intelligent linguistic behaviour. The challenge remained popular for decades, and in 1991 a Turing test-like competition called the Loebner Prize was announced, asking chatbot designers to create a system that could fool judges into thinking they were communicating with a human. It had mixed success.

In the years since, despite AI researchers conceiving of their work in many different ways (see Table 3), and despite the criticisms by Searle and Dreyfus in Chapter 1, AI became an aspirational but flexibly defined program with a concept powerful enough to drive desiring machines that attracted communities of researchers and funding, despite some periods of so-called AI winters. But in the 2010s AI applications such as image and speech recognition, medical diagnosis, fraud detection, music recommendation and personalised advertising demonstrated a new generation of techniques for training software to identify patterns in the world by invoking AI models built with massive training sets gathered from the internet. In the 2020s, AI language models like OpenAI's Generative Pretrained Transformers (GPT-1, 2, 3, 4 and beyond) implicitly challenged readers to distinguish the text they generated automatically from text written by a human.

By the 2020s, recurrent neural nets were achieving greater success in natural language processing and could perform passable simulations of natural language translation and open-ended conversations. In November 2022, OpenAI released ChatGPT, which demonstrated a capacity to generate original text in various

Table 3 Metaphors of Machine Intelligence

Invocation	Characteristics
Calculator	Performs numerical calculations and mathematical operations. Blaise Pascal's seventeenth-century mechanical calculator was designed for applications such as tax collection.
Engine	Babbage's nineteenth-century designs for the Difference Engine and Analytical Engine envisaged the 'execution' of calculations of numbers and data by steam (Jones, 2016; Swade, 1991).
Weaving	Ada Lovelace used automated looms as a metaphor for the operations of Babbage's machine: 'We may say most aptly that the Analytical Engine weaves algebraic patterns just as the Jacquard loom weaves flowers and leaves' (Kim & Toole, 1999).
Behaviour	Turing's 'Computing Machinery and Intelligence' (1950) suggests machine intelligence is proven if the 'average interrogator' could not reliably tell the difference between a human and a machine.
Nerve cells and brains	Von Neumann's *Computer and the Brain* (1958) directly compares the design of the computer with human nerves and organs.
Symbol manipulation	Traditional AI uses algorithms to mimic human thought, based on the assumption that intelligence can be understood and replicated with logical steps and rules.
Expertise	Expert systems (usually a form of symbolic AI) apply systems of rules to model reasoning processes, simulating expert practices of solving domain-specific problems such as medical diagnosis.
Emergent behaviour and evolution	'Artificial life' researchers create simulations of simple organisms that interact in complex ways within an invoked environment. Through 'evolutionary' processes of variation and selection, they claim to produce best adaptations and emergent intelligence (Langton, 1996; Emmeche, 1994).
Embodied intelligence	Rodney Brooks (1991) proposes to design robots with 'bottom-up' intelligence using simple robots with sensors and motors that allow them to behave in intelligent ways in interacting with their environment.
Machine learning	Machine learning involves systems that learn from data and make predictions or decisions without being explicitly programmed.
Neural networks	Artificial neural networks are a special kind of machine learning algorithm modelled after the structure and function of the human brain. They consist of interconnected 'neurons', which are used to process and transmit information (Guerney, 1997).
Language	Language models such as GPT-3 and GPT-4 are a form of neural network trained to generate text based on patterns and structures in large datasets of human-generated text. They can perform tasks such as text completion, translation, question answering and summarisation. Their goal is to generate text semantically and grammatically similar to the text in the training corpus.

genres based on a simple text prompt. This invoked a language model based on a vast training set of examples of other peoples' writing. In another medium, DALL•E 2, Midjourney and Stable Diffusion created images that passed as original artworks. Still, again, this inhuman creativity was based not on copying other peoples' work but on invoking it from an AI model trained on the uncredited creative works of millions of writers, photographers and visual artists.

AI should never be considered a replication of human intelligence, buts its invocation through a diversity of techniques. Computers might have been roughly modelled on von Neumann's image of the brain, and they might perform some forms of labour previously performed by humans, but they are not equivalent to humans. They are invocational assemblages. Invoked intelligence is only one set of many invocational projects. Undoubtably, AI and invocational media more broadly have led some to question the unique status of the human. As computers have taken up powers of perception, surveillance, labour and control, these machines have often engendered feelings of being under threat.

1948: Big Brother's data processor

Contrary to the doctor's advice, George Orwell sits up in bed in a small cottage on a remote Scottish island, typing the final manuscript of another novel (Meyers, 1985). He has yet to decide on its title. It will either be *The Last Man in Europe* or *1984*. In this novel he develops an image of a dystopian world in which technology serves a totalitarian regime. In the world of the novel every room has a two-way telescreen that watches the residents and supplies an endless stream of images. Every utterance, every movement, every thought takes place under the eye of Big Brother. This image of totalitarian control draws from Orwell's own experiences in boarding school, his observations of bureaucracies and political movements, the histories of fascism and Soviet communism (Meyers, 1985) and Samuel Butler's (1863) speculations about the human species being succeeded by machines. The novel *1984* provided a nightmare vision of centrally managed and technologically augmented oppression based on a doubled asymmetrical invocation: the invocation of the image of Big Brother and the invocation of the individual, observed and being fed images through the two-way telescreen device.

Across the Atlantic, in January 1948, IBM launched the SSEC, a showcase machine built in less than two years after its initial plans were drawn up. This was a hybrid electronic and electromechanical computer with the innovative capacity to operate in random sequence (McPherson, Hamilton & Seeber, 1982 [1948]). It was one of the first large-scale commercial computer systems, and although it was a one-off, it would be seen as a precursor to the IBM 701, IBM 650 and System/360 that sustained three decades of IBM's domination of the computing industry. While the SSEC's design was not as influential as EDVAC's, and it was never produced in numbers like UNIVAC, it was the first electronic computer built without involvement from a university. The SSEC's most potent influence, though, was on the popular image of this machine (Bashe, 1982).

The SSEC was a public spectacle installed in a store window on the corner of Madison Avenue and 57th Street in New York City. Its bulky components and the flashing lights of its memory registers were visible to all passers-by. For IBM, it stood as a metonym for American science and progress. The company allowed scientists to use the machine for worthy purposes. Among the tasks it performed was calculating the earth and the moon's relative positions for years ahead. NASA later used these calculations in planning and executing the Apollo moon missions. However, the SSEC had more menacing undertones for some of the people on the street. The mysterious giant brains of governments and corporations seemed to be electronic incarnations of Big Brother.

Over the following decades, computers and robots became symbols of anxieties about technocratic domination. Without directly using invocational media, people were ambivalent, aware of their possibilities but wary about their inhuman power. The punch card's famous inscription 'Do not fold, spindle or mutilate' spoke in the paternalistic and mildly threatening voice of big government and big business. The cards and paper tapes used in these early large-scale invocational systems were a legacy of industrial-age surveillance and control technologies: the Jacquard loom (1805), Babbage's design for the Analytic Engine (1832) and the Hollerith Tabulator used for counting the US census (1890). In 1911, Hollerith's company merged with three others to form International Business Machines (IBM). His electromechanical card equipment continued to be the core of IBM's business well into the 1960s, when cards were still used as a means of computer input, output and storage. Many computer workers' jobs involved the tedious job of moving decks of cards between special-purpose machines that punched, sorted, collated, verified or multiplied the details stored on the cards. They then read the results from dials on each machine, screens or printouts (Shurkin, 1996 [1984], pp. 66–92). Many operators' work was not much different from work on a production line that made cars or weapons.

Another metaphor emerged with the practice of managing data using large stacks of punch cards – that of 'data processing'. This concept constructs data as raw materials comparable to iron ore or cotton fibre in mining or agriculture. The etymology of 'data' is the Latin for 'given', but this is inaccurate, as data are not given but taken. Data for processing are metaphorically raw materials, mined or harvested, refined, analysed and transformed into knowledge in the form of reports. The term 'data processor' was appropriate to the bureaucratic organisations which used these early computers. But there was a trade-off that processors demanded for being able to process data in such volume: all aspects of the world needed to be defined according to the positions of holes on cards. In Heidegger's (1977a) terms, all aspects of the world become standing-reserve. Anything unique or qualitatively different was discarded from the calculation or translated to the nearest available value. The 'data processor' performed as industrial equipment for handling transactions, manufacturing operations, prediction models, people's attributes and many other phenomena. But unlike raw materials, many records are not interchangeable, and their handling can enable social domination.

Orwell himself seemed to believe in the technical perfectibility of oppressive technologies. His nightmare vision supposed that mechanisms of total control – political, technological and psychological – were possible, if not already in place (Bolton, 1984). *1984* became the definitive totalitarian dystopia, often invoked to resist technologies or totalitarianism (Davies, 1992). Anxiety about the social risks of technology was heightened because many computer-related institutions had a guarded culture that maintained strict policies of secrecy (Edwards, 1996). Government, the military and corporations depend on security systems to maintain secrecy from criminals, enemies and competitors.

The systems criticised for breaching privacy in the 1960s and 1970s were trifling compared to the infrastructures available from the 2000s. Batch processors of the 1960s lacked the real-time invocational relationship that came with the interactive systems that emerged gradually from the late 1960s. Long-term storage was held in linear devices like punch card stacks and magnetic tape. The real magic of invocational media came with 'real-time', 'live' interactive computing, which took thirty years to move slowly out of the military into the mainstream.

From the 2000s, the 'big data' concept was taken up with new vigour. Unlike the smaller industries of traditional local databases with standard ways of querying the data, big data brought next-generation AI technologies to extremely large volumes of unstructured data. These data are accumulated in networked invocable domains in a world saturated by invocational assemblages, from the biggest cloud service to the most remote mobile device. Big data are the purview of economic, military and political power. Thatcher, O'Sullivan and Mahmoudi (2016) propose a new metaphor: that big data should be considered a form of dispossession. They argue that rather than accepting the celebratory myth of the 'frontiers' of technology, we might acknowledge forms of colonial violence implicit in its extraction. This violence has involved both corporate and state power.

While the twenty-first-century tech sector is presented as an icon of the free market, invocational media owe a significant debt to government funding, universities and the military–industrial complex, a debt that grew during the Cold War.

1952: Panic stations: SAGE and real-time computing

16 April 1952 – Hundreds of US Air Force pilots scramble to their jets. Gunners run to anti-aircraft batteries. There is a general alert called after reports from Alaska and Maine of unidentified aircraft approaching. Confusion and fear shake the chain of command. Telephone and telegraph links aren't giving commanders an adequate picture of the evolving situation. It turns out to be a false alarm. Still, this incident intensifies a desire within the military to automate the invocation of command and control over defence systems and the nuclear missile arsenal. It is emblematic of the structure of feeling of the Cold War, anti-communist paranoia and the constant sense of threat in the atomic age.

Over the previous two decades, leaders had turned to technology as never before. Military needs had driven technological innovation many times before but never at such a scale or pace. The Manhattan Project's design of nuclear weapons was the most high-profile invention, but its associated milieu contributed to the establishment of computers for cryptography, trajectory calculations and modelling nuclear reactions, as discussed in the previous section. ENIAC was built primarily for producing artillery firing tables for the US Army. John von Neumann was among the most prominent men in the early development of nuclear weapons and computers (Aspray, 1990; Aspray & Burks, 1987; Macrae, 1999; Rheingold, 2000 [1985]). He led a team that used ENIAC to calculate the geometry of implosive lenses in the atomic bomb (Aspray, 1990, p. 28) and used the Air Force's MANIAC computer to simulate the chain reactions in hydrogen bombs (Aspray, 1990, p. 47). As a consultant and 'Cold Warrior' in the late

1940s, he encouraged several branches of the military and government to build more computers, including the RAND Corporation's JOHNNIAC, University of Illinois's ILLIAC and ORACLE at Oak Ridge, Tennessee (Aspray 1990, p. 56). Contributing to developing the hydrogen bomb, he strongly advocated its use against the Soviet Union.

Defending against Soviet nuclear weapons became a technical and political spur to build computer-based 'active defence' systems that extended perception beyond the horizon and accelerated command. Following the Japanese surrender, it had seemed that the atomic bomb and rocket technology from ex-German scientists would give America nearly unlimited global military power. Nuclear weapons gave US commanders godlike destructive power. In the mid-1940s, Colonel Gervaise Trichel, an amateur classics scholar, named the 'Nike' missile after the Greek goddess of victory, setting a precedent for naming missiles, rockets and computers after mythological figures – Atlas, Apollo, Triton and so on (Bruce-Briggs, 1988, p. 47). However, there were non-believers: after the first test of the atomic bomb in New Mexico in 1945, codenamed Trinity, Oppenheimer famously invoked the *Bhagavad Gita:* 'Now I am become Death, the destroyer of worlds' (Goodchild, 1985). Even President Eisenhower (1961) warned about the influence of the 'military–industrial complex', saying there was a 'potential for the disastrous rise of misplaced power'.

And yet, the inertia of the associated milieu of wartime innovations, fuelled by fear of nuclear annihilation and a desire for economic development, became irresistible. Calling for active defence was not just an invocation of technology as saviour but also an invocation of the threat of communism to justify rearmament and corporate welfare. The Air Force's requirements were set by the fear of hundreds of nuclear bombers flying from the USSR over the Arctic Circle. Commanders insisted that weapons systems needed to work inside a slender window of time and across the extensive space of a global exchange of nuclear weapons. To sense low-flying bombers, there was a need for many interconnected radar stations. These requirements drove the development of reprogrammable real-time digital computing applications and complex communication infrastructures. As well as being a weapons system, this was a medialogical process, '*media driven* and *media dependent*', that invoked images of enemies' presence and analysed them in new ways (Packer & Reeves, 2020, p. 6).

The flagship project of the era was the SAGE, a massive computerised defensive system commissioned by the US Air Force and built between 1952 and

1961, costing four times more than the Manhattan Project. It used huge IBM computers at multiple sites to manage continental air defence, invoking data in real time from multiple radar installations to sense enemy aircraft and to issue commands to fighters on where to intercept the attackers (Edwards, 1996, p. 94). SAGE was designed to invoke a unified symbolic domain that create a real-time convocation of perception and action for commanders. It supposedly reduced the intercontinental battlefield to data and fields of action to commands. Some observers within the military were sceptical when SAGE was first proposed because of its seemingly magical claims. They argued that defending the entire United States from Soviet nuclear attack was impossible because of the scale of the continent and the speed and number of incoming bombers and missiles. General Hoyt Vandenberg complained:

> the hope has appeared in some quarters that the vastness of the atmosphere can in a miraculous way be sealed off with an automatic defence based on the wizardry of electronics. (as cited in Edwards, 1996, p. 95)

Despite some resistance, SAGE was funded and sold to the press and politicians as a 'shield of faith' (Bruce-Briggs, 1988). Faith indeed. The US government spent $8 billion in the project's first ten years (Winkler 1997). The legacy of miniaturisation and networking for SAGE eventually became commoditised as integrated circuits, the internet and many other technologies (Bruce-Briggs, 1988; de Landa, 1991; Edwards, 1996; Winkler, 1997).

Although there was never a nuclear attack from the Soviet Union to test it, it was unlikely that SAGE would be very effective as a defence system against ICBMs. The influential US military strategist Bernard Brodie saw SAGE as a grand tribute to the general faith in technology:

> That is not to say that effective active defences against the missile are technically impossible, or that their development should not be pursued; it is only to point out that one must have extraordinary faith in technology, or a despair of alternatives, to depend mainly on active defences. The relevant problems are political and social as well as technological. (as cited in Bruce-Briggs, 1988, p. 431)

The faith in active defence, alongside a preference for deterrence, drove the massive government investment in weapons in the United States and the USSR for decades. Computer-based systems came to analyse satellite-gathered intelligence images and triangulated positions of multiple objects on a global battlefield. Electronic battlefield systems developed from the end of the Vietnam War modelled battlefields in real time. By the 1990s and 2000s, commanders in the wars in the Persian Gulf and Afghanistan could observe virtual effigies of the forces and territories. The dream was to overcome the 'fog of war' by mapping the field of battle as real-time simulations. The commander could invoke a master view through which to perceive and act in this virtual field.

In the 2010s, DARPA claimed that this 'master view' approach was too rigid and proposed the 'Mosaic Warfare' concept that used distributed and interconnected 'sense-decide-and-act systems across a wide number of platforms' (DARPA, n.d.). Imagining solutions of covering the battlefield with a flexible mosaic of randomly chosen elements, rather than a puzzle that needs to be laid across the map and solved, this approach suggested a more decentralised and semi-automated cloud computing paradigm. Command would operate invocationally to draw upon sensors and processors distributed across the battlefield and convocationally to communicate tactical and even strategic decisions to dispersed forces. This apparently aesthetically and ethically considered reconfiguration of the imagined battlefield is just another iteration of the military–industrial complex turning to invocational media for potential for organised violence.

At another level, despite its unprecedented scale and its instrumentalism, SAGE's invocations reflected an older desire among leaders for magical perception and ritual command. Functionally, technologists are modern equivalents of shamans and magicians. Despite their very different training and culture, and the efficacy of their technologies, they serve the power of the state by offering special and secret knowledge of materials and techniques in return for resources and respect.

If magic and high technology have so much in common, why is there such an apparent distance between the two? This categorisation is recent, as alchemy, magic, magnetism and electricity were indistinguishable from science until well into the nineteenth century. This may be why modern scientists firmly positioned themselves as adversaries of magic and superstition. As we saw in Chapter 2, Latour (1993) refutes this distinction between magic and modern beliefs. He argues not that scientific modernism should be resisted, nor that we are beyond the modern era, but simply that modernity never actually happened. He argues that the Western modernist project created two 'Great Divides', the first separated 'Nature and Culture' (p. 99). Objective knowledge of science was partitioned from other forms of knowledge, which became diminished as cultural and subjective. Scientists claimed authority over this special type of knowledge by forming special

Invoking Histories

relationships with non-humans: technological apparatuses in the laboratory such as the vacuum flask and special methods such as the experiment.

The second divide identified by Latour was even more significant. It separated the West from all other cultures, distant and past:

> They do not claim merely that they differ from others as the Sioux differ from the Algonquins, or the Baoules from the Lapps, but that they differ radically, absolutely, to the extent that Westerners can be lined up on one side and all the cultures on the other. (1993, p. 97)

The moderns drew a fundamental opposition between technologies like SAGE and missiles, on one side, and magical seers and shamans, on the other. At best, primitive magic was an anthropological curiosity; at worst, it was evil primitive superstition. This essentialising of the superiority of modernity and the Christian mission justified colonialism and racism. Latour advocates a symmetrical anthropology that eliminates the epistemological breaks between nature and society, subjects and objects and modern and ancient technologies. Ritual practices are ritual practices, he says, whether their efficacy is judged in magical or scientific terms. This is not to say that SAGE is technically comparable with the magic of seers, but both can be compared without an uncrossable line. Their difference is in scale and speed, not kind.

The technological imaginary is close to the magical imaginary. Modern 'scientific' methods may be larger and more reproducible than magic, but the pragmatic, political, ritualistic, affective dimensions of primitive artefacts still inhabit the new technologies. Like modern technologies such as SAGE or the digitised battlefield, a leader's use of the magical imaginary responds to fears of enemies, anxiety about mortality, wishes for protection and guidance and desire for effective command. To cleanly partition off modern practices from the primitive is to downplay the political complexity, messiness, irrationality and sheer horror of contemporary war. We can also see links between magic and technology in popular culture such as science fiction and video games. For example, *Dark Messiah of Might and Magic* players choose magic over sheer firepower because it is more effective in the game. Weapons in *Final Fantasy XIII* include both science and magic. On the one hand, there are 'gravity bombs', and on the other, there are 'manadrives' that perform powerful natural magic. Here tropes from both militarism and magical thinking are in play.

Despite the automation of weapons systems, maintaining command relies on removing resistance from those to be commanded. The will and charisma of a commander call on highly ritualised practices tuned to retain cohesion and responsiveness in the face of crisis and chaos. Military discipline is established through rites of institutionalised humiliation, honour and camaraderie. Before soldiers can be trained, they must be broken down. A motto in basic training in the US Marine Corps is: 'One must first be stripped clean. Freed of all the notions of the self' (Gabbard & Saltman, 2011, p. 8). These conditions were as true in the development of SAGE as they were for rulers in the Middle Ages when magic and science were relatively indistinguishable.

The most significant legacy of SAGE was fostering associated milieux for the future development of invocational media. For example, SAGE established the groundwork for making core memories, which ensured IBM's broader dominance of the industry (Ceruzzi, 1998, p. 53). Many of SAGE's components – real-time computing, networking, projectile tracking – were applied elsewhere. This investment also fostered cultural and social capital. Bureaucracies and chains of command developed into networks of collaboration and competition in the civil world.

A key question for contemporary culture is the extent to which this legacy of the military taints contemporary invocational media. Are today's technologies marked by the material, ideological and mental legacies of the technologies and structures of feeling formed in the development of computing? Crogan (2011) argues that war, simulation and technoculture are implicitly interwoven, as seen in the hardware, software and aesthetics of many contemporary video games. He points to the links between the military–industrial complex and the military–entertainment complex. In the case of SAGE, the influence on the wider culture was quite direct, as MIT's intellectual work was put to work in an online reservations and transactions system called Semi-automated Business Research Environment (SABRE) for American Airlines (Beck & Bishop, 2016). Invocational assemblages would soon be moving from centres of calculation into public and domestic spaces.

1965: Seductions of the mini

18 September 1965 – Captain Tony Nelson, a NASA astronaut, is forced to eject from his Mercury-type spacecraft when the third-stage rocket misfires. The telemetry systems tracking the ship's re-entry malfunction, and the ground station loses sight of the capsule. It lands on an island in the South Pacific, and the

Invoking Histories 105

astronaut is stranded, outside of communications range. Waiting for the search and rescue team, he explores the area and finds an exotic and ornate bottle. When he picks it up and rubs it, a strange pink smoke emanates from the stem and materialises into a blonde woman in a harem pants. He has rescued the bottle's inhabitant, Jeannie, from a 2,000-year-old curse. She kisses him passionately, but at first, he can't understand her, until he mumbles that he wishes she could speak English. His wish is granted, and she responds in English. His next wish is for a rescue helicopter, and one appears immediately. Realising he couldn't explain this to his superiors, he sets Jeannie free. However, she insists (for some reason speaking in medieval English), 'Thou hast set me free, master. Now I belong to thee.' She returns to her bottle and surreptitiously smuggles herself back to the United States. This strange juxtaposition of ancient magic, space age technology and middle-class suburban lifestyle became the pivotal premise for the 1960s sitcom series *I Dream of Jeannie*. Jeannie's naive love and secret magical powers constantly show up the plodding bureaucratic high-tech world of NASA.

Jeannie herself was a tame version of the jinnis in the original story known as 'Ala al-Din and the Wonderful Lamp'. The story is one of many that circulated for centuries in oral cultures in the Middle East, but these were translated into French and English in the late nineteenth century and published as *One Thousand and One Nights*. The story of Aladdin became a favourite in children's books and Hollywood movies. By the time it reached network television, the genie had mutated from 'an Ifrit of terrifying appearance [that surged] out of thin air . . . his vast black head scraping against the ceiling' (Mathers, 1949, p. 538) into a blonde woman in a pink midriff top. Television had transformed the huge, black, male, Arab figure of the stories into a petite woman in pink and maroon pantaloons. Magic was no longer the dangerous, foreign and fearful prospect it once had been. The prime-time TV show proposed that magical technology could control the natural (and supernatural) world. Magic was depoliticised, domesticated, feminised, decontextualised and transformed into a safe male fantasy (even if Jeannie often got her own way). What remained was a residue of magical desire, embodied in an idealised white woman. Not only could Jeannie summon up ancient magical powers, but when Tony got home, she had dinner prepared. When aired on commercial television, *I Dream of Jeannie* was interspersed with advertisements about revolutionary labour-saving consumer products. The promises made by advertisers sat naturally alongside Jeannie's magic. In the mid-1960s it seemed the world (or the United States) was moving towards a state where middle-class desires would be fulfilled almost without effort. Futurists worried about how society would cope with so much leisure (Veal, 2019). Advertisers promised more and more products that were constantly improving. Although the ads contained significant elements of fantasy, many viewers lived in a world materially changed by economic prosperity and consumer devices.

Lifestyle and consumption were central to the structure of feeling of the early 1960s. In the post–Second World War economic boom in the United States, there was a product to address every household problem, if not the war in Vietnam or civil rights. Consumer devices took effort out of daily tasks. Fridges created ice for drinks; TV dinners cooked in minutes. The TV took central place in the living room, offering sanitised images of worlds outside. The world of objects was becoming charmed: everyday life increasingly involved using a series of specialised technical devices, each of which supposedly required minimal effort. Objects had handles, wheels, buttons or other invocatory controls. However, despite the advertised ease of use, women's unpaid housekeeping labour was generally unacknowledged. Baudrillard (1996) points out that in a world where daily life involves dealing with a series of technological controls and readouts, the experience recalls magic: 'Something is revived here of the ancient habit, prevalent in a world of magic, of inferring reality from signs' (pp. 57–8).

By contrast, the sitcom represents the world inside NASA's security perimeter as disenchanted and gently ridicules the practices of command, science and progress. These practices belong to Captain Tony Nelson's workplace, a place of nine-to-five rationality. Computing is masculine, instrumentalist and scientific. Computers perform logical, mathematical command tasks, transforming orders into actions and summoning results with superhuman accuracy and speed. However, in the second season of the series, the private world intrudes on the workplace. Major Nelson and his colleague Healy are assigned to use the Electronic Rapid Input Computer (ERIC). Realising the Jeannie does not know her own birthday, Nelson decides to use ERIC to calculate it, discovering it was 64 BCE. However, this personal use of technology is disturbed when Healy and Nelson are caught out, and the psychiatrist Dr Bellows confiscates the computer printout. NASA has the most powerful technology of its time, but its day-to-day office life is bureaucratic, banal and petty. The high-tech romanticism of rockets and computers is contrasted with the mundane routines of work. The performance of the technologies proves to be patchy, and the workplace is ruled by hierarchy and office politics.

Outside of work, though, everyday life is more magical. Jeannie personifies the unacknowledged influence of the irrational suppressed in technoscience. Her

Invoking Histories 107

promise 'Thou can ask anything of thy slave, master' offers a kind of power that engineers can only dream of (Sheldon, 1965). She summons events with pure force of will and a simple gesture. She makes things appear and disappear. Her effortless command over the world mocks the lumbering weight of NASA's Big Science. But her powers are tainted with irrationality, insanity, desire and foreignness. The Jeannie character reflects gendered and Orientalist stereotypes: she seems naive and unpredictable. Over time, though, she blends in with conventional suburban patriarchal whiteness, domestication and repressed sexuality.

Tony Nelson constantly denies and conceals Jeannie's powers. There is no place for her magic in NASA's high-tech bureaucracy, which rigorously polices the great divide between science and magic. Much of the comedy and tension comes from his attempts to hide her magical actions from the military bureaucracy and to attribute rational causes to her bizarre actions. In one scene in Episode 92, 'The Used Car Salesman', Jeannie is herself mistaken for a computer: Nelson is forced to explain that a car magically controlled by Jeannie, which seems to be driving itself, is being driven by an experimental NASA computer. As Margaret Wertheim (1999) points out, sitcoms and other television shows served as cultural preparation for the arrival of cyberspace:

> We who grew up with *Bewitched, I dream of Jeannie, Gilligan's island*, and *Get Smart* – are we not already participating in a vast 'consensual hallucination'? (p. 243)

In the same year that *I Dream of Jeannie* debuted, the magic of invocational media was coming closer to the domestic world. On 22 March 1965, Digital Equipment Corporation (DEC) released the Programmed Data Processor 8, or PDP-8 minicomputer. As the first computer retailing for under $20,000 it would be considered the 'Model T' of the computer industry. It was the first 'portable' computer, even if it was the size of a small fridge. When one was stolen, the DEC marketing department was quietly happy, promoting it as the first computer small enough to suffer this fate. At around US$18,000, depending on the configuration, the PDP-8 was a commodity product, far cheaper than the IBM computers that had dominated the market for over a decade. It was dubbed a minicomputer, a term credited to John Leng, head of DEC's operations in England, who sent a sales report that started: 'Here is the latest minicomputer activity in the land of miniskirts as I drive around in my Mini Minor' (Powerhouse collection, n.d.). For its day, the PDP-8 was wildly successful, selling more than 50,000 machines before its phase out in

1970. This did not mean it was easy to use. It was initially controlled through a panel of switches and lights that required mastery of arcane assembly language. However, the PDP-8 has an ongoing life. Just as there are fans of old television programs, there are still fans of old computers. Several groups around the world have restored PDP-8 models to working order. Programmers have created and shared software simulators. The success of the minis established the associated milieu to support the uptake of smaller, cheaper and less powerful microcomputers with embedded microchips in the 1970s, beginning with the Altair 8800 in 1972.

The minicomputer and time-sharing systems at universities helped drive a cultural shift through which the dark magic of invocation and its extraordinary powers of command began to be domesticated. High technology moved towards low culture. For example, DEC was approached by a television station for help in developing a new quiz show, starring the PDP-8. Hosted by a former New York DJ, 'Dandy' Dan Daniel, *The Computer Game* pitted a panel of celebrities against the computer in a challenging word game. They competed to beat MINI, the minicomputer. The contest was hardly fair: the computer had an entire dictionary loaded into it, so it couldn't lose, but the producers hoped it might make great TV. The show opened with a close-up of the machine. As the station announcer started his banter, the camera zoomed out to reveal the whole machine. Its tape reels started rocking and rolling in time with the cheesy theme music. Dandy Dan leapt out and the show began. Unfortunately, perhaps, the show didn't get beyond this pilot. But forty years later, in 2011, IBM's Watson computer system appeared on the US TV quiz show *Jeopardy*, beating two of the show's human champions. Like the 1946 demonstration of ENIAC, demonstrations of invocational media in the media have often presented them as marvellous but somewhat inscrutable.

The PDP-8 was becoming closer to popular culture in other ways, too. Copywriters advertising the PDP-8 tried to counter perceptions that computers belonged only within engineering cadres. The intimidating connotations of giant brains, Big Brother and military command needed to be softened before consumers would feel comfortable with them. While the PDP-8 was not a consumer device, DEC's documentation of the time showed some effort to 'humanise' the computer. For example, a guide to the FOCAL language started with the example of a program that could calculate bank interest rates (Digital Equipment Corporation, 1969). This was not a conventional piece of technical writing. The first example program asked, in typically dry terms:

HOW MUCH MONEY DO YOU WANT TO BORROW ?

Invoking Histories

But the writers offered a rephrased version:

> Let's write a computer program which is quite personal in nature and see how the computer could be made to be personal.
> This time let's run the program before we explain it:
> HI THERE, GOOD LOOKING. HOW MUCH MONEY DO YOU WANT TO BORROW ?:300. (Digital Equipment Corporation, 1969, p. 6)

Their little joke completed, the writers returned to a straighter version of the dialogue. They warned:

> One problem though; the computer doesn't know who it is working for – male or female; young or old; pleasant or grouchy; single or married. How would you like a computer flirting with your grandmother? Maybe it really is best to keep the computer impersonal!!

The brochure's friendly tone and the humour in its cartoons reflected the anti-authoritarian mood of the time. Its illustrations looked like cartoons from *Rolling Stone* or the Beatles film *Yellow Submarine*. The brochure deliberately positioned computers as accessible and 'personal' – a long way from the culture of command typical of earlier computers. This anticipated a breezy style of advertising for the commodified microcomputers that appeared in the 1970s and 1980s. Ted Nelson's (1974) *Computer Lib/Dream Machines* adopted a similar casual and enthusiastic style advocating the wider embracing of computers while riffing off the women's liberation movement: 'By Computer Lib I mean simply: making people freer through computers. That's all' (p. 70). He directly contests the accusation that his projects of advocating and designing computer systems are Orwellian:

> Some people have called my ideas and systems 'Orwellian', which is annoying for two reasons. Firstly, it suggests the nightmare depicted in Orwell's book *Nineteen Eighty-Four*, which I want no association with. But hey, do you remember what the world was like in 1984? The cryptic wars against ever-changing unseen enemies, government spying, and the manipulation of language? To paraphrase Huey Long: 'Of course, we'll have 1984 in America, we'll just call it 1972'.

> Secondly, it reduces Orwell, the man, to just the world of '1984', ignoring his lifelong efforts to uncover oppressiveness in human institutions everywhere. In honor of Orwell's commitment to human freedom, I would be proud if my systems could be referred to as Orwellian. (p. 70)

In the same year that Jeannie and the PDP-8 appeared, the destiny of computer power was declared a natural law. Gordon Moore, the founder of

Intel, prepared a speech in 1965 where he observed the doubling of transistor density on a manufactured die every year. On this basis, he framed 'Moore's law', which asserted that computer power per dollar doubled every eighteen months. This was not so much a natural law as an engineering challenge and a marketing plan for an industry with excellent prospects for growth. His prediction became a self-fulfilling prophecy, inspiring the development of the sociotechnical bases of the invocational assemblage of the following decades (Mollick, 2006).

In 1997, the telephone company AT&T revived the Jeannie character, contracting Barbara Eden, the actor who played Jeannie, to make a commercial promoting their responsive customer service. In this advertisement, things have changed for Jeannie. She materialises as a help desk operator answering customers' phone calls. Her desire to please her master has been transferred to pleasing customers. The camera zooms out to reveal the whole call centre inside Jeannie's bottle. But Jeannie is not alone. There are dozens of identical desks, with dozens of identical Jeannies answering queries. She is no longer only in the home: she is connected to everywhere. Invocational media had become a mass-produced part of everyday life, no longer secret and available to all. Techno-magic had reconfigured bureaucracy. Each operator gave instant satisfaction to customers' demands. Computing was ubiquitous.

1984: Invocational media for the rest of us

The television viewers of the 1984 Superbowl between the Oakland Raiders and the Washington Redskins are witness to a melodramatic TV commercial. It portrays a totalitarian world in which Big Brother has transformed its population into mindless drones. Rows of men march through a futuristic maze-like corridor and into a large auditorium. A massive close-up of a grim-faced man stares down from a big screen. The grey, identically dressed figures shuffle into row upon row of seats and look up at the screen.

Intercut with these images is a running woman, bathed in light, coming from the back of the auditorium. She is wearing a T-shirt and shorts and wielding a sledgehammer as she bounds down the central aisle towards the screen. A group of riot police gives chase. As she approaches the screen, she swings the hammer around her body and releases it. The camera tracks the hammer as it tumbles

Invoking Histories

through the air. The screen explodes, lighting up the stunned faces in the crowd. As the camera tracks past them, text scrolls up the screen: 'On January 24th, Apple Computer will introduce Macintosh. And you'll see why 1984 won't be like "1984"' (Levy, 1994, p. 170).

The good Apple, Macintosh, faces off against the evil tyranny of IBM. The woman in the Macintosh advertisement is Jeannie with a sledgehammer. She is Lassie coming home. She is one of the Muses. She's an angel of information. She confronts Orwell's Big Brother – big government and big business and, most directly, the computing monolith of IBM. She also heralds the commodification of the computer as a fully fledged consumer product.

This utopian fantasy introduced a device that tightly integrated hardware and software. It was, said Apple, a general-purpose computing machine and an information appliance. This concept was a leap of faith, which would gradually seem to be vindicated but never in quite the manner envisioned by its creators. Where microcomputers had been associated with hobbyists, and IBM computers with workplaces, the Macintosh was saturated in popular culture. New magazines started to support it. A personality cult grew around the company's CEO Steve Jobs and his charismatic 'reality distortion field'.

As a system, though, it was something different, because it was designed to create its users rather than requiring them to be formally trained. It was promoted as 'a bicycle for the mind', a metaphor that invoked a space for mental exploration. The most significant feature Macintosh popularised was the invoked spatiality of the GUI, prototyped by Engelbart and Xerox. This differed from command-line interfaces like Microsoft's Disk Operating System (DOS), in which users typed, memorised and composed invocations. With DOS, to copy a text file from a floppy disk onto a hard drive, a user had to invoke a command such as 'copy a/ chris.txt c:\ docs\chesher /v'. This would copy an ASCII file 'chris.txt' into a directory 'chesher' in the 'docs' directory on the 'c:' drive and verify that copy. Each invocationary act was performed discretely and had to be syntactically precise, or it would produce an error. Using the Macintosh, users performed the invocationary action of clicking on a document icon and dragging it onto a folder icon. When the mouse button was released, the file was copied. Entering textual commands to logical entities was replaced by embodied invocationary actions within the graphical space of desktop, icons, files, folders, alert boxes and buttons. User invocations no longer needed to be performed one at a time in a machine's language but could be performed as gestures using icons in a magical invoked environment. As Bolter says in *Writing Space* (1991), the graphical interface paradigm invoked a richer cultural imaginary:

> The word 'icon' is more appropriate than programmers may realise. For like religious relics, computer icons are energy units, which focus the operative power of the machine into visible and manipulable symbols. Computer icons also remind us of the use of Hebrew letters in the Cabala or the use of alchemical and other signs by Renaissance magi like Giordano Bruno . . . such magic letters and signs were often objects of meditation (as they were in the logical diagrams of Raymond Llull); they were also believed to have operational powers. But electronic icons realise what magic signs in the past could only suggest, for electronic icons are functioning representations in computer writing. (p .53)

The magic of the GUI was soon accompanied by software and hardware components that increasingly resembled other media devices, such as radio buttons, play and pause buttons and video screens. Into the 1990s, 'interactive multimedia' emerged, offering combinations of text, graphics, sound, animation and video, usually delivered by CD-ROM. Filmmakers were puzzled by the term because they had been combining film, sound, text and animation since before the talkies in the 1920s and to far better effect than any of the day's multimedia presentations. Before the 1990s, the term 'multimedia' signified orchestrated public performances using multiple media (usually tape recording and triggered slide shows, sometimes with lights and even smoke machines). The computer industry commandeered the term to refer to applications which used the computer to deliver entertainment or education content. But in this context, 'multimedia' was a misnomer. The whole point of computer-delivered texts was *monomedia*. What had required a video recorder, slide projector, audio tape player, CD player, sampler, synthesiser, for example, might now be possible with invocational media. But as a medium, the multimedia computer of the 1990s was both less and more than the media parts converging on it. On their own, none of the parts approached the standards of the medium from which they were extracted: videos were jittery and small, audio was tinny and interaction was slow. But the machine was more than its parts because media elements became invocable. With interactive media, users directed narratives, explored virtual spaces and played games. Invocations become increasingly evocative as they invoked entire media environments. If computers were multimedia, then it was in a different sense – through software and hardware peripherals, invocational media invoked any number of other media forms: writing text,

Invoking Histories 113

manipulating images, communicating with one or many people and so on. In this way, computers were not one medium but many media.

Among the invocational cultural forms that emerged in the early 1990s were CD-ROM multimedia, which experimented with techniques for interacting with invocational media. Several multimedia encyclopaedias were released, including Microsoft's *Encarta* (1993), based on the content of Funk & Wagnalls Encyclopedia. Starwave collaborated with The Jim Henson Company to create *The Muppet CD-ROM: Muppets Inside* (Starwave and Jim Henson Interactive, 1996). In this work, referencing the medium as an invoked space, several muppet characters get stuck inside a computer and travel across the 'bitmap' on a 'databus' to find a way out. Musician Peter Gabriel released *Xplora1: Peter Gabriel's Secret World* (1993), allowing users to explore the music production process, including mixing Gabriel's songs on a virtual mixing desk and selecting musicians in multiple genres to create remixes – a common feature of invocational music. Developers worked around first-level limitations such as processor speeds, limited computer memory and slow data rates and access speeds. CD-ROM was an optical storage medium initially developed for audio, making it challenging to reproduce conventional screen language. It was only possible to include simple animations and low-quality videos a fraction of the size of the screen. Without the impact of full-screen movement, designers preferred static graphical interfaces or collages of elements on a surface, sometimes integrating videos. The favoured development environment, Macromedia Director (later Adobe Director), adopted a moviemaking metaphor, with a linear timeline. However, it also supported the invocational scripting language called Lingo. Unlike other software, which Apple expected should follow rigid design principles, each CD-ROM title established its own, often poetic, conventions for navigation and interaction.

The classic CD-ROM *Puppet Motel* by Laurie Anderson, for example, adopts a distinctive gothic aesthetic that resists the standard computer interface paradigm. The home screen resembles a dark corridor receding into black distance, with animated clocks in the foreground. A time-based menu on the wall on the left shows a series of unlabelled icons that fade in and out. Each icon accesses a different room with a cryptic interactive vignette. The space is littered with charmed technologies: empty chairs, telephones and aeroplanes. There is a strong theme of magic and mysticism, a contemplative temporality and a tactile mechanic. For example, there is a palm-reading room that explores the fluidity of language and translation. In another scene there is a Ouija board, with the pointer becoming a planchette while Anderson gives a monologue about reincarnation and living previous lives. Unlike in the standardised avocations of GUIs, where users understand what they are invoking, in *Puppet Motel*, they cannot anticipate the evocations. The user's cursor stumbles around darkened spaces, occasionally coming across artistic jokes and playful interactions, such as reversing the movement of the cursor or recording the user's voice. While CD-ROM interactives lasted less than a decade before being outmoded, their influence is still seen in the spaces of games and websites.

1993: Journeys into cyberspace

Space 1: Text and images gradually populate an empty grey page. The content comes from anywhere in the world that can be addressed with a uniform resource locator. Some of the text appears as blue hyperlinks, which invoke further pages from any other location. It had ambitiously been given the name 'World Wide Web', and the web browser window becomes its portal.

Space 2: An ancient book falls against a star-speckled sky, landing with a thump and a glowing magical aura. Clicking on the first page of the book triggers a postage stamp video fly-through across a deserted steampunk island. While this CD-ROM game presents a game world from a first-person viewpoint, the pace is slow as the protagonist moves around this island to unlock clues and solve puzzles.

Space 3: A grimacing soldier's face, the barrel of a gun and demonic monsters fill the screen. The world is also seen from a first-person view, but the pace is rapid as the player moves frantically through a dungeon-like 3D immersive space, seeking health packs, avoiding hazards and blasting enemies.

These three well-known pieces of software mark 1993 as a year when invoked spaces became prominent in popular culture: (1) Mosaic was the first graphical web browser; (2) *Myst* was a reflective puzzle-solving game set on an uninhabited steampunk island, with photorealistic 3D graphics and atmospheric sound; (3) *Doom* was the breakthrough game in the first-person shooter genre. These heterogeneous sociotechnical apparatuses, experiences and clusters of meaning contributed to the emerging invocational vocabulary, grammar and experience by which invocational media could be portals into invoked spaces.

In science fiction, parallel dimensions and worlds 'through the looking glass' were familiar themes, so it was no surprise that advanced computer systems might invoke fantastic spaces. The term 'cyberspace' appears first in the novel *Neuromancer* (Gibson, 1984) and in its sequels *Count Zero* (1987) and *Mona Lisa Overdrive* (1989). The cyberspace William Gibson invokes is more a contemporary nightmare than a utopian projection. The world of the novel combines romanticism, mysticism, corporate power, cyborgs, drugs and mental illness in equal measure. But the art of 'voudou' in *Count Zero* is quite a pragmatic image of technology-magic:

> 'Vodou isn't like that', Beauvoir said. 'It isn't concerned with notions of salvation and transcendence. What it's about is getting things done.' (Gibson, 1987, p. 111)

In Gibson's world, corporations have taken almost absolute control over life on earth. The 'matrix' is an invoked space rapidly outshining the decaying physical world. It is a space inhabited by warring artificial intelligences and vodou magicians.

Ironically, 1980s sci-fi nightmares inspired 1990s VR designers. John Walker from the computer-aided design software company Autodesk started a 'cyberspace initiative' in 1989 to build a technology based on Gibson's dystopia (Sherman & Judkins, 1992). But the imagined worlds they initially created for its head-mounted displays were more rudimentary than Gibson's nightmares. For example, one of the early VR demos shown to journalist John Perry Barlow (1990) sees him immersed in a nondescript office featuring a bookshelf and no ceiling. His 'corporeal self is a glowing, golden hand', and he can interact by making a fist to pull the book from a shelf. This synthetic world reflected a high-tech nostalgia for a pre-tech world of books. The 'virtual reality' dream implied that technology could provide a way of returning to spatial and direct experience. Even though computers were synthetic and non-spatial, VR inverted these limitations by claiming that the systems created a *better* experience and a *new kind* of space (Chesher, 1994).

So, while PCs in the 1990s proliferated in offices and homes, the potential significance of computers and networks remained hard to envisage. When smokestacks and speeding trains transformed the landscape during the Industrial Revolution, change was undeniable, even if progress was unevenly distributed. Robber barons prospered while Luddites resisted and labour organised, but no one could avoid seeing the change. The 'information revolution' lacked such conspicuous material manifestations. In the 1950s, the classic image of the computer in the United States was the SSEC, with its panels of flashing lights, spinning tapes and flipping cards. The multimedia computer was a more modest artefact but still hard for many to understand, particularly when it connected to the internet. From the 1980s, artists, designers and games developers created representations of the logical worlds of computers as 3D spaces, sometimes inhabited by blocky human or animal figures. Spatial concepts and images promoted computers as mediators of new spaces. Info-bots on surfboards shot down superhighways that spanned glowing hallucinatory landscapes.

One of the first cinematic uses of computer graphics to represent the space inside a computer was Disney's *Tron* in 1982. In this film software engineer Kevin Flynn finds himself inside the machine, fighting a Big Brother figure, the 'Master Control Program'. He is forced to fight deadly gladiatorial games on the 'game grid' but escapes to hijack a spaceship in a sequence resembling a video game. Similar images appeared in countless films, such as *Lawnmower Man* (1992), *Ghost in the Machine* (1993), *Ralph Breaks the Internet* (2018) and even the opening sequences in the romantic comedy *You've Got Mail!* (1998). All reinforce the impression that computers are spatial worlds.

These techno-spatial metaphors in science fiction, cinema, television and human–computer interface design also appeared in political rhetoric. Some adopted the discourses of colonialism, invoking narratives of discovery and exploration such as those propounded by John Perry Barlow:

> Today another frontier yawns before us, far more fog-obscured and inscrutable in its opportunities than the Yukon. It consists not of unmapped physical space in which to assert one's ambitious body, but unmappable, infinitely expansible cerebral space. Cyberspace. And we are all going there whether we want to or not. (Barlow, 1994)

Here Barlow quite uncritically compares cyberspace with a heroic history of westward expansion. His libertarian technological utopian vision presented these developments as inevitable and desirable. But this imagery was a myth that puts white male Americans at the centre. His cyberspace was a colonialist invocation of an irresistible individualist manifest destiny.

Some early cyberspace designers saw an opportunity to establish private infrastructures of virtual property. In *Cyberspace: First Steps*, one of the first books theorising cyberspace, architect Michael Benedikt (1992) describes a system for creating usable invoked spaces. He proposes principles of dimensionality, continuity, curvature, density and limits, claiming that these will create virtual spaces with a 'reassuring uniformity' (p. 132). His cyberspace resembles a neon-glowing urban grid – a matrix of cells, each of which represents an institution. Users in a 'probe' can cruise over the rows of thousands of data cells. Benedikt's vision of cyberspace reasserted property relations: each cell is 'owned and maintained in some way . . . it corresponds to the idea of property, of real estate' (p. 202). This shape of cyberspace is unapologetically political: '[j]ust as in the real world, the size of a plot of cyberspace is itself information: about the power and size of the institution that owns and operates it' (p. 203). Its ontology is conservative, precluding any possibility that invoked worlds might escape the constraints of conventional spatial dimensions or power relations. Benedikt's instinct is to impose on cyberspace a phenomenal uniformity that can be controlled, mapped and commodified. While 'cyberspace' would not turn out to follow Benedikt's designs, it has reasserted notions of buying, making, selling and protecting property, such as in *Second Life* (2003–). Mark Zuckerberg's proposed metaverse includes dedicated commoditised spaces of Horizon Worlds, Horizon Workrooms, Horizon Venues and Horizon Home that can be explored using Meta's head-mounted displays.

But not all visions of internet space were so commercial. In contrast to Benedikt's vision, Berners-Lee, Cailliau, Groff and Pollermann (1992) offered the World Wide Web as a '[d]ream . . . to bring a global information universe into existence using available technology' (p. 52). This practical initiative from the CERN research centre introduced the first-level standards of HTTP and HTML, a second-level experience of hypertext (a concept that preceded the web) and the grand third-level concept of the web. This initiative lacked the corporate backing that supported several commercial online services available at the time, such as CompuServe, America Online, Prodigy and Apple's eWorld. And unlike these, and the bulletin board systems favoured at the time by hobbyists, the World Wide Web was native to the public, non-proprietary internet.

The web assemblage reached a point of singularity on 22 April 1993, when the University of Illinois' National Center for Supercomputing Applications released the first popular graphical web browser, NCSA Mosaic 1.0. This software invoked a multiplicity of spaces at several levels: sociotechnical spaces of protocols, domain names and directory structures; an extensive space of connections to distant servers on a global scale; material and semiotic spaces of windows in a GUI inside a screen; spaces of authors and readers in their sites of production and consumption; and a multimodal sequential textual space of 'pages' tied together with hyperlinks and forward and back buttons. Mosaic's breakout success was based on calling up an assemblage connecting all these spaces. It is notable that, like much of the software on the early internet, it was freely available. The take-up of software was expedited because the assemblage to a large extent did not invoke patented standards, licensing or rent.

The early internet worked largely as a gift economy until about the time that Netscape, the company established to commercialise the browser, floated on the stock exchange in August 1995, signalling the start of the 1990s dotcom boom. Soon after, Netscape released its Navigator browser supporting Secure Sockets Layer (SSL), the first low-level encryption standard for the web. With the growth of the web, a new form of scarcity became prominent: the limited namespace for the internet's invocable domains. All domain names must be unique, and there are practical limits to the length of an address. Companies scrambled to reserve .com domain names associated with their brands because .com was the default. There was also frantic speculation to buy the most attractive non-brand addresses like sex.com, toys.com and hotels.com.

As search engines became the more popular way of invoking internet content, users no longer needed to remember domain names but could invoke what they desired by searching in natural language. Upon each search, the user's invocation called up results ranked algorithmically based on an assessment of their ranking. This produced another form of invocational territoriality as publishers sought to improve their site's rankings through tactical avocations. The vocation of search engine optimisation sought to refine a site's content to court Google's algorithms. The whole of language had become a commercialised invocable domain.

Space remained a central metaphor in internet discourse and was imported directly into public policy in the rhetorical rollout of the 'information superhighway' in the mid-1990s (Gore, 1993). US vice president Al Gore warned of avoiding 'bottlenecks', ensuring 'public right of way' and establishing 'road rules'. His historical reference to the 1950s freeway system (which his father had championed as a senator) claimed a leading role for the US government in building computer networks in the 1990s. Among the initiatives of the National Information Infrastructure legislative program was to enable government surveillance through the proposed mandatory 'Clipper chip', which could intercept user invocations. The superhighway automotive metaphor had cleared the rhetorical path for a virtual highway patrol. While the attempt to introduce the Clipper chip failed by the end of the 1990s, governments worldwide invested in the interception of 'signals intelligence' on an enormous scale. By the 2000s, the US National Security Agency (NSA) came to monitor the communications of over a billion people (Pasquale, 2015). The Chinese government instituted mass surveillance through cameras, mobile devices and internet infrastructure. The new media assemblages that in the 1990s seemed open spaces for unfettered

Invoking Histories

freedom of speech and political organisation gradually became some of the most observable spaces in human history.

Two other very different spatial media appearing in 1993, mentioned earlier, were the games *Doom* and *Myst*. These became the archetypes for two audiovisual and spatiotemporal paradigms in gaming. Each presented an immersive first-person perspective within a three-dimensional computer-generated space, but each offered a very different style of experience. *Myst*, created by Cyan, Inc., was a narrative puzzle CD-ROM game with high-resolution pre-rendered images invoked at a slow pace. The protagonist navigated from one lush 3D-rendered scene to another, following pathways and entering buildings on a deserted island, discovering and unlocking invocatory devices (keys, wheels, doors, ratchets, books, etc.). Solving a puzzle often invoked animations of steampunk mechanical devices in action as a reward, uncovering narrative traces of historical events in the game universe. The mood was reflective and the pace slow, and the puzzle game mechanic recalled the invocational legacy of cryptography, rendering the player as a human computer.

The game world of id Software's *Doom*, by contrast, was a lower-resolution monster-filled maze nightmare encountered at speed. Building on id's 1992 Wolfenstein 3D, *Doom* popularised the first-person shooter genre characterised by intense invocationary action. The player was cast as a space marine who must destroy demons on each of nine levels to move from the moons of Mars to Hell itself.

The aesthetic differences between *Myst* and *Doom* emerged from different solutions to the constraints of the invocational platforms of the day. Each game favoured different invocable domains. *Myst* privileged the large capacity of optical media to invoke hi-res rendered images and meditative soundtrack, whereas *Doom* favoured the invocation of fast silicon circuits and low-level algorithms in the game's engine. However, both offered compelling and evocative spaces, moods, soundscapes and visuals while working within the limitations of the platforms of the day. *Myst* and *Doom* could be emblematic of a controversy for scholars in the emerging field of games studies in the early 2000s. The contentious question was whether games are primarily stories or games. *Myst's* unfolding narrative architecture contrasted with the minimal backstory in *Doom*. The narratology versus ludology 'debate' dominated the early years of the emerging discipline. Scholars such as Aarseth (1997) and Frasca (1999) sought methods and formalisms to understand the properties of the emerging medium of games. Murray (2005) claimed there was no actual debate, as the terms had been defined by the advocates of ludology. Though this debate was never settled, scholars developed richer readings of the specificity of invocational media and particularly the invocation of space.

These examples from 1993 have illustrated the strong presence of spatial tropes with invocational media: science fiction, architecture, cinema, interface design, public policy and games.

The complex but critical questions about the spatiality of invocational media relate to relationships between physical space, embodiment, mental space and invocable domains. Inputs can be calibrated to capture data about physical objects sensed and imagined by humans. Objects and spaces can be modelled virtually and transformed through calculations and simulations for spectacle in games or prediction in simulations. Digital networks connect people and objects across physical space, as in a telephone call, and produce virtual space as in a multiplayer game, or a physical space, as with telepresence. There is no necessary connection between objects invoked, mental or physical. In Chapter 4 I further explore how spatial relations are mediated through the invocational assemblage.

2000: Networks, openness and the power law

In December 1999, 150 participants cram into a bunker built in the lower floors of a former warehouse at 353 Broadway, New York City. Each participant has access to a tiny Japanese-style sleeping capsule equipped with a mattress, an alarm clock, a video camera and a TV monitor. The cameras are on for twenty-four hours daily, capturing everything participants do. The shared areas are captured too: a banquet hall, a shower in a clear geodesic dome, publicly viewable toilets and even a shooting range with various weapons. The TV allows participants to watch the feeds, and there is a central control booth from which anyone can see everything. *QUIET: We Live in Public* is an expensive art happening and social experiment designed by the eccentric internet millionaire Josh Harris. It aims to document what happens to people in an environment of total invocability and no privacy (Kaplan, 2009; Smith, 2012, 2019). On New Year's Day 2020, the building is raided by police and fire units, and the experiment ends abruptly.

What makes this story curious today is how unremarkable living in public seems in a contemporary structure of feeling where sharing images and information in invocational media seems normal and is even celebrated.

Invoking Histories   121

Influencers, livestreamers and reality TV stars who achieve fame and sometimes money from hyperconnected self-exposure are only the most visible and invocable. In 2023, well over half of the world's population uses social media. This is not to say that peoples' presence at multiple public convocations is uncontroversial. Invocability has been legally and culturally regulated. For example, unlike the United States, the European Union's General Data Protection Regulation has attempted to give people invocational rights, such as the right not to be invocable – 'the right to be forgotten' (Krzysztofek, 2021, p. 15). The EU recognises control over one's information as a human right.

David Lyon (2018) identifies the emergence of surveillance culture in which peoples' experiences with everyday surveillance practices have engendered a surveillance imaginary that has changed how they picture themselves and their relationships with others. In some contexts, he observes, people respond tactically to unwanted surveillance, such as by using encryption or by opting out of credit card loyalty programs. In other contexts, he says, they may initiate their own surveillance practices such as installing a dashcam, reading other people's social media profiles or self-surveillance with fitness monitors in the interests of a 'quantified self'. Lyon highlights the complexity of contemporary surveillance.

In a surveillance culture, then, people negotiate both voluntary and involuntary invocations. Even within a voluntary invocation, such as watching a YouTube video, you are performing involuntary invocations that use your clicks and mouse movements to profile your consumption tastes and offer recommended videos and ads. As I will argue in Chapter 4, there is a paradox in invocational media. Users are graced with invocational power by embracing input devices like keyboards, cameras and microphones, which historically have been surveillance technologies. In many cases, the difference between voluntary and involuntary is not clear, and the increasingly obligatory use of invocational media means subjecting oneself to a surveillance culture. However, in some critiques of surveillance culture there is a risk of identifying invocational media as a corporate conspiracy and of portraying peoples' lived experiences with invocational media as somehow delusional.

For example, Dave Eggers (2014) takes a very gloomy view of the surveillance imaginary in the satirical speculative fiction novel *The Circle*. A company called The Circle is presented as fostering a utopian corporate agenda advocating complete transparency and full access to information, with the motto 'ALL THAT HAPPENS MUST BE KNOWN' (Eggers, 2014, p. 99). Eggers chooses even more outrageous corporate slogans that echo the style of *1984*: 'SECRETS ARE LIES, SHARING IS CARING, PRIVACY IS THEFT' (p. 449). Whereas in *1984* mass surveillance is conducted by the Big Brother state, which uses technology to control all information and truth, in *The Circle* the tyranny lies in a monopolistic corporate conspiracy to profile and control populations by convincing them to use technology to share all their truths in public.

A dystopian polemic, *The Circle* is a provocative critique of big tech and a defence of the value of privacy. However, it depends on extending to absurdity a caricature of a manipulative ideology of compulsory openness and abandonment of all privacy, infantilising its characters as foolish and deluded in succumbing to it. In doing so, it dismisses the changes in everyday life, social relationships and other cultural practices brought about by network media. In some sense, it speaks to disillusionment in collective hopes in the 1990s for the possibilities of networks.

Some of these hopes were manifest at the heart of capitalism, driving speculation on tech stocks in the dotcom boom. In a climate of exuberance, many believed that internet companies somehow escaped all previous assumptions about wealth creation. For most of these speculators, disappointment came dramatically. After peaking at 5,048 on Friday 10 March 2000, the NASDAQ Composite stock market index continued dropping, eventually to 1,114 on 9 October 2002, representing a 78 per cent decline.

For those with interests outside the market, the experience of participating in convocations such as discussion forums and mailing lists, sharing free software and creating personal homepages and blogs demonstrated the more progressive possibilities of invocational media. Many hoped these network-like dynamics might support even more radical non-hierarchical modes of organisation and resistance to power. They were attracted to Deleuze and Guattari's (1987) concept of the 'rhizome', which suggests that there are alternatives to state-like, hierarchical, tree-like 'arborescent' structures to be found in practices and even institutions that are more horizontal, intermeshed, self-organising, grass-like networks.

Castells (1996, 1997, 2000) takes a sociological approach to the rise of networks, arguing that networks have always existed and in many ways are ethically and politically preferable to hierarchies. However, in an environment of pre-invocational media, they didn't scale well, so hierarchies prevailed in large-scale societies. He argues that the rise of information technologies created conditions where networks work better to manage globalised social and organisational complexity.

Castells is not utopian, as he subtly analyses the qualitative changes in economic, social and experiential conditions associated with the network society. These conditions include what we may refer to as invocational relationships to time and space. Drawing on Innis, Castells observes that even older media technologies, such as the telegraph and the telephone (invocatory and modulatory technologies), had fostered an experience of simultaneity and closer everyday relationships with distant events and processes. With modern networks, this is only intensified. They support 'unprecedented temporal immediacy to social events and cultural expressions' (p. 491). Meanwhile, time is experienced as a hypertext, a collage, giving a sense of timelessness: an invocational relationship to time. As discussed earlier, this invocational time sense is inherent to the near immediacy of events, with the invocational assemblage calling to distant and past events at the user's whim. Castells argues that these media also affect relationships to space, lessening the influence of the local 'space of places' and increasingly favouring 'spaces of flows' of goods, information and command.

Into the 2000s, with the rise of networks, the previously marginal fields of network theory in mathematics and social science came to prominence in academic and popular literature (Barabási, 2002; Watts, 2003). The rise of the network imaginary owed much to invocational media. First, the emergence of computer networks foregrounded the experiences, discourses and imaginaries that arose out of these networks. At the same time there was a rediscovery of the literature from older network studies, such as Moreno's (1934) work on 'sociograms' – formally diagramming how relationships formed social networks. Second, technical networks provided abundant data on networks, such as phone calls, instant messages, chat rooms, academic citations, movie databases, power transmission records, financial transactions, crime statistics and even the growth of bacteria. These provided data that mathematical network theorists could employ (Watts, 2003). Third, invocational media provided tools to automate modelling, analysis and visualisation to offer insights into network effects present in large datasets.

Some of this research challenged assumptions that networks intrinsically tend towards the horizontal and democratic. On the contrary, the models of network theorists like Barabási (2002) and Watts (2003) found that many networks followed the 'power law'. The power law says that even where networks are initially random, the nodes that make more connections early tend to accumulate even more connections over time, while those less connected initially languish in relative obscurity. In a 'scale-free' network the rich inevitably get richer. Barabási (2002) argues that according to the power law, the inherent qualities of each node are less important than their relative position in networks. While these conclusions have some promise in modelling social inequalities, this branch of network theory is highly formal, mathematical and empiricist, reducing heterogeneous fields to nodes and connections. At its worst, it tends to lose historical specificity and social context.

A narrative in which the power law comes into operation can be identified in the aftermath of the dotcom crash. While many dotcom companies went out of business, the development of network technologies did not slow. With the introduction of broadband and mobile media, invocable domains became simultaneously more geographically extensive and closer to everyday life. People could invoke and remain invocable almost everywhere. Additional undersea fibre optic cables improved the reach, speed and economy of global invocable domains. A panoply of interactive websites popularly known as Web 2.0 appeared in the mid-2000s. Where most previous websites were relatively static, Web 2.0 sites ran on dynamic invocational platforms offering more complex applications of interactive avocations. Among the popular genres were blogs, microblogs, web bookmarks, reviews, news, images, videos, discussions, downloadable files, meetings and social networks. These services typically allowed holders of free accounts to communicate with others and share resources. Wikipedia provided an exemplar of a popular, non-profit, community-managed, high-quality resource.

Early theories of networks were typically insensitive to the role of protocols and software in conditioning events in invocational network transactions. By taking a software studies approach, it's possible to address relations between technical standards, software, networks and culture. For example, while Galloway (2004) acknowledges Castells's analysis of networks, he stresses the significance of protocols in regulating network interactions. The concept of a technical protocol was, of course, a metaphor drawn from social protocols: the formal and often unwritten rules governing social interaction, diplomacy and worship rituals. All invocations are bound by sociotechnical protocols at all three levels of invocation, for creating structures, establishing forms of agency and controlling events.

Technical protocols that mediate invocable domains – such as the internet's TCP-IP and HTML – are invoked automatically in first-level invocations. However, these protocols also govern aspects of second-level user experience, such as how quickly a web page loads or what is called up from a database.

Galloway's (2004) detailed reading of TCP-IP shows how these standards, despite being highly distributed, still enable forms of social control. He links technical protocols, materials and hardware configurations with forms of management. Rather than entering an imagined virtual space, the invocational infrastructure provided an architecture that overlaid an information space upon physical space, augmenting everyday spatial experience.

2007: Hurricane Katrina and the power of mapping

On 23 August 2005, a storm associated with a tropical depression forms over the Bahamas. In the following days, it grows in strength and moves towards Florida, passing over as a Category 1 hurricane. As it crosses the Gulf of Mexico it intensifies such that on 27 August it is Category 3. It crosses the Louisiana coast with an eight-metre storm surge. While the storm does not directly pass over New Orleans, a city of over 1.2 million, much of the city is below sea level, relying on levees to hold back the water. Overwhelmed, the levees break, and on 30 August, 80 per cent of the city is under water. Many houses are under water, and thousands of people are in need of rescue. Around 30,000 seek shelter in the Superdome sports stadium. Thousands are dead or missing. The shamefully slow government response to the disaster brings accusations of racism and incompetence (Elliott & Pais, 2006).

In 2007, users of the 3D world map application Google Earth noticed that the aerial photographic images of Louisiana had changed. Instead of showing the state as it appeared in the aftermath of the hurricane, they saw images of it beforehand. It seemed that this historic trauma had been erased from the online record. Congressman Brad Miller wrote to Google, arguing that 'use of old imagery appears to be doing the victims of Hurricane Katrina a great injustice by airbrushing history' (Miller cited in Claburn, 2007). The director of Google Earth and Google Maps, John Hanke, defended the company, pointing out their effort during and immediately after the disaster in updating the maps with the latest imagery (Claburn, 2007). He cited a voicemail from a user that commended Google for helping the rescuers. He explained that the mistakenly uploaded images were attempted 'data enhancements' and promised that the site had already been updated (Claburn, 2007). For those in New Orleans using Google Maps, though, this was a doubled alienation from control over physical and invoked space, or what Crutcher and Zook

(2009) refer to as cyberscapes. Masking the trauma was read as, once again, a racialised production of the cyberscape.

This incident reveals the real-time convergence between landscape and cyberscape in services like Google Maps. Where the spatial simulations in games of the 1990s created illusions of spatial experience largely detached from physical space, Google Maps established indexical and iconic relations to actual space that gave users the impression that they could relate directly, cartographically and visually to geographic space. Google drew on thousands of satellite images, aerial photographs and mapping data to offer an almost seamless invocable map that seemed to encompass the whole world.

With Google Maps included on the newly released iPhone, the mobile map phenomenologically encompassed the territory of the whole earth (particularly with GPS introduced in the iPhone 3G in 2008). Recalling 'On Exactitude in Science', a short story by Jorge Luis Borges (1985) about an empire that produced a full-scale map as large as the territory being mapped, Google Maps locates mobile users at their exact position on a map that encompasses the whole world. Where travellers with paper maps use multiple maps with diverse content and styles, Google Maps' seemingly homogenous representation erases all differences between the world's spaces and places. Its invocable domain offers a unified image of the planet, another monopoly of invocation: a centralisation of the means of knowing, imagining, experiencing and advertising across a global space.

In April 2007, the social media platform Facebook had a respectable 14 million users, but it was growing fast. It established a platform for mapping networks of 'friendships' that paralleled Google Maps' mapping of space. Where Google Maps curated places and spaces to make them invocable, Facebook did something similar for people and their relationships. Unlike the heterogeneous and distributed networked spaces of newsgroups, personal homepages, forums and blogs from earlier internet paradigms, Facebook centralised the managing of users' experiences into a massive proprietary set of invocable domains. Over the following years, its user base grew steadily into the billions. It would become a monopoly of invocation that demographically profiled its users in unprecedented detail as targets of customised advertising.

Facebook users were subjects of constant experimentation to tune the site's invocations. In 2007, Facebook introduced the News Feed, a controversial feature because it aggregated updates from all of a user's friends into one screen. In 2011, it modified the News Feed to curate the order in which messages appeared rather than leaving them in chronological order. These features aimed to keep users on the site, pushing a continuous mix of customised news and advertising. People's time on social media displaced their traditional media consumption, sucking resources away from expensive journalistic investigation in print and broadcast media. Avocational texts such as 'clickbait' and 'fake news' proliferated. User profiles and analytics revealed much about users, allowing Facebook to segment populations according to their data signatures.

2020: Streaming to the coronavirus

After visiting a wet market in Wuhan in China's Hubei Province in December 2019, several people fall ill with a mysterious respiratory disease. People are dying from it. Over the following weeks, the disease spreads to other regions of China and to Thailand, Japan, South Korea, Italy, Spain and the United States, and worldwide. Scientists announce that it is a previously unknown virus and name it SARS-CoV-2 and name the disease it causes Covid-19. The only available response against the virus is to get whole populations to stay home and avoid close physical contact with others. Governments worldwide close their borders and mandate that people remain in isolation. Streets fall quiet. Cafés, restaurants, cinemas, museums, theatres and workplaces sit empty.

As people are shut up in their homes, they turn to invocational media as never before for work, entertainment, education and connection with family and friends. The situation intensifies the use of almost ubiquitous sociotechnical communications infrastructures worldwide. The video chat application Zoom sees a thirtyfold increase in daily downloads from a year before, counting 300 million daily users in April 2020 compared with 10 million during the previous December (Warren, 2020). Twitch's online game streaming platform reaches over 4 million concurrent viewers and sees over 1.2 billion hours of content consumed in March alone (Galloway, 2020).

These practices were supported by broadband infrastructures that had been consolidated over the previous decade. The internet was increasingly widespread: households using the internet grew from less than 7 per cent of the world's population in 2000 to nearly 60 per cent by 2020 (World Bank, 2022a). Mobile phone subscriptions grew even more dramatically, from around 738 million in 2000 to over 8.2 billion in 2020 (World Bank, 2022b). Over 80 per cent of the world's population have a personal invocational device.

In the early days of the pandemic, many cultural practices usually associated with places where groups assembled were translated into invoked spaces. Funerals and weddings were livestreamed. At least one couple conducted their wedding in the game *Animal Crossing: New Horizons* (Antonelli & Haasch, 2020). With physical performance venues closed, musicians lost their livelihood but could still reach audiences online. On a small scale, local musicians used Facebook Live, YouTube, Instagram, TikTok and livestreaming platforms to perform, sometimes supported through tips to online payment sites. On a larger scale, Lady Gaga curated a globally telecast benefit concert in April that featured musicians performing from their living rooms in support of healthcare workers and vaccine developers. In June, the UceLi Quartet performed Puccini's 'Crisantemi' at Barcelona's *Gran Teatre del Liceu* opera house to an 'audience' of 2,292 plants. After the concert, the plants were donated to health workers. The livestreamed event marked a re-emergence from lockdown after Spain had recorded over a quarter of a million cases of COVID-19 and 30,000 deaths (Guy, 2020). In July, Rave Family Block Fest was a four-day online festival of over 850 artists performing on stages inside the networked game *Minecraft*.

The shared experiences of domestic isolation, modulated with anxiety and trauma, saw a proliferation of invocational micromedia events. Craft practices flourished as people had time to kill at home, and creators used the internet to share their handiwork. Popular activities included baking sourdough, knitting and gardening. In isolation in the South Island of New Zealand, actor Sam Neill turned to Twitter and YouTube, trying his hand at new art forms: "'I'm hopeless on the ukulele. I can't paint for nuts. I certainly can't write poetry, but I'm giving them all a go," Neill says' (Chenery & Gordon, 2020).

Along with the intimate and the domestic, invocational media continued to operate on the larger stage of activism and politics in a climate that would become increasingly socially divisive. Amateur phone videos of George Floyd dying under the knee of a Minneapolis police officer in May 2020 triggered a series of massive protests in the United States and around the world. The tag #BlackLivesMatter became an online convocation of affiliation and an avocation for participation. Zappavigna (2015) argues that hashtags often function not only to classify a message's topic but also to enact relationships: 'They may also be used to invoke, often as a form of interpersonal emphasis, the notion that there are people who feel the same way as the microblogger' (p. 289). The refrain 'Black Lives Matter' echoed as a multimedia event that passed through invocational vectors, voices in the streets and images in mainstream media.

Invoking Histories 129

By 2020, the invocational media platforms were central to how politics worked. Starting during the 2015 Republican primaries, Donald Trump heavily used the Twitter platform until he was finally banned from it in January 2021. While Dunn (2020) argues that his use of Twitter was built on a persona he established in the reality TV show *The Apprentice*, Trump took this much further. His use of Twitter could be compared with previous presidents' uses of the invocatory and modulatory medium of radio, which had the same advantage of projecting a relatively direct voice to the electorate without the mediation and commentary of the press. Many US presidents used radio, including Coolidge, Hoover, Roosevelt, Reagan and Clinton (Han, 2006). President Obama gave weekly radio addresses and made them available on YouTube. While Obama used Twitter, it was at nowhere near the scale at which Trump would use it. Over twelve years, Trump tweeted around 57,000 times (Madhani & Colvin, 2021). Ott (2017) argues that his tweets flourished in the Twitter media ecology with their 'simplicity, impulsivity and incivility' (p. 60). Starkly different in tone from Roosevelt's reassuring 'fireside chats' on radio between 1933 and 1944, Trump's tweets were often confrontational, abusive and self-aggrandising. Towards the end of his presidency, his posts became increasingly erratic and provocative such that social media companies began tagging some of his tweets with warnings that they made unsubstantiated claims. After Trump incited his followers to storm the Capitol building, Facebook and Twitter banned him from their platforms altogether. Social media companies, which had long claimed to be simply technology platforms, had come to acknowledge that they were functioning as media companies.

2022: Chatting with AI models

Every year, the Colorado State Fair awards an artist a prize for the best Digital Arts/Digitally Manipulated Photography. On 29 August 2022, Jason Allen was awarded the $300 prize for the work 'Théâtre D'opéra Spatial'. The image showed a massive hi-tech cavern with three human figures in flowing dresses looking into the distance through a large round hole in the cavern wall; it evoked a mixture of science fiction and renaissance imagery. But other artists in the competition were upset because rather than spending hours using tools like graphics tablets, digital cameras, Photoshop and 3D modelling and rendering software, Allen had created his work with a textual prompt using the recently released Midjourney AI image generator. This was not art, they argued, and

Allen was not an artist, as the image had been invoked by AI. The judges stuck by their decision, saying there was nothing in the rules that prohibited it from winning but acknowledging that the question of whether someone could create art with text-to-image AI systems needed to be debated for the next year.

The controversy made news around the world, as this event marked a threshold moment for AI when a short piece of text could invoke visually sophisticated and evocative images that passed for human creativity. These services became an internet sensation, and millions of people began using Midjourney, DALL•E 2 and other image generators to create their own artworks. Beyond the impressive performance of the technology, though, there were significant legal and ethical questions about who owns the images, how they were created and the implications for the careers of artists.

For one thing, it was ambiguous whether text-invoked images qualified as human creativity. Legal opinions suggested a computer-generated image could not be copyrighted as it was not created by a human artist. The image would simply be in the public domain. Allen argued that creating the prompts had been a highly creative practice that took many hours of refinement before he created a satisfying image. He also needed to take the effort of printing, framing and submitting it to the competition.

Over the months following the release of Midjourney and many other text-to-image generators, the algorithms and features were refined, and the practice of writing prompts became more sophisticated. As Midjourney ran on a Discord chat server, other users' prompts and images could be seen by other users in real time, serving as instructional avocations on the best strategies for creating effective prompts. The practice of writing descriptions for image generators became known as 'prompt engineering'.

Yet there were much more significant legal and ethical issues with the text-to-image generators. Critics observed that developers created their large image models by extracting information from billions of images collected from the internet without permission. The AI generates images by starting with random noise and then modifying and refining them with information from the AI model to match the users' text prompts. This image-generation process depends entirely on the labour of millions of artists and photographers whose work was invoked to create the models. This led to several as yet unsettled legal disputes over whether the generated images are considered derivative of the original training images, requiring permission from the creator, or if they are considered transformative and therefore original.

Invoking Histories 131

There are also questions about artists' moral rights when users of image generators can invoke their names in their prompts. For example, Greg Rutkowski, recognised for his fantasy images, had his name invoked by thousands of his fans creating their own images in his style. Rutkowski argued that his reputation as an artist had been exploited; his characteristic style had been pastiched; and his own work had been devalued as it disappeared into a sea of fake images bearing his name (Heikkiläm, 2022).

Rutkowski'sproblem was only one example of a larger question of how the text-to-image AIs might affect artists' livelihoods. Image generators did more than earlier invocational media, which augmented human creativity. Image generators seemed to give people with no artistic training the capacity to create usable images on their own. In doing so, the AI seemed to challenge the special status of creativity as distinctly human. Here we might recall Turing's prescient questions about machine creativity in his 1950 essay on 'Computing machines and intelligence' in which he asked whether computers would ever create something new. He cites Lady Lovelace's objection to machine creativity. She said that Babbage's famous early design for the computer-like Analytical Engine could only 'do *whatever we know how to order* it to perform' (p. 450, italics in the original). For Turing, this left open the possibility that the machine could learn to be creative.

So are image generators based on deep neural networks a step towards the kind of creativity Turing anticipated? Perhaps not, as these AIs are not creative in a human sense. The image models invoke giant image training sets consisting of millions of uncredited images and texts. The generated images themselves are created by invoking these models. The user plays a key role in performing the invocations that initiate the production of the invoked images, while the collective creative labour behind them remains unacknowledged. The creative process of Midjourney bears little resemblance in matter, form and substance to the embodied practices in traditional artistic assemblages, and AI will be meaningful only as it becomes part of these assemblages.

On 30 November 2022, OpenAI announced another service called ChatGPT (Chat Generative Pre-Trained Transformer), which could respond to users' invocations by composing surprisingly human-like texts. Like the text-to-image services, it worked by invoking an AI model trained on over 8 million documents. In the process of creating the text, ChatGPT worked step-by-step to match the prompt. At each step it calculated the most statistically likely next word, gradually creating a credible piece of text with the appropriate content and style. Because it was trained on a very diverse range of sources, it could create original texts in many genres: songs, poems, movie scripts, essays, computer code, reports and texts. ChatGPT attracted more than a million users in the first few days of its release and was commercialised within three months.

For many, though, ChatGPT and Google's 'Bard' caused even more alarm than the image generators, particularly for teachers. It could 'write' quite sophisticated answers to complex questions on a wide range of topics. Many schools banned it on the spot. Some teachers considered abandoning the usual ways of assessing student work. Journalists asked whether this would put writers out of work.

But ChatGPT had many limitations (as did Google's 'Bard'). While it could write essay fragments that teachers considered comparable with those of mid-level students, it exhibited some giveaway stylistic qualities for given prompts – certain turns of phrase, laboured expression and a tendency for repetition. It often made factual errors and even fabricated facts entirely. Even as its performance improves, it will be understood better as a component in invocational assemblages rather than as an intelligent agent with no context or associated milieux.

Conclusions: Third-level invocations

After seventy years, invocational technologies have become several orders more powerful not only in technical specs but also in their mediation of markets, social relationships, knowledge, media and social control. Going far beyond their computing functions, they have subsumed virtually all other media for command, control, audiovisual production and communication. Big tech platforms based in the United States have built an almost global invocational and convocational media ecology that is unprecedented in history, while a largely separate but equally oligopolistic – and more autocratic – invocational environment has grown in China from the 2000s.

Invocational media continue to invoke intelligence, data, defence, communication, territory and presence. While not yet invoking a brain that passes as human, they have proven more than capable of performing a wide range of invocationary acts and actions. They make decisions, perform speech acts, recognise faces and voices. As chatbots and social robots they engage people almost interpersonally and emotionally. We have become accustomed to quite baroque invocationary spaces – the spatial compression of cyberspace, the reformation of spatial experience in virtual reality and the live mapping of bodies in space. We are co-present with one another in many convocations. Zoom brings us together through video and audio bitstreams across indeterminate distances, reconstituting us as talking faces on screens. We allow ourselves to be traced with GPS, visualised in on-screen maps and made addressable with messages or phone calls. We find it no problem to invoke multiple spaces simultaneously, such as being physically located at home; playing an online game; appearing as a video image on other peoples' screens; chatting on Discord; and changing tracks on Spotify. Amid this complexity, new forms of sociality, performance and economic production have emerged in the matrix of all these spaces (Woodcock & Johnson, 2019).

Many developments in invocational media were not thoroughly planned or even anticipated. However, they were influenced by the prevailing structures of feeling and a constantly reconfigured set of associated milieux. As this chapter has suggested, invocational assemblages have adopted many voices. The shifting identities of the invocational assemblage reveal its radical abstraction. It is a technical lineage characterised by a capacity to become something else again and again. It is the universal invoking machine. However, the invocational assemblage is not outside of history. It is abstract but not so abstract that its components carry no baggage. Quite the contrary: as the following chapter will show, all the sociotechnical components of the invocational assemblage – command, memory, connection, code, decision, time and force – are very much part of the times and places in which they emerged.

4

Invocational machines and assemblages

The technical components of digital computers are well known: inputs, memory and storage, software, clocks, processors, outputs and networks. This chapter is structured around this set of components. But it expands the focus from the individuated components to consider each in relation to the interconnected social, technical, semiotic, aesthetic and ethical machines invoked. Taking an expanded sense of the machine from Guattari (1995a), who argues we should 'consider the problematic of technology as dependent on machines, and not the inverse' (p. 33), I will argue that each component is associated with a particular sociotechnical machine. There are machines of command, memory, archiving, code, decision, temporality, force and connection. Each of these machines has a complex, often controversial history and must be understood by examining actual computers operating in everyday physical and social contexts – invocational machinic assemblages.

This reconceptualisation of computer components as machines in their own right invokes Guattari's (1995b) more extensive conception of machines, which discovers the contexts of technologies in invocational assemblages – people, ideas, interactions, experiences, thoughts, ethics, meanings and histories – all of which are integrated into machines that operate within and beyond the technical components:

> [W]e will attempt to discern various levels of ontological intensity and envisage machinism in its totality, in its technological, social, semiotic and axiological avatars. And this will involve a reconstruction of the concept of machine that goes far beyond the technical machine. For each type of machine, we will pose a question, not about its vital autonomy – it's not an animal – but about its singular power of enunciation: what I call its specific enunciative consistency. (Guattari, 1995a, p. 34)

I argue that machines of command, archiving, code, decision, temporality, force and connection pre-existed invocational media but were drawn irresistibly into

136 *Invocational Media*

the invocational abstract machine to take on invocational forms. Once digitalised, these machines invoked not just the purely technical (first-level) components but also the psychological and experiential (second-level) and institutional and discursive (third-level) actors and processes. If the buzzword 'convergence' has any meaning, it is in how invocational media bring together these machines and events into integrated media assemblages. Table 4 identifies the computer's technical components, the machines they mobilise and the peculiar invocational operations with which they are associated.

It is not only the selection of these components that defines invocational assemblages but also their distinctive arrangement. This arrangement of components can usefully be considered as an 'abstract machine' (Guattari, 1995a, p. 35). The term 'abstract machine' in computer science discourse refers to a precise and detailed analysis of how a computer system works. It is a formal way of understanding all the inputs, outputs and operations of a computer.

But let's take Guattari's (1995a) expanded conception of the 'abstract machine'. We can identify a more expansive, constantly changing diagram of machinic

Table 4 Technical Components and Machines in Invocational Assemblages

Technical Components	Machines	Machinic Invocational Operations
Inputs	Command machines	Capture invocations by sampling the physical world for commands, control and data
RAM and storage	Memory and archiving machines	Extend the duration of invocations to inform future invocations
Software	Code machines	Inform events in all the other invocational machines, invoking software machines and protocols
Processor and real-time clocks	Machines of temporality	Synchronise, record and regulate the temporality of invocations
Central processing units, GPUs	Machines of decision	Interpret code, performing arithmetical, logical and control operations and mediating decisions
Output devices	Machines of expression and force	Give semiotic and material expression to decisions by performing statements, spectacles, sound and movement
Networks	Machines of connection and convocation	Extend invocations across physical and social space to mediate communication in networks, communities and other sociotechnical formations

Invocational Machines and Assemblages

relations that operate in a transverse way between technological, semiotic, psychological and social levels.

> When we speak of abstract machines . . . They are montages capable of relating all the heterogeneous levels that they traverse . . . The abstract machine is transversal to [all the levels], and it is this abstract machine that will or will not give these levels an existence, an efficiency, a power of ontological auto-affirmation. (p. 35)

We can say that beyond technical interconnections, invocational abstract machines are the implied diagrams that connect all the other machines, particularly through the decision and code machines that transversally connect all the other machines. As I will show, the configuration and mobilisation of these machines and their connections with wider universes are the basis of the formation and operation of invocational assemblages.

Let's take an example and begin with a simple narrative that can be described purely technically: accessing and liking a photo on Instagram on a smartphone. Most of these events involve first-level (technical) components in an invocational assemblage. A user launches the app, which uploads images into their feed. When they choose an image and tap the heart icon, the pressure of their finger on the app icon is registered as an input. The input initiates logical events in the smartphone's CPU to modify some variables and change the colour values of pixels on the screen to turn the heart red. These changes are transmitted across the internet for others to see. This is a complicated event, but it is not particularly complex. It would theoretically be possible to trace every first-level invocation. Instagram itself tracks and records many of them.

Instagram is, of course, more than hardware and software operations. It is an invocational machinic assemblage driven by all the machines in Table 4. The user is amused by the expression on a friend's face, generating an affective reaction – a laugh or a smile – and inspiring them to show that they appreciate it. The outlined heart icon is more than a graphic: it is a desiring machine – an avocation that invites the user to make a cognitive, aesthetic or emotional judgement about the image. When they tap on the heart icon, the decision is registered as a command that evokes a satisfying animation of the heart filling with red. The person who posted the image is pleased when they see the 'like'. Instagram is not popular for its first-level invocations, even if these are necessary for higher-level invocations. The app's popularity reflects how the accumulated intensities of such everyday relational events can engender in people a desire or compulsion to keep using the app. Instagram is a means of self-expression (command), a potential witness to everyday events (archiving) and a set of conventions and algorithms (code) to socially connect with my followers and those I am following (invocable domains and convocations). As my image joins billions of others in Instagram's enormous, distributed archive of faces, objects and scenes, the software (code) extracts sets of images based on follower relations or hashtags to have special resonance for socially defined friends and for fans of the Instafamous (Lee, Lee, Moon & Sung, 2015).

Overview of the machines in invocational assemblages

This chapter examines, in turn, machines of command, archiving, code, decision, temporality, force and connection as they have been incorporated into invocational assemblages – computers in their everyday context. In such contexts, the invocational machines connect with other machines – artistic, bureaucratic, educational, military and so on – to interoperate with other broader assemblages. This chapter explores the deep technological and cultural heritages of the invocational machines. These often displaced previous machines. For example, in offices, invocational media gradually outmoded the operations and ritual uses of typewriters, filing cabinets, paper publications and physical mail, transforming the overall assemblage but not totally revolutionising it. Previously heterogeneous technologies and processes were translated into configurations of invocational machines. I will begin by quickly outlining the machines found in invocational assemblages and then consider them more deeply.

Command, control and capture machines

Command, control and capture machines are sensitive to events and patterns in the environment. They accept input events in a variety of ways. Some configurations capture discrete events, like keystrokes or mouse button presses. Some operate continuously, for example, tracking mouse movements. Others capture blocs of sensation in space (a digital camera, for example) or over time (a sound recording). While each of these events can initiate commands, software must first call them to act, and not all commands are humanly intentional.

Archival machines

Memory and archiving machines hold and store traces of events over time for future invocation. Memory machines like human short-term memory and

Invocational Machines and Assemblages 139

random-access memory are volatile and transient but crucial to engaging with immediate activities. Archiving machines like human long-term memory, paintings on rocks in sacred places, manuscripts in monasteries, printed books in libraries and audio tapes in archives, hard drives and SSDs are more durable but also susceptible to many forms of failure.

Even notepads or paper napkins might be convenient as temporary places for mathematicians, bureaucrats or journalists to record information. Large-scale record-keeping and archives before the advent of invocational media required substantial dedicated physical space, bureaucratised, manual classification and indexing and arrangements for physical security. Invocational assemblages incorporated a diversity of material technologies to store data in archival invocable domains. In random-access memory, archives are even more ephemeral than a napkin until their traces are committed to storage devices. Building databases at scale (in corporate systems and lately in the 'cloud') made many physical archives obsolete. Yet, they required new kinds of social and algorithmic order: database architectures, social processes for managing data entry and security measures for regulating invocations. Control over invocable archives is unevenly distributed, reinforcing social, economic and geographic dominance and marginality.

Code machines

The emergence of digital computing owed much to the practices of code-breaking in the Second World War, and encoding and decoding processes remained key to the operation of invocational media. However, invocational code also provides instructions to perform complex algorithmic invocations that establish spatial, temporal and semiotic order in space and time. With the choice in the 1940s to store programs and data in the same archiving devices, code could be easily accessed and changed. Software code can be compared to spells or recipes, in that it stores the steps for machines of decision to execute; data can be compared to ingredients to be included in the assemblage's quasi-magical operations. However, these are not just any kind of magic; they are invocational magic. While magicians/users initiate many events, most steps are automatically invoked through the agency of code, invocable domains and decision machines. Software directs the articulation of invocations and evocations, determines how archiving is organised, and establishes connections and convocations. With new software, a general-purpose invocational device magically becomes a different device, reconfiguring how all other components relate to users and the world. To understand the politics and aesthetics of invocation, we must turn to the human and non-human decision-making involved in developing and executing algorithms and software.

Machines of temporality

There are two kinds of machines of temporality in the invocational diagram: processor clocks and real-time clocks. Processor clocks establish the rhythm at which invocations cycle, determining the temporal threshold limit for activities mediated by invocational assemblages. The constant cycling of primary and secondary invocations at the clock speed of the processor is oriented towards the present moment. The multi-gigahertz speed of invocational media might seem faster than human awareness, but there are many contexts in which invocational sequences experience a perceptible delay, glitch or freeze. Invocational media establish a distinctive form of the present that sustains a constant ontological tension in the cycling between primary invocations that open puzzles or desires and secondary invocations that seem to resolve them, only to return to generate further desires and puzzles. Whether playing a computer game or recalculating a spreadsheet, this tension can be sustained for as long as the invocational assemblage remains, somewhat precariously, 'live'.

The second clock is the real-time clock that supports scheduling future events, reminding users of their commitments and creating timestamped records. With cloud computing, scheduled events can have a sense of liveness that makes shared commitments more tangible in peoples' electronic diaries. As I will argue, real-time clocks have regulated everyday experience for centuries, allowing coordination and scheduling of events. However, the emergence of the live processor clock has supported practices such as 'microcoordination' (Ling & Lai, 2016), using mobile media to organise and reorganise physical and social connections rather than relying on the real-time clock to plan events.

Machines of calculation and decision

Just as invocational media constitute all inputs as commands, they constitute all events as decisions. In this section I will argue that the CPU is the key component in general-purpose computers responsible for controlling operations and performing mathematical and logical events: doubled invocations that produce decisive actions. To oversimplify once again, triggered by the clock, the primary invocations in the fetch-execute cycle call up code fragments from the instruction register. Based on this interpretation, secondary invocations perform decisive connections to invocable domains. Over many of these rudimentary operations, decisions invoke meaningful events of input, recollection, inscription, arithmetic, logic and output.

Machines of expression and force

Outputs are technologies of spectacle, exposure and force that give semiotic and material presence to the patterns and events established in the other invocational components. Historically, they have invoked the screen cultures of television but also radar screens that betrayed the presence of distant actors. They recall the printing press, public address systems, radio and other technologies that expose publics to information and propaganda. Outputs give material form to invocationary acts and actions, serving as the points at which commands, texts, sensations and emotions are articulated and evoked.

Machines of connection and convocations

Like the means of transportation and communication of the past: legs, wheels, air, telegraphy, radio and telephony, invocational networks extend objects and voices (and other controlled actions) over space through networks. The moment that an invocation establishes a connection, it also clears a space and configures an architecture for communication, often including a space for social convocation. Just as the physical architecture of a hospital or school helps arrange people into social categories, so convocations connect and arrange people into distinctive relations to one another: managers, email correspondents, social media friends, or participants in a metaverse. Convocations establish more or less flexible relations of enunciation and audibility, social roles, architectures and expressive modalities. Even something as basic as email convocations can mediate more than one-to-one convocations. It can also operate as a one-to-many convocation or many-to-many with a mail exploder. Some convocations establish a synchronous live connection, while others are asynchronous and archival. In this section I explore the dominant conceptions of convocations: communities and social networks. I argue that both terms carry too much baggage. Networks and communities mediated through invocational media are convocations with different architectures, avocations, algorithms, input and output machines.

For the remainder of this chapter, I will go into more detail about each of these machines. Of course, while this chapter engages with these machines one at a time, they are always working together. They are interacting components in assemblages drawn together with the invocational abstract machine.

Command, control and capture machines (input devices)

Built from materials and components selected for their sensitivity to patterns in the physical world, invocational inputs sense events and encode them to perform commands, exert control and capture things in the world. Inputs are deterritorialising machines, extracting and encoding patterns from an environment for distant and future use. The most common sensors are those that measure physical force, light photons and sound vibrations, but anything measurable can be used as an input. Depending on the device and the software, inputs can trigger invocationary acts, track invocationary actions and record sensations.

There are three basic modes of input, each producing different event:

- An invocationary act is a discrete programmed event, such as typing the letter A, that invokes a single invocational event.
- Invocationary action is a continuous event extended and controlled over time and space, such as moving a mouse or holding down a modifier key.
- An act of capture digitises blocs of sensation such as movement, sound, image or video.

In many cases, the same input device can perform each of these three modes of action. For example, a series of keystrokes can control invocationary action, and this sequence can be captured, stored and visualised as a graph. An act of capture such as a camera with biometric software can perform invocationary acts – such as recognising a face and opening a secure door.

Inputs may or may not manifest human intentionality. Often input events can be involuntary, like stepping on a landmine or inadvertently mousing over an advertisement. Inputs can be non-human, such as when a sensor picks up environmental sounds or movements. In other contexts where the identity of commanders, controllers and capturers is critical, invocational assemblages incorporate mechanisms like passwords and encryption to verify the identity attached to input events.

Command and control for invocational assemblages can be materially and ethically complex. For example, drone operators in the military get a high degree of immediate power by using invocationary controls to pilot a drone, identify targets and fire missiles. However, once a guided missile is released, the operator loses control and automated targeting takes over. At this point, the targets control the missile against their will. In their appearance and movement, the missile's control systems sense their controlling invocationary action. In their final moments, the targets are the unwilling commanders of their own destruction.

Machines of surveillance and creativity

The history of earlier assemblages that command, capture and control the world is multifaceted, as the same machines have had different associated milieus. For example, many of the input components used within machines of surveillance can also be seen within machines of creativity. Typewriters, cameras and microphones capture keystrokes, images and sounds but to different effects. For example, from the late nineteenth century, typewriters could be found in police stations typing up dossiers and in writers' garrets typing up novels. Each expresses command over language (bureaucratic and creative writing) and command over populations (police records and bestsellers). Cameras and microphones, too, generated moving images and sound in Hollywood for the judgement of audiences and in the FBI for the judgement of juries and judges. Yet the tables can turn, as even your creative writing can be used against you.

Before computers, surveillance was already a principal mechanism for securing social order. Foucault (1991) is the pre-eminent theorist of the disciplining of subjects through a 'state of conscious and permanent visibility . . . [that] assures the automatic functioning of power' (Foucault, 1991, p. 201). Developing the concept of panopticism, he investigates how 'disciplinary' societies collectively manage fields of vision that make people, events and objects visible to power. Historically, institutions have managed the visibility of subjects by arranging them so that they may be observed and disciplined, such as in the famous prison with a central watchtower (Foucault & Gordon, 1980, pp. 146–65; Foucault, 1991, pp. 195–230). Hospital beds were arranged into wards to allow doctors to examine patients efficiently, while patients were separated to avoid contagion (Foucault, 1963). Schools disciplined students as a group while tracking them individually and singling out deviance. However, the distinctive feature of panoptic assemblages is controlling subjects through their constant perception that they may be being watched.

Disciplinary institutions use trained human labour, technical apparatuses and bureaucratic procedures to organise panopticism. But before computers, the input components were heterogeneous and loosely connected. Typewriters, prison watchtowers, clinics, interview rooms, folders, filing cabinets, tape recorders, cameras, fingerprint pads and so on were relatively inefficient and bound to bureaucratic assemblages, specific locations and material objects. Institutions captured records and traces of subjects, but all of this was partly a bluff, relying on the subject's awareness of the possibility of being observed.

With the emergence of invocational media, many of the diverse technologies and techniques of modern disciplinary assemblages could be translated onto the invocational diagram. Watchtowers became CCTV cameras. Filing cabinets became cards in tabulating machines and, later, digital databases. Invocational media increasingly displaced this variety of command and archiving technologies, adapting them to the quasi-universal forms of invocationary acts, actions and recordings.

Societies based on invocations operate at a different speed, reach and granularity than those reliant on previous generations of technology. Deleuze usefully identifies a historical transition in the twentieth century from disciplinary societies to societies of control. He argues that where disciplines moulded subjects by passing them through a series of enclosures – school, military, workplace and hospital – control operates through constant modulation. He argues that people change from being individuals in masses to become 'divided individuals' (Galič, Timan & Koops, 2017, p. 20) or '*dividuals*' (Deleuze, 1992, p. 5) who lack individuals' depth and consistency. Deleuze observes that dividuals are controlled by names and passwords rather than influenced by watchwords and slogans.

However, control society does not operate with analogue modulations but through digital invocationary command, control and intelligence. Invocational societies could simultaneously disperse and centralise control. Unlike modulations, invocations can be circulated, assessed, multiplied and replicated across multiple invocable domains almost indefinitely. Databases for taxation, policing, advertising and so on have been linked according to an invocational imperative. It has become easier to deal with businesses and the government, and we casually accept their terms of service, but this ease of input to their centres of calculation affords institutions higher degrees of control. Invocable domains and invocability trump enclosure and visibility.

Our invocationary actions are also free labour that generates value and builds invocable domains for corporations and government. Using social media is unpaid work of media production and advertising consumption (Fuchs, 2015). Zuboff (2019) argues convincingly that corporations such as Google and Facebook gather user data to extract 'behavioural surplus' that allows them to predict and even control peoples' future behaviour.

The tech industry has grown through this invocational imperative that advocated translating as many social and technical operations as possible into invocationary actions. It is a war machine with its own logics and relationships with state forms. Invocational assemblages have infiltrated everyday life through charm and coercion. While this imperative has been resisted passively by individuals and actively by social movements, its force has been irresistible in many institutions.

The paradoxes of invocational work and pleasure

Despite the ubiquity of surveillance, invocationary action is typically not coerced. People are often charmed by invocational media. In practices of convocational socialisation, gameplay and vernacular creativity, invocationary action can be empowering and fun (Gauntlett, 2011). People use social media because they are occasionally self-affirming or instrumentally valuable, despite being products of capitalist commodification. The work of coding, design, media production and play is often rewarding before it becomes gruelling. Strategies of gamification try to make work fun. However, the fun of gamification depends on the direction from which it comes. Woodcock and Johnson (2017) argue that gamification can come from above and from below:

> Gamification-from-above is the imposition of systems of regulation, surveillance and standardization upon aspects of everyday life, through forms of interaction and feedback drawn from games (*ludus*) but severed from their original playful (*paidia*) contexts. By contrast, gamification-from-below represents a true gamification of everyday life through the subversion, corruption and mockery-making of activities considered 'serious'. (Woodcock & Johnson, 2017, p. 543)

The instrumental success of strategies to encourage playfulness depends on authentically capturing the engagement and investment of users. However, there is no easy distinction between false and genuine playfulness. For Jenkins, Ford and Green (2013) the contexts of creative practices such as amateur media, fandom and participatory culture give play its meaning. They give the example of the early adopters of amateur radio early in the twentieth century before it became commercialised. They point to the establishment of an African American press to contest the racism that was propounded in the film *The Birth of a Nation*. They argue that amateur media establish intrinsic values before their capture by the market. However, they argue that this agency from below continues to operate even after that institutionalisation:

> [W]e will struggle between conflicting and perhaps contradictory pulls – between a corporate conception of participation (which includes within it a promise of making companies more responsive to the needs and desires of their 'consumers') and a political conception of participation (which focuses on the desire for us all to exercise greater power over the decisions which impact the quality of our everyday lives as citizens). (p. 156)

Invocational media have created fertile environments for ambivalent cultural dynamics. Invocations can be simultaneously magical and diabolical. For example, Facebook began with relatively simple algorithms that performed various forms of the avocation of users' social actions: complete your profile, connect to friends, post your status and so on. People adopted the platform out of curiosity, and Facebook's avocations invoked unexploited externalities – using users' existing relationships, everyday experience, images, knowledge and so on. Over the following years, Facebook introduced more and more complex compound invocations that diverted and multiplied users' invocational voices, simultaneously serving the interests of users, advertisers and the corporation. Meanwhile, the diversity of other invocational platforms with different invocational repertoires was policed or became irrelevant.

One of the implications of the invocational colonisation of everyday life has been the translation of a diversity of social and professional practices into a relatively narrow invocational repertoire. As many people with vocations in writing, graphic design and typography more or less willingly abandoned their physical typewriters, rulers, pens, metal type and so on for the unified and powerful invocational environment, they sought to translate traditional practices into the new medium: another form of invocation. Many of the avocations of new software were grounded in prior arts, as suggested in the language of fonts, kerning, leading (or line spacing) and so on. Yet the veneer of familiarity in these avocations, and the aesthetics of the invocational imperative, masked a certain rigidity and homogeneity of rearticulating work as invocationary actions. Where the sign writer's art was displaced by PDFs, the copywriter's art is complicated by ChatGPT.

The three input modes: Commands, control and captures

Now I will return to the formal distinction introduced earlier in this section that identified three distinct modes of operation of inputs: commands that trigger events, controls that determine paths and speeds and sampling that captures and records patterns in the environment (see Table 5). In the flow of using invocational media, these device modes are often used in combination and even cross-translated. These three input modes preceded the invocational assemblage. For example, the assemblage of a human driver and car has similar features: an accelerator and brake to trigger speed changes, a steering wheel that controls direction of movement and a field of vision for human perception, which recognises the sensory world. The invocational assemblage mediates and automates aspects of users' capacity to command, control and capture phenomena. As can be seen in Table 5, commanding, controlling and capturing are typically used in combination, but they represent distinct forms of intervention in the flow of events.

Triggering is a discrete invocationary act that marks a logical binary change at a critical moment. For example, keys on a computer keyboard work as binary switches triggering a discrete and singular value as part of the typical QWERTY set of 66, 72 or 88 physical keys. When the user hits the letter 'A', it triggers a switch to change quickly between the default off state to the on state and back again. The computer registers the Unicode value 'U+0001' and records it in memory. In the case of auto-repeat, the key effectively has two states and after a moment moves into a mode of control. Yet, triggering is discrete and decisive, such as in weapons design and manufacture, where the goal is to eliminate mechanical error at the moment of need. Many switches toggle between two opposing states, and this is foundational to invocational media, with low and high voltages signifying a logical one or zero.

Controlling input devices like dials, joysticks and mice perform ongoing invocationary action, changing values continuously across two or more

Table 5 The Three Modes of Operation of Input Devices

Social Action	Technical Practice	Disciplinary Origins	Events	Invocation	Examples
Commanding	Triggering	Engineering	Decisions in time	Act	Button, keyboard, trigger, brake
Controlling	Curves and vectors	Mathematics	Direction and force in space	Action	Steering wheel, mouse, trackpad, joystick, touchscreen
Capturing	Sampling	Science and art	Sensation	Acts of recording	Scanner, digital camera, digital microphone, digital video, thermometer

Invocational Machines and Assemblages 149

dimensions. It might be as simple as a dial that increases volume linearly. Or a user might move a mouse to move a pointer in two dimensions across the screen. Using vector graphics programs such as Adobe Illustrator involves analysing mouse movements to mathematically map points, lines and curves. While the points a user creates are mapped onto Cartesian coordinates, the lines and curves can be extrapolated and calculated mathematically. This makes the shapes highly manipulable and scalable. The objects and calculations that connect them get more complex in a three-dimensional space like a game or a 3D graphics application. For example, a driving game-like *Drift Hunters* simulates the movement of a vehicle on the road by modelling its geometry, trigonometry and physics and those of many other game objects, each with meshes of thousands of polygons. When the player experiences the game, the sensation of invocationary action is based on simulation models in apparently continuous variation.

Capturing input devices like digital cameras, microphones and video signals capture blocs of sensation in the environment and convert them into digital bitstreams and files. As with controllers, these inputs are continuous, but rather than controlling and modelling movements along mathematical paths, they extract samples of analogue data from the environment and record them in digital form. This involves a sampling scheme defined on a given number of pixels per inch for an image, samples per second for sound or frames per second for moving images. A digital microphone invokes the pressure values of sampled sound vibrations, measuring a certain amount of information for each sample (such as 8, 16 or 24 bits) at a specific sampling frequency (22kHz, 44kHz, 48kHz, etc.). Samplers, therefore, capture details in the noisy empirical world, but their recordings are not continuous vibrations but matrices of digital values. These data can be invoked as sound through the evocative outputs of amplified speakers. Once invocable, audio data can be graphed intermodally as images: waveforms or frequency maps. However, captured data do not scale well. This is a relatively rigid deterritorialisation. The invocable sound file can be transformed with algorithms, but such operations risk losing data.

Similarly, images captured by a scanner or a digital camera are 'raster' images: arrays or maps of rows and columns of pixel values. The quality of the image depends on the number of pixels and the amount of information for each pixel. Raster images can capture photographic quality much better than vector images can. They are real rather than ideal.

150   *Invocational Media*

Data collected through command, control and capture are regularly combined and cross-translated. Continuous inputs can act as switches, for example, when a microphone triggers an alarm as the sound level reaches a certain threshold. Many programmers command their code with keyboards, but others control it with visual coding to describe invocational processes through illustration. For special effects in games or movies, CGI artists capture actors' movements with cameras and other sensors and convert raw movement data to 3D models that replay the actors' motions as animations viewable from any perspective. But raster images are often used to add detail 'wrapped onto' the surfaces of the models. In the final instance, the animations are rendered as rasterised digital video. Games development requires constant movement between designing models, working with scripts and gameplay experience. In evaluating invocational media products, it is unclear whether the code is the true artefact or the compiled software is.

Code and action, intellect and intuition

Software is experienced in two ways: a programmer's invocational code and the invocationary action when the program runs. This difference relates to Bergson's (1998 [1911]) distinction between intellect and intuition. He sees these as two sources of knowledge of the world that are complementary but different. He argues that the intellect is best for studying inert objects because it can use concepts, symbols, abstraction, analysis and fragmentation to understand the spatial world. However, he argues, intellect misses the crucial phenomena of movement and time. He says these dimensions of reality can only be glimpsed through intuition. And this is crucial because 'movement is reality itself' (p. 169). Bergson's work was highly influential in the early twentieth century but is relatively marginal today. However, its influence can be seen in common-sense thinking about intuition today. Programmers or someone in software studies might usefully analyse a video game by its code and its formal features, but for most users it is experienced more intuitively by how it is experienced as it 'runs'. Bergson argues that by ignoring knowledge gained though intuition, both ancient and modern philosophical approaches miss the essence of reality, which appears only in movement.

The techniques of invocational command, control and capture in computational media can be seen as manifestations of the dominant philosophies of space, time and movement that Bergson critiques. In appraising philosophers'

Invocational Machines and Assemblages 151

attempts to use intellect to understand movement, he argues that the dominant philosophical approaches try to capture motion by taking 'snapshots' of objects before and after a change in position. He describes this as the cinematographic illusion (1998 [1911], p. 306), which reconstructs movement by taking a series of still images. He argues that however fast the images are captured, each image remains static. The impression that these pictures capture movement is an illusion. In all their accuracy, they exclude duration itself. This sampling strategy is a principal modern way of understanding time and space.

However, Bergson considers that while modern and ancient philosophies are both problematic, they are distinctively different in their approach. The ancients (Plato and Aristotle) and the moderns (Galileo, Kepler, Descartes) try to comprehend movement by measuring the change an object has undergone between immobile points. But the two traditions choose their points differently: ancients look for privileged moments, while moderns focus on samples:

> What is behind this difference of attitude of the two sciences toward change? We may formulate it by saying that ancient science thinks it knows its object sufficiently when it has noted of it some privileged moments, whereas modern science considers the object at any moment whatever. (Bergson, 1998, p. 330)

He says ancient science defined movement by capturing 'privileged or salient moments' (p. 330). For example, if ancient observers wanted to track a falling object, they chose the moment at which the object is released and the 'culminating point' at which it hits the ground (p. 331). They observed that the object follows a naturally curved path between these two points. They saw this movement as an instantiation of an ideal curve. Even if the object is blown off course a bit, this deviation represents only a degradation of a mathematically true geometrical path. In this conception, movement takes place through a transition from a privileged point, through a series of ordinary points, to another privileged point. As Deleuze paraphrases, ancient movement progressed from 'pose' to 'pose' (1986, p. 4).

Input devices that select and control invoked points, curves and polygons continue in this ancient tradition of defining movements by capturing poses. A click on the mouse button defines a salient moment – it strikes a pose. In a vector graphics program like Adobe Illustrator, users draw lines by clicking at one privileged point and dragging to another point. They draw circles and curves by choosing an appropriate 'tool' and clicking and dragging to form a circle or a curve. While this is mapped onto Cartesian coordinates, the curves themselves can be calculated to shapes with a higher resolution. These figures are considered 'perfect' (Naiman, 1988, p. 549), recalling Plato's argument that the world is divided between by 'Ideas' or 'Forms' that are the essences of things, while objects or matter in the physical world are merely imitations. In this case, the object in memory is mathematically defined and perfect, but what appears on the screen is an imperfect lower-resolution rendition.

Modernity never entirely replaced ancient methods. As can be seen in the distinction between vectors and raster graphics, the two coexist in invocational assemblages. They rely on both Euclidean and Cartesian geometrical principles. Mathematicians continue to study Plato's Forms, Newton's gravity and Einstein's relativity. Mathematician Roger Penrose (1989) explicitly acknowledges his philosophical allegiance to Plato, with his belief that mathematical concepts have a fundamental reality and exist independently of human minds. He argues that the physical world is ultimately based on mathematical principles and that the universe follows its laws. He also believes that the human mind has the capability to understand and access this mathematical reality, much like Plato's belief in the existence of a realm of abstract forms that is separate from the physical world. Platonism continues to inform the thinking of many programmers (Agre, 1997, p. 49), especially in symbolic AI approaches, which attempt to build models of objects in the world and the 'rules' by which they interact. Even for those who don't directly study ancient philosophy, its methods and concepts are part of the Western cultural conceptual and technological toolbox.

We can see the influence of both modern and ancient philosophical concepts in invocational animation applications such as Adobe Animate. This application uses a timeline that presents the animator with a series of equal 'frames', somewhat like cinema. Animators can draw images using lines and shapes one frame at a time. When these stills are invoked rapidly in sequence, they create an illusion of movement like cinematic animation.

However, several of Animate's features have an ancient heritage. In Plato's (1974, p. 312) dualist ontology, 'intelligible' entities exist in a different reality from 'visible' entities, which are lower-level instantiations of the original Form. In Animate, symbols are like intelligible objects, held in the 'library' environment, which is separated from their visible existences on the 'stage' of the final multimedia work. Designers can change or distort instances by manipulating their properties, but the original symbol remains sacrosanct. Yet when the symbol is changed, all these changes are 'inherited' by all the instances.

Invocational Machines and Assemblages   153

Animate can also model *movement* in a classical way. A feature called 'motion tweening' moves an object from one 'key frame' to another 'key frame'. That is, it does not change each frame but moves between 'privileged moments' (Bergson, 1998, p. 330). The program uses 'tweening', calculating the movement between these frames and attaching them to a motion path. In this case, it performs a 'regulated transition from one form to another, that is, an order of *poses* or privileged instances, as in a dance' (Deleuze, 1986, p. 4,italics in the original). The program smoothly transforms objects in position, scale, rotation and even colour, as the playback head that marks 'now time' passes between the two key points.

An object approach is not unique to graphics. The philosophy of object-oriented programming also reflects an invocational construction in which objects are invoked as instances of classes and methods (actions). Subclasses inherit features from their parent classes, and further objects can be based on these. Objects send messages to invoke actions in instances of other objects. This mode of representation is an enrolment of a dualist philosophical conception of objects, instances and events.

Sampling input devices discussed earlier take a more modern approach to capture real-world objects and their movement. These take a series of measurements of their surroundings at 'any-instant-whatevers' (Deleuze, 1986, p. 3). They are more subject to noise than switches and vectors. Their purpose is to capture regular samples from the noisy and unpredictable details of physical events like environmental sounds, images and movements. In direct contrast to the formally modelled systems of meaning in objects and their poses, bitstreams are chaotic. Input devices such as microphones and cameras open onto the world with a sensitivity to specific types of variation – sound waves, photons and so on. In the data capturing mode, input devices extract a single set of measurements of the movements around them from their immediate surroundings and convert them into matrices of discrete values.

Bergson sees both ancient and modern scientific methods for capturing movement as illusions (1998 [1911], pp. 272–370). Neither the poses approach nor the any-instant-whatever approach captures change in itself, only static snapshots on either side of it. Change is the 'open', which always occurs between the immobile sections. It is pure duration, an 'infinite multiplicity of becomings' (p. 304).

However, critics have called into question Bergson's claims that the technological techniques fail to seize the world in some manner. Deleuze (1986) argues that Bergson underestimated cinema's capacity to capture movement. In his two *Cinema* books (1986, 1989), he carefully analyses Bergson's rejection of the cinematographic illusion and uses some of Bergson's concepts to argue that cinema in fact does present images of movement and time. He develops a theory of how the cinematic apparatus creates not an illusion but an immediate image of movement. Much of the cinematic image's impact is virtual – something apparently between the frames. The cinema image is 'not the photogramme [but] an intermediate image to which movement is not appended or added; the movement on the contrary belongs to the intermediate image as immediate given'. The cinema image is not a series of stills but a 'movement image' (Deleuze, 1986, p. 2).

The change sample

The invocational assemblage is not cinema, even if it sometimes invokes cinema. But where cinema captures pure images of movement and time, invocations capture pure samples of change. Sampling input devices collect samples of 'any-instant-whatevers' using a method similar to cinematic movement images. Both the film camera and the sampling computer input device capture 'blocs of space-time' (Deleuze, 1986, p. 61). Samplers apply a similar principle to cinema's regular 24 frames per second but in a far more rapid and more abstract process: sound samplers typically capture 5,000–48,000 samples per second. Video samplers capture and compress thousands of pixels for each frame.

Cinema frames are different from samplers because of what each captures. The film camera optically captures the scene within a frame, distinguishing 'saturated' and 'rarefied' regions. It manifests a point of view and defines an 'out-of-field' (Deleuze, 1986, pp. 12–18). By contrast, digital video files are masses of data, using various resolutions, colour systems, frame rates and compression schemes. They may produce movement images, but technically they are clusters of change samples – pure samples of change. Change samples must be invoked, decoded, and output to be played back. They can be transformed with mathematical or AI techniques that perform changes that are experienced intuitively, such as reverb on sound or photomontages of images.

The granularity of the individual invoked change samples gives digital bitstreams and files their abstraction and versatility. Sampling can be multimodal, capturing not only temporal phenomena like sounds but also spatial forms like

Invocational Machines and Assemblages 155

digitised images. An invocational image is captured by sampling pixels (picture elements) one row at a time. Each pixel typically records red, green and blue values on a scale from saturation to rarefaction for a colour image. These data are stored in invocable domains in memory archives. In earlier computer generations, though, this technique of scanning change samples was expensive in terms of processor and storage resources. It produced very large, 'dumb' files, and for a long time distributing audio or televisual content at scale was technically and economically unviable. However, by the 1990s, programmers had had great success using compression techniques such as JPEG and MPEG to reduce image file sizes by eliminating redundant information. Rather than recording all the raw samples, algorithms could invoke fields of differences that could be sensed, encoded, transformed and invoked indefinitely. By the late 2010s, with faster processors, networks, better compression and cheaper storage, networked invocational media had become competitive with the programming of broadcasting and portable physical media such as Blu-ray discs and CDs. Internet streaming was becoming the dominant way of fulfilling desires for audiovisual content.

However, invocational media experiences were never limited to linear samples. Applications such as computer games, virtual reality and augmented reality incorporated diverse mixtures of code, images, 3D models and interface elements. These various configurations of sampled and algorithmically switched and vectorised content created highly versatile and abstract entities in invocable domains. Invocational systems are a metamedium that invokes not only single samples but entire media forms.

At this point, we can be more precise in the claim that invocation is the genetic element for digital computers. For Deleuze, *montage* is the 'genetic element' in cinema (Deleuze, 1986, p. 83) – the elemental force from which more complex compounds are created. For invocation, the dynamic remains constantly immanent in invocational media. Once input devices command, control and capture data, they become indefinitely reconfigurable with further invocations. Invocational events in circuitry complete operations that would never be computed by human hands. They automate practices from mathematics and logic which capture formalised images of change. But more than analysing these samples, they reconstitute these change samples as evocations through outputs, creating sensations of movement, light or sound that are experienced intuitively.

The invocational interval recalls the film editor's point of decision, constantly and automatically. It maintains a state of indeterminacy, so what is invoked is

156 *Invocational Media*

never only a repetition. The invocational medium is constantly performing invocations and redrawing the next screen. Like a folded-up and automated operator in Bergson's (1988) 'central telephonic exchange' (p. 30) (one of his analogies for the brain), the CPU is constantly called on to decide what to connect next from a range of possible events. What is invoked moment by moment is conditioned by automatic transformations in the current state of the digital machine based on what is available in the invocable domains of memory, storage and networks and what vibrations are recorded on input devices.

Unlike cinema, invocational media can be open through inputs and conditional branching to invoke substantial variations from moment to moment. In cinema, the final work is in the sequence fixed once the film editor and director have completed it as a whole work. In invocational systems, users usually have some command and control over what is revealed moment by moment. User input devices are the agents for initiating change and control. This is how users decide what will happen next. This privilege is granted because computer designs incorporate spaces for possible users: pauses, stand-ins and sensors opening onto the world to detect users' manifest intentions.

This section's focus on command, control and capture must now be supplemented by an analysis of archival technologies – the components in the invocational abstract machine that secure the ongoing availability and organisation of traces of commands, data and programs over time.

Archival machines (memory and storage)

Memory and archives are integral to invocational assemblages as they give invocations duration. In Innis's (1986) terms, they are 'time-binding'. The memory and archiving components in invocational assemblages, such as random-access memory, SSDs, hard disks and tapes, work at different speeds. They can hold memory traces from imperceptibly short periods to indefinitely long ones. They establish complex invocational relationships to time, memory and the archive. The fastest memory domains are CPU registers, which supply the instructions for the first stage of the fetch-execute cycle. They are the temporary stores for data that are almost immediately destroyed and reused. Each first-stage invocation forms a second-stage invocation which calls to other invocable domains – all the machines I address in this chapter. Many second-stage invocations access

Invocational Machines and Assemblages

archival bits either to read or transform them. Over the history of invocational media, these practices of invocationally inscribing and recalling data have displaced many other forms of memorisation and archiving.

The invocational imperative makes it desirable to have the fastest, largest and most comprehensive invocable domains of memory and archives possible. However, there are always technical and financial limits, so different components add different amounts of invocational distance and delay. The next fastest archival components constitute random access memory (RAM). Slower and further away are the storage devices such as SSDs, hard disks and even tape, which hold data even when not powered. Over computing history, engineers have developed archival technologies that retain traces of invocations by exploiting the physics of cardboard, mercury, sound, light, magnets and semiconductors. The intangibility of these media and the possibility of copying data indefinitely can create the impression that information persists across a limitless range of materials, fostering an indifference to materiality itself. When data are in the cloud, their physical material location is sometimes considered irrelevant, but it is not.

In *Archive Fever*, Derrida (1996) argues that changes in archival technologies – media of inscription – change the future and the past. That is, how we store records today affects how we understand the past and therefore influences the future. Today's emails, Instagram posts and other records become legacies committed to the future. When we use archiving technologies we are determining how we will experience and imagine the past. This is why memorials are created, war artists are commissioned and photo albums are produced. We are necessarily also destroying much of the present. We often exclude or renegotiate our historical trauma. Accessing records from the past affects our present actions.

Invocational media record the present in new ways, automating some of the writing of history and storing it in different ways. They also change how we access past knowledge. Rather than visiting the library, we might invoke our history in ten-second blurts from our voice assistant or in a fragmented set of results from a search engine. Invocational archiving dramatically diverges from previous practices of human mental work and recordkeeping. Written records have for a long time been stored as near-permanent marks on a surface read directly by the human eye. Now, they are inscribed and copied through invocable domains using the diversity of materials just discussed. Records are not indexed by spatial relations at the scale of the human body (pages, binders, shelves, filing cabinets) but in peripheral hardware. In a physical archive, each object is located *at an address* (a particular physical place). In invocable domains, virtual objects are located by being *addressed* – in the form of quasi-speech. Archival traces can be called up from first-level technical spaces and expressed as outputs in second-level material expressions on screen or on paper. This split between levels makes the invocable data seem immaterial and indestructible but only until the machine crashes or the material storage device is lost, damaged or corrupted. At this point, data become more inaccessible than ever.

The shifts from traditional archiving to invocational media have been culturally and socially transformative. Historical materials are traditionally stored as physical archives and histories are told as narratives, but databases organise historical traces differently. Manovich (1999) observes that where a narrative 'creates a cause-and-effect trajectory of seemingly unordered items', the 'database represents the world as a list of items which it refuses to order' (p. 85). A database doesn't have a moral – not in the same way as a narrative – although in some ways it does implicitly say that these entities are like one another and have some importance and validity. Where physical archives must be arranged using one form of order, a database offers an array of searches, automated visualisation and summary tools to create new interpretations of the data. A database report has no natural beginning or ending. It does not impose the teleology or sense of closure that is expected from narrative accounts of a series of past events.

Sociotechnical changes to archiving have also involved changes in business models. The tech industry constantly seeks strategies to make invocable domains available in exchange for purchase, attention or rent. Again, there are trade-offs for speed, security and flexibility. While most personal computers have in-built local memory and storage, cloud storage has become a convenient, secure and liquid invocational commodity that is not actually held by the user. Many people's records and memories are now held in the cloud in repositories or on social media. The imperative for convenient universal invocability has made a large subset of the cultural record available on demand. By comparison, knowledge offline seems local, vulnerable and inflexible , but also material, contextualised, auratic and authentic.

There is a hidden violence in this utopian project of making all human knowledge instantly invocable anytime and anywhere. Google's mission statement 'to organise the world's information and make it universally accessible and useful' (Google, 2020) is undoubtedly a manifesto for data colonialism (Couldry & Meijas, 2019). If, as Derrida (1996) argues, archiving is a violent practice that consigns the diversity of what is given to an exteriority, then Google does damage with its secret methods of capturing, indexing and ordering all that information. It builds a proprietary repository of the world's intellectual labour by drawing from a diversity of everyday places where traces can be captured and homogenises them as lists of ranked equivalent search results. In sorting them with secret algorithms, Google displaces a diversity of physical and cognitive practices of discovering and organising knowledge and presents it alongside custom advertising. The quasi-universality of the Google archive represents an unprecedentedly centralised monopoly of knowledge. Despite the many exabytes of data captured in Google's data centres, there is an infinity of givens that are relatively inaccessible: the uninvocable. What can be invoked is commodified, structured and framed in Google's terms. What is not recedes as the forgotten and the outside.

Google increasingly compensates for these gaps by offering results that anticipate users' desires by profiling them using big data and AI. Unlike a conventional database query, so-called unstructured data are not arranged in fields and records but can be analysed through deep learning. Manovich (2018) proposes an approach to criticism of texts and images using unsupervised machine learning that he calls cultural analytics. He claims that this avoids the practice in cultural theory of analysing cultural texts by imposing concepts defined by the analyst: 'be they "modernism", "narrative structures", "images of the working class", "selfies", or "amateur digital photographers"' (p. 37). Instead, he claims, it is possible to invoke meanings that emerge, without reduction, from the data themselves:

> Unsupervised machine learning methods allow us to discover new categories for which we don't have names and to see connections we were not previously aware of. Thus, rather than reducing cultural data to familiar categories, unsupervised machine learning can expose limitations of such categories and suggest new ways of seeing culture. (p. 37)

As well as conducting his own cultural analytics research on large image datasets, Manovich points to the emergence of recommendation engines such as in YouTube, Spotify and Netflix that analyse users' media consumption patterns through AI analyses of cultural objects, using features such as the media content, associated texts and consumption patterns of other people with a record of similar tastes. We could argue that such recommendations offer word of mouth in convocations, responding to the user's invocations and invoking associated genre and intersubjective patterns in media and audiences. As Manovich (2018) points out, these categories are not grounded only in genre names ('blues', 'shoegaze', 'ambient') but also in clusters of similarity that emerge from AI analysis. These recommendation systems not only provide practical guidance to users but also serve as agents in the constitution of clusters of taste. Where box-office figures, focus groups, questionnaires or Top 100 music charts map the taste of a small sample of consumers, records of media invocations seem immediate and accurate to the level of the individual, allowing deep learning methods to statistically analyse the relationships between cultural objects, identities, consumption and taste.

The limits of invocability

Despite the implicit promises of techno-optimists that we would all have universal invocational power, many factors limit the invocable domains we can access. Some resources have never been made invocable. Some invocational infrastructures technically fail. Some invocations are restricted and encrypted, while others are commodified and must be bought, rented or offered with the involuntary invocations of advertising.

First, most things in the universe have never been exposed to the inspection of input devices and have never been captured in accessible invocable domains. Some of these natural absences are omitted because their holders want to keep them offline. Otherwise, invocability is unevenly distributed, to the disadvantage of the geographically, economically and socially marginal. There is a digital divide in the inequitable distribution of narratives, images, datasets and other invocable cultural resources (Graham, 2011). Even things that are made invocable reflect the practices of digitisation of sampled and switched data. The resolutions and perspectives at moments of input reflect the values of those commanding them into being invocable.

Second, records become uninvocable because of failed first-level invocations with incompatible or unsupported standards, file corruption, hardware breakdown, power failure, network faults and so on. Failures can be difficult and expensive to resolve, and there is a generally hidden labour in the sustaining of a viable capacity for invocation. Critics raise the possibility that our era will become a digital dark age because of the poor long-term durability of invocational recordkeeping.

Third, many invocations are restricted by institutional policies, for better or worse. Commercial and government secrecy and copyright are habitually secured by systems of physical, invocational and contractual control. On the other hand, there are attempts at constraining invocational power in the public

Invocational Machines and Assemblages 161

interest. The most significant example is the European Union's General Data Protection Regulation (GDPR) (Intersoft Consulting, 2022), which came into force in 2016 and which might be interpreted as establishing invocational rights. They enact liberal principles that hold that invocations of personal data should be lawful, fair, transparent and consensual. Invocable and invoking subjects should have invocational rights to be informed, access, rectify, erase, restrict and copy their own data. They have the privacy rights to become uninvocable or to restrict their being subjected to automated decision-making and profiling. These kinds of policies can be algorithmically embedded in software, automating their enforcement – at least until hackers break into these repositories.

Fourth, there are many ways in which invocations have been commoditised and monopolised. IBM controlled the market for institutional invocational power by offering long-term equipment leases with regular upgrades. A new business model emerged with personal computers, when Microsoft famously secured a deal with IBM to licence the DOS operating system for the IBM PC. This allowed Microsoft to sell 'shrink-wrapped' licensed software that gave users conditional rights to invocation. In the 1990s, the internet became the dominant distribution and communication medium, with Secure Socket Layer standard from 1995 and Transport Layer Security from 1999, helping transform what was previously a strictly non-commercial network into a global marketplace. Over the following decades, much of the tech sector changed its business model to holding users' data, profiling them and selling advertising to give them access to their own data.

Finally, with the consignation of culture to the 'cloud', the material and energy costs of the medium itself are rendered invisible. Data and algorithms have physical existences in expensive gadgets, signals on optical fibre networks and servers in data centres. These are all quite material: using energy, consuming space, degrading physically (Borning, Friedman & Logler, 2020). Many of the material components have environmental costs, as some are toxic during manufacture and after disposal. There are human costs, also, as labour conditions in manufacturing, call centres and content moderation operations are notoriously poor. Yet, these costs are often rendered invisible.

Code machines (software)

While the term 'code' has become commonly adopted to refer to the texts that programmers write and compile to create software, the term has a much older,

162 *Invocational Media*

secretive legacy in cryptography, as explored in Chapter 3. Codes and ciphers were used by the Roman Empire and later in the Arabic-speaking world, such as the first known book on cryptology by Baghdad polymath al Kindī (Al Kadit, 1992) published in the ninth century. Of course, cryptographic techniques attempted to allow those in power to ensure that commands and other messages are successfully communicated. In the Dark Ages in Europe, cryptography came to be perceived as something foreign and magic. But in the Renaissance, Europeans rediscovered cryptography, and by 1600 most nations had 'black chambers', whose work was to create and break cryptograms (Dooley, 2013). As cryptographers competed to develop schemes to encrypt and decrypt messages, each countered the others' efforts with more and more complex techniques.

As twentieth-century technologised militaries took up telegraphy, radio and cryptographic machines, the strategic importance of encrypted communications fostered a secret battle between invocatory devices. Most famously, as discussed in Chapter 3, the evocatively named Enigma machine, an electromechanical invocatory device used by the German military from the 1930s, was cracked by a device called the *bomba*, attributed to Polish cryptographer Marian Rejewski, and a similar one credited to Turing, the bombe (Copeland, 2006; Dooley, 2013). However, the cracking of a German high-speed enciphering machine attached to a teleprinter using the so-called Tunny code is attributed to the development of the first special-purpose digital electronic computer, Colossus (Budiansky, 2006). While Colossus was designed to break codes, it did not yet operate with programming code, as inputs were madewith switches and patch cables.

The first general-purpose computers after the Second World War were programmed manually or with machine code. The development of coding languages in the 1950s began offering users avocations to perform invocations using more familiar higher-level codes. By 1950, the Eckert–Mauchly Computer Corporation had developed 'Short Code' for the UNIVAC computer, which allowed users to enter equations as coded higher-level invocations rather than addressing hardware components (Schmitt, 1988). This represented one of the first steps in recoding first-level invocations as second-level avocations – that is, the lower-level machine operations were recoded to support users' prior experience and education in other codes. In the process, computer languages and the code itself became ideological (Chun, 2011). Designers of programming languages came to tailor these avocations towards groups with specific

Invocational Machines and Assemblages 163

ideological orientations. For example, FLOW-MATIC and its descendent COBOL were designed to resemble business-related English so that computers could be marketed to corporate customers (Marino, 2020).

As institutions came to inscribe their processes in software, the relationship between software code and socially regulatory codes came into focus. In pragmatic terms, this was more than a metaphorical relationship, as software code governed how institutions operated. Lawrence Lessig (2006) drew attention to the implications of this form of inscribed agency:

> In real space, we recognise how laws regulate – through constitutions, statutes and other legal codes. In cyberspace we must understand how a different 'code' regulates – how the software and hardware (i.e. the 'code' of cyberspace) that make cyberspace what it is also regulate cyberspace as it is. As William Mitchell puts it, this code is cyberspace's 'law'. 'Lex Informatica', as Joel Reidenberg first put it, or better, 'code is law'. (p. 5)

The political influence of code demanded some new methods to examine it in detail. The critical code studies approach that emerged in the 2010s is grounded in applying hermeneutic approaches to code itself, based on the premise that code reveals things before and beyond the functionality it will invoke. Montford et al. (2012) argue that a textual critical examination of code helps reveal not only how a program works but also the contexts of its production and the aesthetics and politics of its developers. The book focuses on a simple single-line maze-generating program for the Commodore 64 microcomputer. It analyses the BASIC language in which it was written and the hardware on which it runs, which makes this also an example of platform studies. Their work is convincing not only because of its reading of code but also because it explores the assemblages in which the code participates: the hardware, developers and institutions. However, this close reading approach may not scale well.

When the source code becomes an object to be examined by human readers rather than just compiled for execution, as discussed in the previous section, it can reveal things not apparent in the compiled software. As Marino (2020) observes, there can be many audiences beyond the programmer and the machine: other programmers, project managers, conference attendees, corporate bodies and courts. In some cases, code is a kind of performance, as with the hacktivist art project Transborder Immigrant Tool, a phone app purportedly designed for people crossing the US–Mexico border. It could guide people to water and read them poetry to keep their spirits up. While this code was never invoked by its intended users, the concept and the code succeeded as a disruptive political intervention: its creators and their code attracted the attention of Congressman Duncan Hunter, Fox News and one participant's university workplace (Marino, 2020). Code can serve as a provocation as well as an invocation.

Examining code can help reveal how software, once it is executed, distributes agency between humans and non-humans (Mackenzie, 2006). Code extends the encoded or performed voices of programmers, corporations, governments, artists and so on in ways governed by its hidden affordances. Code can make the attribution of agency clear, for example, by giving different classes of users or individuals privileges to access different fields and operations in a database. However, this must be designed carefully within the code. Without a strategy, the agency for invocations can quickly be lost.

While critical code studies often aim to demystify the operations of code by revealing how it was written by humans and how it operates in detail (Montford et al., 2012), the performance of code 'in the wild' quickly becomes impossible to trace, considering the interaction between system layers, code libraries, a diversity of users and so on. Much code is also inaccessible, as corporations and governments keep their proprietary programs secret and protected. For Chun (2011), the source code of software often serves to obscure as much as it reveals, becoming a form of 'sourcery':

> As our machines disappear, getting flatter and flatter, the density and opacity of their computation increases. Every use is also an act of faith: we believe these images and systems render us transparent not for technological, but rather for metaphorical, or more strongly ideological, reasons.
>
> As stated earlier, this paradox is not accidental to computing's appeal, but rather grounds the computer as a useful and provocative, indeed magical, model. Its combination of what can be seen and not seen, can be known and not known – its separation of interface from algorithm; software from hardware – makes it a powerful metaphor for everything we believe is invisible yet generates visible effects, from genetics to the invisible hand of the market; from ideology to culture. (Chun, 2011, p. 17)

So, code itself may not reveal the abstract processes by which the magic operation of invocational media is performed. Understanding algorithms – the equivalent of magical spells, tricks or formulae – may reveal more than the code that implements them:

When enacted, symbolic logic can effect procedural alterations to reality . . . The key term here is 'enacted'. This book uncovers how the humble vehicle of computation, the algorithm, has its roots not only in mathematical logic but in the philosophical traditions of cybernetics, consciousness, and the magic of symbolic language. (Finn, 2017, p. 2)

Algorithms and procedures are the principal resources for invocationary acts, informing events in invocational assemblages. They 'must be understood *both* as a formalised account of computational possibilities and as a practical tool, and the relationship between these two is not fixed' (Dourish, 2016, p. 6). However, Dourish argues, they are often inscrutable to serious examination compared to human processes, which might be traceable. Pasquale (2015) points out that many corporations closely guard their algorithms to avoid the scrutiny of regulators. He calls for public attention to algorithms and whether they support privacy, fairness and accountability. One of the key principles behind the move to adopt free and open-source software is to make algorithms more transparent.

On the other hand, Bogost (2015) sees belief in and fear of algorithms as a kind of mystification:

Our supposedly algorithmic culture is not a material phenomenon so much as a devotional one, a supplication made to the computers people have allowed to replace gods in their minds. (Bogost, 2015)

Bogost may be correct that the veneration of code, algorithms and software has obscured and stupefied public discourse about invocational media politics. Perhaps this is one of the most critical political struggles around this technology: contesting the power and obfuscations of monopolies of invocationary action.

Machines of temporality (the two clocks)

The interplay between CPU and memory in the invocational interval is regulated by two timekeeping components establishing an invocational time sense. One is the system time that is measured in ticks. The other regulates the rhythm of processor operations in billions of pulses per second. These two clocks, each with different functionality, history and ontology, generate complementary and contradictory mediations of time. The real-time clock (based on system time) works to synchronise and coordinate events globally and to locate future and past events, translated into years, months, days, hours, minutes, seconds and milliseconds. The other regulates invocationary action at high speed to mediate human and non-human decisions in the present. These clocks are metonyms for invocational temporalities in societies that have adopted invocational media.

Calendar and clock time have regulated time for centuries more or less precisely, but the real-time clock inside the computer has enhanced their operation's precision and degree of connectivity. For example, invocational events such as changes in a database are typically timestamped automatically, allowing sequences of events to be reconstructed. Lewis Mumford famously argues that '[t]he clock, not the steam engine, is the key-machine of the industrial age' (Mumford, 1967, p. 14). This machine helped discipline workers within factories by allocating and policing working hours. An industrial way of life arose, in which capitalists controlled and coordinated work more rigorously than ever. Clock rhythms reached beyond their cogs and springs into the material, social and psychological worlds they governed. Where previously craftspeople had worked at their own pace on various skilled tasks, the Fordist and Taylorist production line rationalised labour into a series of simple tasks suited to less skilled work at higher speeds. Labour time became another input resource in production, as jealously guarded and contested as any other. Capitalism fostered an ethic of time-thriftiness, differentiating productive work from leisure time, which became increasingly dedicated to consumption.

Invocational media support even more precise time accountancy. Processor time in the device are typically reduced to one value: the 'tick'. Ticks are synchronised time divisions that allow tasks to be tracked within fractions of a second; each device translates the universal value of the tick into the user's local time and date. Rather than using the Gregorian calendar and standard time zones, ticks are counted from an arbitrary moment set by the original programmer of an operating system – the beginning of an 'epoch'. For example, the epoch of the UNIX operating system began on 1 January 1970 at 00:00:00 Universal Time. Each operating system uses a different epoch and resolution (in seconds, milliseconds or nanoseconds). Because the number of possible ticks is a finite value in memory, every epoch has a start and finish date. These values are sufficient for most purposes, but for UNIX, for example, there will be problem on 19 January 2038, when, if the system is not updated, the signed 32-bit integer will overflow, and the system will revert to 13 December 1901. This is reminiscent of the notorious Y2K bug at the turn of this century, which it was feared would bring down systems when the clock ticked over to 2000.

Invocational Machines and Assemblages 167

These limitations illustrate the risk of programmers making arbitrary decisions and the impossibility of invoking the infinite span of time and space. Invocable domains are, by their nature, finite.

While the real-time clock manages real time, the other key timekeeping component in the invocational assemblage, the processor clock, changes the present. Real-time system clocks register the passing of real time; processor clocks regulate the speed and rhythm of invocations, measured in millions (MHz or megahertz) or billions (GHz or gigahertz) of pulses per second. This is not only a drumbeat that regulates machine operations but also a new ontological state of being. At these speeds, the flow of invocations secures the consistency of platforms. Constant repetition of decisions and non-decisions maintains an interactive openness to invocationary action at speeds above the level of perception. Virilio (1993) sees these changes in temporality as deeply disturbing disruptions to the previously familiar temporality and presence:

> What is becoming critical here is no longer the three spatial dimensions, but a fourth, temporal dimension – in other words the present itself . . . technologies of the real time . . . kill 'present' time by isolating it from its presence here and now for the sake of another commutative space that is no longer composed of our 'concrete presence' in the world, but of a discrete telepresence whose enigma remains forever intact. (p. 4)

While Virilio's assessment of the death of present time is hyperbolic, there is no doubt that the clocks in invocational media mark a transformation in individual and collective time sense. The cycles of the processor clock are a structuring force for what Castells (1996, p. xl) refers to as 'timeless time . . . a systemic perturbation in the sequential order of . . . social practices'. Patterns of invocational bursts and jumps bring everything invoked and invocable to states of liveness. This high-speed performance of invocations is the enabler of Deleuze's (1992) control society 'modulations', engendering the serpent-like corporation that supersedes the slower disciplinary rhythms of industrial capitalism:

> Of course the factory was already familiar with the system of bonuses, but the corporation works more deeply to impose a modulation of each salary, in states of perpetual metastability that operate through challenges, contests, and highly comic group sessions. (Deleuze, 1992, p. 4)

This transition from shiftwork to invocable labour offered corporations much finer-grained spatial and temporal control over labour. With timestamped

168   *Invocational Media*

and location-tracked invocational events, workers could be microcoordinated and made accountable as never before. A case in point is the gig economy. Corporations such as Uber transformed their workers from employees into contractors, making them independent of traditional labour conditions, including regulated hours. Uber claimed this gave workers/contractors flexibility and autonomy to work whenever they liked. Rather than being paid by the hour, workers were summoned 'just in time' to earn fares for pickups, drop-offs, distance travelled and so on. Uber implemented surveillance and rating systems for every aspect of the work and discontinued those who failed to measure up. This was not a good deal for workers. In one extreme case in Sydney, Australia, in 2020, an Uber Eats rider was killed by a truck. The company checked its records and determined that the rider was not working at the time of the incident, so it initially refused to honour insurance benefits for his family (Begley, 2021). In any dispute, companies are favoured because they command, control and record invocationary acts.

Interconnecting some of these machines

Now we can draw together the politics of the invocationary machines so far examined. With inputs, differences in the environment can be invoked to constitute commands, controls or captured data. The configuration of these inputs serves to regulate invocational powers through physical access and security systems. Many invocational assemblages are asymmetrical: providing command over populations by limiting the most potent invocations to centres of calculation while extracting inputs that are charmed (social media), involuntary (security cameras with AI) or coerced (police databases) from these populations. The invocational assemblage also stores up invoked data and algorithms for the future in a manner informed by the perspectives, pragmatic constraints and ideological judgements of system owners. For example, Amazon analyses users' behaviour purportedly as a service for its customers but mainly to lubricate transactions. Similarly, the mediation of social relationships in convocations is conditioned by those who design and own interaction architectures. These convocational spaces offer various types of command and control, articulated as posts, tweets, photos and so on, that are perceived immediately or on delay by those addressed. All these components are subject to everyday invocational temporalities, regulated by the two clocks in combination, mediating events at a temporal granularity that is locally below the threshold of consciousness while being globally synchronised in a quasi-universal simultaneity and coordination of distributed events.

Machines of calculation and decision (CPU)

The next component to examine is often taken to define the medium: the central processing unit. As I have argued, the CPU is the nexus that mediates the fetch-execute cycle. It performs the two-step dance: a primary invocation that starts by gathering what is given in the first instance and then the secondary invocation that generates something new by addressing invocable domains of input, calculation, logic, memory, storage and output. When an invocation brings command and memory together under the regulation of the two clocks, the results are decisions. For mathematician and philosopher Norbert Wiener, decision-making is central to communication and control:

> The fundamental idea is the message . . . and the fundamental element of the message is the decision. (Wiener, as cited in Hayles, 1999, p. 52)

Decision is the killer app of the invocational assemblage. It is the calculation that draws from inputs, data and code to make binary choices – a zero or a one, the opening or closing of a circuit. Invocations to non-human components delegate what was previously a human capacity to make decisions. Every step executed on a digital computer invokes a decision. Flows of bits in logical flip-flop circuits are essentially choices, of which a small fraction are human. Whereas analogue media operate through flows of variation (modulations), invocational media operate by articulating sequences of decisions. Decisions read the data written into archives. Decisions also store new things back into archives. Decisions express events on output devices. Users contribute to these decisions through input devices. In most modern computers, by far the most common decision is barely a decision at all: the program counter is incremented by one, and the next instruction in a programmed sequence is invoked. At some points, though, a program encounters a point of branching, when the next event is determined by states of other programs and variables. Users' inputs may inform many decisions, but programs execute most actual decisions autonomously. For example, when I type a key on my word processor, I cause the event, but the autocorrect software automatically makes decisions on my behalf. The CPU automatically chooses the course of action based on data and algorithms in memory and storage devices.

Decision-making has a diverse cultural legacy. It is deemed crucial in law, military tactics and strategies, business, politics and everyday life. Decisions have been performed with mixtures of faith, ritual, habit, intuition, psychology, courage, policy, reason, calculation, risk assessment, gambling, heuristics, empirical research and statistics. However, a much narrower model of decision theory from philosophy, logic and mathematics is embedded in the architecture of invocational assemblages. At the third level of invocation, electronic invocations invoked concepts from the Western rationalist tradition that constitute a patriarchal mythology of the fathers of computation.

Writing in the mid-nineteenth century, George Boole (2017 [1854]) took problems of logical decision from the discursive domain of philosophy and into the mathematical domain of algebra. In his investigation into the laws of thought, he positioned the 'empty class' on one side and the universe on the other. He labelled these 0 and 1 – nothing and all things. From this point forward, logical equations could adopt these two symbols. Thanks to Shannon's (1938) translation of Boole into information theory, the principles of Boolean algebra became manifest not only as symbols but also as switches and variations of voltages in circuitry (Nahin, 2017). In their implementation as invocations, each relay, valve or transistor would conduct a higher or lower voltage, depending on the state of the other components connected. Data transformations in the technical first level of invocation are invoked with logic gates that return 1 or 0 depending on two input values. The simplest operations of logic gates are AND, OR and NOT. These assess input signals and produce outputs based on this assessment. For example, an AND gate will produce an output of 'true' only when all of its inputs are true. In combination, more complex logical operations are possible, such as NAND, NOR, XOR, XNOR, MUX and DMUX. End users are most familiar with Boole when they invoke his name in generating Boolean searches through databases.

Physicist James Clerk Maxwell is remembered for his work on magnetism and electricity, which was foundational in the development of electrical power and electronics. He is also recognised for his speculations on the power of decision. In his famous thought experiment of 1867, he dreamed that the material world might be transformed with decisions alone (Leff & Rex, 2003). Maxwell proposed to break the second law of thermodynamics – the universal tendency in the universe towards noise and disorder, also known as entropy. According to this law, the universe is slowly but inevitably degenerating towards a homogeneous state of disorganisation. Maxwell imagines a way to work against entropy, envisioning an experiment in which two vessels filled with gas initially at different temperatures. The vessels are connected by a small hole. Under normal circumstances, once this hole is opened, the hot and cold molecules will mingle until the difference between the two is cancelled out. However, Maxwell proposes that entropy might be reversed by putting a mechanism of decision into the system: a notional molecule-sized decision-maker – 'a very observant and neat-fingered being' – that allows hot molecules to pass only in one direction and cool molecules in the other (Krajewski, 2018, p. 175). If this works, these decisions would produce negative entropy, and the temperatures in each container would diverge. Popularisers like Lord Kelvin embellish the story, anthropomorphising this actor as a 'demon' that 'can do as much for atoms as a pianoforte player can do for the keys of a piano – just a little more' (Krajewski, 2018, pp. 174–5). While many of Maxwell's assumptions continue to be controversial, in the late 1920s Leo Szilard (1964 [1929]) takes up Maxwell's hypothesis, proposing that an inanimate intelligent actor might make decisions at the molecular level: 'a simple inanimate device can achieve the same essential result as would be achieved by the intervention of intelligent beings' (Szilard, 1964, p. 309). This imagined device could sense the most basic quantum of information: the absence or presence of a single molecule. This establishes a conception of what would be fundamental in computing: the binary digit, or bit (Leff & Rex, 2003), which leaves no room for doubt at a decisive moment. All logical and arithmetical operations could be broken down to such decision points.

In the mid-twentieth century, practitioners of computational logic turned to 'real-world' scenarios in the domains of politics, economics and science. Game theory sets out to calculate mathematical proofs that determine the optimal strategies for players in a logically defined game. It always starts with a strict set of assumptions about the situation, such as: there are two (or more) opponents; each wants to beat the others in the game; the initial conditions are finite; the possible moves must be made in formally defined 'steps'; and all goals are measurable. Most early game theory work dealt with 'zero-sum' games, in which if one player wins, all the others lose. Von Neumann (1944) mathematically proves that the best strategy in many circumstances is to follow the 'minimax' principle of minimising losses and maximising gains, but his real contribution is to reduce decision-making to an agonistic, mathematically formalised process outside of discourse, politics and social relations. He applies game theory not only to parlour games but also to biology, economics and geopolitics.

Game theory became a highly politicised intervention in public policy. Its advocates claimed was more obective and rational than discursive and interpretive understandings of society. Game theory became institutionalised in many contexts. Abraham Wald generalised von Neumann's approach with his work on 'decision theory', synthesising game theory principles with statistics and weighted risk functions (Beniger, 1986, p. 52). By the mid-1940s, decision theory was being applied at a high policy level to deal with a wide range of problems (Deutsche, 1954). Wald and von Neumann's formalist approaches applied mathematical models to any and every complex phenomenon. In classic rationalist and determinist style, they reduced all change to cause-and-effect events of bifurcation and subjected them to logical analysis and explanation. The principle of mutually assured destruction – a game in which both sides develop an armoury that would make war unthinkable – was the foundation of the Cold War strategies of the superpowers. Computers seemed particularly aligned withimplementing game theory calculations. They also carried the aura of supposedly objective calculation despite being reliant on contentious assumptions and data.

Von Neumann was something of a public figure who was wheelchair-bound until he died from prostate cancer in 1957. It is rumoured that he was a model for the title role in Kubrick's *Dr Strangelove* (Myhrvold, 1999). The plot depicts the ultimate fusion of invocation and commanded destruction: the doomsday device, a Russian bomb that will destroy all life on the surface of the earth if the Americans attack. As Strangelove explains, the designers removed the possibility of 'human meddling' by delegating the decision to trigger the doomsday device to a computer program. Unfortunately for the Americans (and the rest of the world), the Russians have not yet announced the existence of the device, so its deterrence function in this game is not effective. And despite the military's sophisticated command and control infrastructure, they can't contact the rogue B-52 bomber on its way to bomb Russia, which brings about nuclear armageddon.

Von Neumann was also a pioneer in computing research that purported to give programmers the capacity to invoke artificial life. This fleshless invocation of living things involved setting into motion primitive elements in invoked environments with simple rules that produced emergent patterns and behaviours. For example, von Neumann demonstrated that it was possible to model a cellular automaton that gave birth to other cellular automata. However, there is something bizarre about male artificial life researchers claiming to be practising what Langton (1996) called 'synthetic biology'. He insists that

Invocational Machines and Assemblages 173

experimentation *in silico* is 'life made by man (*sic*) rather than by nature' (Langton, 1996, p. 39), claiming he is literally generating life rather than invoking it. Based on a discursive slippage from comparison to reproduction, from simile to metaphor, similar ontological errors are the foundation of many problematic representational claims in computing.

Invoking intelligence

Another set of projects based on a problematic metaphor is AI. Here I would like to return briefly to connectionist AI, which invokes large training sets, rather than symbolic AI, which invokes rules. Connectionist AI purportedly invokes the low-level workings of biological nervous systems and their capacity to learn from sense data. It is empiricist, as it measures statistical 'weights' based on experience and memory rather than passing the program through logical sequences of rule-based decisions, as with the more rationalist symbolic AI tradition (Gurney, 1997).

Developers of neural nets expose their programs to large training sets of real-world data – images, texts, music, video, recorded speech and so on. These data are passed into an invoked artificial nervous system, with millions of layered nodes, to identify patterns within the data. A voice assistant employs multiple forms of AI to pass as a conversation partner, such as natural language processing to interpret users' 'intent'; speech recognition to convert spoken words into text; machine learning to improve its performance; and knowledge graphs to provide answers to questions.

From the 2010s, 'deep learning' approaches were applied to applications such as natural language processing, face recognition, medical diagnosis and social network filtering, with varying degrees of success. With neural nets, developers and users never fully know what they have trained the system to do. Such a system may seem to be working well, but what it is doing remains largely a mystery. Users subject themselves to the black hole of the invocational interval. This recalls the ancient relationships with capricious Muses and other gods, in which belief in the veracity of their decisions was based uneasily on faith. Recent advocates of 'explainable AI' have contended that trust is essential for building a relationship with invoked others (Gunning & Aha, 2019) On the other hand, one solution for connectionist AI is to understand the 'human psychology of explanation' (p. 44) – finding ways to convince users of the transparency of a system while masking its impenetrability.

It is increasingly recognised that deep learning is often unreliable (D'Amour et al., 2020) and has different forms of algorithmic bias (Danks & London, 2017). Its performance is undermined by inadequate training sets, underspecification and biased algorithms. The danger with such applications is that when they confidently or automatically offer decisions that seem credible, they are believed. Invoking decisions is first about pragmatics, not knowledge; about performance, not truth. Once a decision is made, we are still left with questions. Beyond the machine's decision, how should it connect with the human physical and social world? To what extent should people rely on these decisions? Should it be a guide that offers advice, or a carrier that passes decisions on to others, or should a decision machine directly carry out the consequential actions autonomously? The invocational imperative suggests that the most expedient outcomes should be based on the seamless and free operation of invocational events – connecting non-human sensations, calculations, memory and action through output devices. But what levels of error or distortion are acceptable?

In late 2022, when several research groups demonstrated AI applications that generated images, text and video from basic textual prompts, these new invocational media forms were greeted with both enthusiasm and concern. Their outputs seemed surprisingly close to the work of human creators, making concrete some long-anticipated capacities of the technology. Users of the DALL•E 2 image generator, released in September 2022, could invoke images from simple text prompts. The ChatGPT language model, released in November 2022, allowed users to invoke lucid original text on many topics in varied authorial styles, discourses and genres. Most generative AI tools used deep learning models trained on large amounts of data collected from the internet without acknowledgement or payment, raising the question of whether using this data constituted intellectual property theft, breaches of privacy or plagiarism.

Generative AI was certainly seen to be an act of bad faith and a threat to the livelihood of artists and writers. Image generators supported the exploitation of artists' style and identity by allowing users to invoke their names in prompts. Polish digital artist Greg Rutkowski, who creates fantasy artwork, protested against the widespread use of text-to-image AI to create works in his style. Thousands of users used his name as a prompt in creating images. While Rutkowski initially thought it might give his work greater recognition, he found that the internet was being flooded with fake images in his style (Heikkilä, 2022).

Songwriters derided ChatGPT's efforts at songwriting. Australian musician Nick Cave responded angrily to lyrics written by ChatGPT in his style sent to

Invocational Machines and Assemblages   175

him by a fan. He observed that ChatGPT's automated fakery is incomparable to the human creative process:

> What ChatGPT is, in this instance, is replication as travesty . . . Writing a good song is not mimicry, or replication, or pastiche, it is the opposite. It is an act of self-murder that destroys all one has strived to produce in the past. (2023)

This apparent threat to creative labour offends long-standing assumptions about human personal and cultural expression. But there are limitations to the current technology that may be difficult for its developers to overcome fully. The image generators often mangle details such as people's hands. Their depictions of human physical contact and the gaze between subjects – vital details in cinema – are poor. ChatGPT can create text that reads convincingly but is often factually wrong. It also tends to repeat certain formulations and clichés. But doubtless, these new invocational capabilities will develop further and continue to provoke legal and ethical controversies. Of course, AI models are nothing without outputs that interpret and manifest these data.

Machines of expression and force (outputs and evocations)

Outputs are the crucial expressive components in the invocational assemblage: the generators of force, sensations and evocations. These machines exert physical force on the material world, audiovisual force on the senses and language's performative force in social situations. This includes the force of a robotic arm, the vibration of a rumble pack on a video game player's chest, the affective and cognitive impact of evocative sound and images and the performative symbolic force of language acts, as discussed in Chapter 2. Outputs give a location in space and time to invoked texts, sounds, images, light, vibrations, movement and so on. They are machines tuned for reterritorialisation. Output forces are usually experienced immediately as sensations, and almost as quickly, they generate evocations that exceed the technical event. They may elicit pleasure, surprise or intense affect but just as possibly, inattention or indifference. If data are finite values and the images and sounds they invoke are material events, evocations are virtual until they are perceived by someone. Evocations are singular events, even when repeating the same data or material act.

Invocational media are a product and a driver of rampant capitalism, thriving on producing evocative consumer experiences. Monitors and screens output image commodities in many genres: documents, maps, game worlds, photographs, videos, control panels and, with selfie cameras, a kind of mirror. Head-mounted displays immerse users in evocative virtual worlds. Smartphone touchscreens support visual and tactile interaction with icons, buttons and other elements. Augmented reality evokes a charmed world with magical lenses, filters and responsive overlays on the visual field. Social robots produce evocative facial expressions, eye contact and physical gestures that invoke rudimentary interpersonal communication.

Evocational machines are a twenty-first-century development on two earlier generations of media identified by Kittler (1990): print media of the year 1800 and the automatic media of 1900. As Kittler observes, the discourse network of 1800 was dominated by print media and with it the interior voice of the subject, sometimes rational and sometimes, reflecting romanticism, emotional. He sees reading as a form of hallucination of images and sounds evoked by the text. When people ensconced in the world of print media encountered sensational proto-media technologies developed or popularised in the nineteenth century, many appeared confronting, magical and creepy. Associated with conjuring the dead, connecting with those absent, evoking inhuman voices or creating images and illusions. These included steam-powered printing; the magic lantern; mechanical automata; seances; photography; the telegraph, the typewriter; the telephone, the gramophone and cinema (During, 2002; Leeder, 2017; Marvin, 1988).

Kittler argues that by the turn of the twentieth century many of these technologies were becoming demystified mediators of media texts and creators of spectacles for the 'masses'. Speakers in radios, phonographs, telephones and public address systems; photography in prints and posters; and screens for cinema projectors were stripped of their magical connotations. Instead, they were mobilised to communicate with large urban populations. Where the human subject was central to the culture in 1800, Kittler argues, objectivity ruled in the media of 1900, supported by technologies such as the typewriter, which outmoded handwriting, and the camera and the microphone, which seemed to capture moments for objective examination of phenomena that were previously mysterious and fleeting. However, the ideal of objectivity was an illusion, as these apparently transparent evocatory devices came to transform the subject in new mass media formations of propaganda, advertising and globalised entertainment industries.

Guy Debord (2002 [1967]) proclaimed that the centrality of vision and the commodity had produced in the twentieth century a society of the spectacle:

Invocational Machines and Assemblages

the spectacle's job is to use various specialized mediations in order to show us a world that can no longer be directly grasped (Debord, 2002, par. 18). If capitalism caused 'a degradation of *being* into *having*' (par. 17), the society of the spectacle 'is bringing about a general shift from *having* to *appearing*' (par. 17). Debord argues that the mass media, advertising and tourism increasingly present the world as preconstituted images, and this process makes people into spectators, converting their experiences into separated, packaged commodities:

> The spectacle is the stage at which the commodity has succeeded in totally colonising social life. Commodification is not only visible, we no longer see anything else; the world we see is the world of the commodity. (par. 42)

With invocational media we moved beyond the spectacle and emerged into a society of the invocation. While we still love possessing evocative objects, and experiencing evocative events, invocational powers offer a further dematerialisation and an acceleration in the seductive power of commodified objects that imagine, speak and evoke media, personas, workspaces, game worlds and spectacles. In mediating so many transactions, invocation is regularly captured by vectoralist capitalism. A case in point is Amazon's one-click purchasing, which integrates the spectacle, the invocation and the exchange into a singular event. To sketch this dynamic: the avocation tempts the user to interact; the user's invocation accepts, modifies or rejects the offer; a confirmation page concludes the interaction; and the exchange commitment brings debts and accountabilities. In most cases evocations adequately satisfy the desire expressed a moment earlier in the invocation. Unlike previous forms of media spectacle, which sometimes now appear remarkably static, output devices are constantly refreshing, asking users to defer their judgement because they might soon be presented with something new. For users, evocations at the interface are typically unlike physical commodities or public spectacles. Instead, they are customised, privatised, intimate and everyday blocs of sensations that may be meaningful or evocative. Users get a sense of ownership over the evocation because they have called for it (how frustrating is it to watch someone else use your computer?). Evocations often offer a sense of tactility that puts them within the user's grasp, in a manner made literal by touchscreens or printers. When an invocational assemblage operates in real time, synchronised with human duration, a sense of immediacy emerges most intensely.

Evocations are usually not limited to what appears on the interface, but their value is in the transactions that they signify. Swiping right on the dating app

Tinder to say yes to a potential suitor generates a certain frisson of decision, desire and vulnerability because it performs a transaction. Starting a mission to rob a train in the game *Red Dead Redemption 2* sets up an intense series of encounters with train guards and the possibility of game death. These real-time invocationary actions are said to admit users directly into events, unlike the experience of television or cinema. Unlike television viewers, users of invocational media are often directly involved in the co-production of the text (even if television viewers and cinema spectators can be engaged intensively in these media). More than users of traditional media, invocational users are given both immediate feedback and promises of more. Tinder responds to the user's swipe by showing NOPE or LIKE on the screen but then establishes an algorithmic chain of events that might put users in contact with potential matches. Its 'freemium' model allows users to buy subscriptions, 'Super Likes' and 'Boosts' that improve their chances of making a social connection. *Red Dead Redemption 2* offers a repertoire of objects, animals and people evocative of the American West that also serve as avocations for play consumption and indicate possibilities for future action (wearing a hat, firing a weapon, hunting a bear). Its online version allowed publisher Rockstar to offer subscriptions for multiplayer experiences in the convocational world of the game in which the player had already invested hours playing, attracting income beyond the initial game purchase.

Evocations on *Silent Hill*

This evocative power of invocational media is accentuated in many classic video games. For example, *Silent Hill* (Konami) playfully evokes a sense of terror by dropping the player into a town that has been possessed by demons. From the beginning, the game intentionally obscures and withholds the revelation of the whole game world. In the first interactive scene, the user's avatar, Harry Mason, stumbles through a town hidden by mist and darkness, looking for his daughter. He gradually discovers evidence of past violence and then physical threats to his body. In the tradition of cinematic horror, the game constrains the player's senses to present a haunted world of charmed objects, arcane rituals and terrible secrets (Perron, 2012). But this is different from cinema. The experience is not reducible only to the players' sensations but also to their agency to use invocationary actions, to navigate through the disorienting pathways in the game. Players have only limited power within the game, channelled through the controller in

Invocational Machines and Assemblages

their hands and evoked audiovisually through the screen and speakers. While players move their avatar, select objects, shoot, view a map, choose items from an inventory, move a flashlight and read a menu, the game maintains a sense that they are not always in control. There are many unsolicited evocative events – jump scares, cut scenes, non-playing characters and monsters that emerge at unexpected moments in the game's flow. Players can invoke charmed objects in their inventory for moments of crisis – ammo, guns, flashlights, lighters and so on, but most of these have only limited impact. The narrative is revealed only with the work of players overcoming their disorientation. Their action is strategically managed by constraining their invocations according to a set level of difficulty.

Playing *Silent Hill* presents at least three forms of difficulty – mechanical, interpretive and affective (Jagoda, 2018) – that were designed by the programmers, writers and artists at Konami. Some of these difficulties are associated with the lower level of code, which invisibly calculates conditions such as the effectiveness of weapons and the player's health level (Perron, 2012). The player's capacity to control the character is retarded by the weaknesses of Harry Mason's body: his clumsiness, his slow pace of movement, his limited point of view and the obstacles in his environment. He regularly passes out, leaving him wondering if he is hallucinating or experiencing a living nightmare.

The player's experience also involves resolving interpretive difficulties – puzzles that require players to decode culturally bound meanings and archetypes. Jagoda (2018) compares interpretive difficulties with those of readers of poetry or novels facing dense, complex and abstract texts. The player–reader attempts to unravel the backstory of the demonic haunting of the town of Silent Hill and plays out actions in the game world that, with ongoing interpretive and mechanical work, forms a narrative. Unlike the viewer's or reader's interpretation of cinema or novels, though, progressing in *Silent Hill* requires that players do the work of resolving these interpretations for the narrative to be revealed (Aarseth, 1997). Playing reveals the existence of a cult attempting to invoke an ancient demon. The game has multiple possible endings that are resolved depending on the performance of the player. With these invoked narratives, the player is judged, punished or rewarded, depending on their record of mastering the mechanical and interpretive difficulties.

However, the *Silent Hill's* most intense and enduring difficulty is its evocation of affect. This is engendered in images of bloodied bodies and disfigured nurses with knives, the use of disorienting movements and angles of the virtual camera and particularly its use of sound (Merriner, 2017). Early in the game, the player finds a radio and soon establishes that when a monster is approaching, it will begin to crackle, as a monstrous avocation to combat. The game is punctuated with monsters' laughter, screams and moans, in the distance as they approach and as they die. The game builds a sense of the abject and the monstrous feminine (Merriner, 2017). The affectivity evoked by *Silent Hill* is both designed and emergent. As a relatively old game, its graphics, animations and games physics are primitive, and its voice acting is weak, but its narrative, atmosphere and soundtrack retain their power.

Interface and affect

Many of the compelling difficulties that video game players face are intensifications of the affective intensities of invocational media more broadly. While promoters of office software, websites and apps claim that their products are easy to use, many features require significant effort to master and remain largely inscrutable for many users. There are mechanical problems – failing hardware, errors in using software and damage to the body, including repetitive strain injuries and eye strain. Despite avocations and automation, people often have interpretive problems in understanding software features (what do all those formulae in Excel do?). The experience of using invocational media can have the psychodynamics of absorption and flow but also the experiences of obstruction and frustration. For example, in an everyday situation, someone using Microsoft Word might want to add a table of contents to a document. The avocations in a menu suggest that the application can do this, but the feature does not work correctly without the user understanding and using the 'Styles' feature, which takes some effort to master. These and other frustrations bring to bear affective difficulties that, while not deliberately designed, remain a common feature of invocational assemblages.

Many creative practices involve the mobilisation of invocations and evocations, notably the production of hip-hop beats – combining and remixing short music segments from heterogeneous sources to create original musical tracks. Initially, rap music emerged from various 1970s analogue live performative practices such as party DJing, scratching, breaking, mixing, playing synthesisers, drum machines and rapping. However, when samplers emerged in the mid-1980s, hip-hop producers used their invocational powers to create extended beats overlaid with rappers' rhymes. Sound sampling allowed the intensive reterritorialisation and revivification of elements from the sonic archive into new flows. Musicians found their samples through 'digging in the crates' – finding second-hand records for useful sounds (Schloss, 2014, p. 79). By the 2000s, producers could build invocable domains of samples in digital audio workstations that could be performed live or assembled in produced tracks. Sampling repeats, reterritorialises and transmogrifies sounds in new compositions that evoke what is familiar while offering new interpretations. Exarchos (2019) points to the supernatural associations with sampling: 'Rap producers attribute an inherent "magic" to working with past phonographic samples and fans appear spellbound by the resulting "supernatural" collage' (p. 33). But the production of beats is less an evocation of nostalgia for these old recordings and more the virtuosic, selective invocation and transformation of these sources into new sounds and beats. The standards by which they are judged by audiences are in the evocative force and affectivity of the final performances or recorded tracks. However, as hip-hop artists reached a larger audience, the sampling became a new source of income for the artists whose work was invoked (and for their record companies and lawyers) through royalty deals.

The face in the interface

Another intensive form of output is the invocation and evocation of faces. Drawing on the brain's sensitivities to faces, they communicate identity and emotion. In the early days of video games and microcomputers, evocative faces appeared on outputs everywhere. Pac-Man's two-dimensional face slid backwards and forwards, up and down through a maze in a frenzy of munching (Poole, 2000, pp. 190–5). The 'Happy Mac' face greeted users when the Apple Macintosh started up. Later, electronic mail smileys and emoticons apologised for the absence of face-to-face contact. The obsequious animated cartoon paper clip 'Clippy' in Microsoft Office 98 offered unsolicited advice to puzzled users. In the game *Doom*, a grizzling, battered and disembodied face stared defiantly at its players. With Facebook, friends from multiple locations and social circles were arranged in homogeneous Friends lists. On Zoom, live faces were reterritorialised across a grid. Even when there are no faces on a screen, the screen itself is already performing as a face.

The face has always operated as a machine for expressing emotion and identity. Deleuze and Guattari (1987) argue that faces are mechanisms through which subjectivity and signification work together – an 'abstract machine of faciality' (p. 177). They propose that the face is a 'white wall/black hole system'

(p. 180). Using the example of the high-contrast images of early German expressionist cinema, they say that white walls – light regions – are mechanisms of signification. Meanwhile, black holes – regions of shading – are associated with the depths of subjectivity. In combination, the face emerges as something recognisable and expressive of emotion and identity. When a computer screen evokes patterns of dark and light, it is already functioning as a face, in more than just resemblances.

In a world mediated by software, what Kitchin and Dodge (2011) refer to as 'code/space', there is a proliferation of faces. For example, in the airport your mobile phone or your ticket becomes faces that expose you at the self check-in counter. Approaching the security check and customs, you expose multiple faces – your own flesh, your passport image and your ticket – to secure your identity and your authority to travel. Your documents are checked against a database to invoke your identity. Meanwhile, security agents are scanning your face for tells of anxiety or agitation.

For Deleuze and Guattari (1987), faciality operates increasingly as a system of domination by eliminating all meanings that are not facial. Faciality emerges after a generalised 'collapse of all heterogeneous, polyvocal, primitive semiotics in favour of a semiotic of signifiance and subjectification' (p. 180). The white wall of signification translates all meanings into images on the wall, and the black hole positions the subject as autonomous and isolable holes: 'you will be pinned to the white wall and stuffed into the black hole' (p. 181). There is little space for other possible meanings: 'there must not be any exterior' (p. 179).

Outputs mix faces and landscapes. We can observe that computer monitors often function as professionalised or domesticated facial systems. They are mutations of the cinematic close-up, the instrument panel and the mirror. They are where the internal affective states of command, decision and memory are evoked. The screen becomes a surrogate machine mirror face, hypermediated with controls and information (Bolter & Grusin, 1999). This has implications that are both affective and micropolitical. Commodified invocational faces tend to personalise and differentiate mass spectacles, complicating conventional relationships of domination from the outside. Invocational screens reflect images of users themselves, quite literally with the selfie camera, but also in the distinctive rituals of submitting inputs and witnessing outputs. Mouse pointers, digital cameras and sound samplers offer people their own avatars (see Chapter 5). As the images or texts that appear on screen are usually things the user has just requested, audiences are co-producers of any artefact

Invocational Machines and Assemblages 183

or performance, constantly implicating themselves by what they call onto their screen, even though they only have a limited degree of control over the dynamics of that process. As Heim (1993) observes, the facial systems of invocational media recall the ancient Greek interface, *prosopon*, where one face faces another:

> Two opposite faces make up a mutual relationship. One face reacts to the other, and the other face reacts to the other's reaction, and the other reacts to that reaction, and so on ad infinitum. The relationship then lives on as a third thing or state of being. (Heim, 1993, p. 78)

Evocative interfaces also present landscapes. Computer screens create live immersive-world views. Unlike portraits, newspapers or personal letters, which distance the event of composition from the event of reading, computer screens often offer a sense of (almost) liveness and immediacy (Bolter & Grusin, 1999). A video game or virtual reality space creates immersive impressions of a world outside. The webcam offers a live view from some distant location. However, as Latour (2005) argues, it is only through closing off the rest of the world that the view seems to reveal a totality in panorama. Invocation often draws together and abstracts heterogeneous assemblages into concrete hypermediated evocations (Bolter & Grusin, 1999). When stock prices update in real time, when multiple webcams stream or when a message arrives, users experience events tangibly in a shared simultaneous present. This fosters new competencies beyond the face-to-face and, therefore, new subjectivities based on command over interfacial invocations. In the following section, I explore the implications of interfaciality in all the forms of sociality associated with online communities and networks or what I prefer to refer to as convocations.

Machines of connection and convocations (networks)

When users of invocational media seek to connect with others, they do not usually invoke them directly but invoke a convocation – an invoked technically mediated configuration of space designed for social interaction: a phone call, an email client, an online forum, social media or a game. In the traditional sense of the word, convocations are formal assemblies of people for ceremonial purposes, but with the emergence of electrical and electronic communication technologies, people were called to communicate in entirely new ways, each with its own technically formalised spaces and protocols. In this context, a convocation is any invocational assemblage that affords the formation and performance of social connections.

Contrary to Meyrowitz's (1985) argument that people lose their sense of social place in electronic space, many enduring convocations give experienced users a firm sense of place and identity and an appreciation of the norms and values that apply there. This is not to say that convocations are never sites of conflict, nor to say that all systems designed as convocations succeed. Convocational assemblages work at all three levels of invocation: technical, experiential and institutional–conceptual. Those that become self-sustaining, or autopoietic, tend to be emergent media and cultural forms with a sense of purpose, investment and continuity. But no convocation is identical. Players in an online game space expect a different range of features and social actions than those in, for example, a tax department chat forum or an online classroom. Different convocations summon people according to any number of configurations of metaphor, framing and affiliation.

There are many different families of convocation, each with its own modes of self-presentation and embodiment, forms of social action, spatial architectures, algorithms for transactions, social norms and structures of feeling. In this section I will briefly discuss some of the most common forms of convocation:

- Telegraphy and telephony
- Time-sharing
- Play spaces
- Bulletin boards and Usenet groups
- Virtual community
- Virtual ethnography
- Public sphere
- E-commerce
- Networks
- Social networking
- Social media

Marvels of late nineteenth-century engineering, the telegraph and telephone systems established the first forms of invocatory communication, invoking the marvellous experiences of writing and speech at a distance. Both required new protocols and rituals for initiating connections and communicating over the medium. The telegram convocation encouraged short messages, as they were transmitted in morse code and charged by word or character. Using the early telephone involved negotiating an operator and using an apparatus that gave a sense of living presence without physical presence.

As discussed in Chapter 3, the first decades of computer convocations belonged to the closed worlds of the US military and business. A very different ethos emerged in university-based time-sharing systems built in the 1960s. While they were predominantly designed to share valuable computing time, these systems gradually supported sociality, such as in the development of email at MIT in 1965 and 'multi-terminal conferences' at Dartmouth College in the early 1970s (McGeachie, 1973). These convocations were comparable to a conference phone call in text, with multiple participants speaking over one another, a style of communication that would recur in many text-based chat environments. Among the first uses for the Dartmouth online conferences was a multiplayer simulated poker game (McGeachie, 1973).

In fact, games and play spaces became some of the most intensely developed convocations. A game convocation can establish a special space for play that Johan Huizinga (1949) famously identifies in *Homo Ludens* as 'a play-ground marked off beforehand . . . a consecrated spot . . . the magic circle' (p. 10). The earliest video games, such as *Space War* and *Pong*, were inherently social, tending to establish physical spaces where multiple players came together. Text-based spatial, social environments, such as multi-user dungeons (MUDs) and object-oriented MUDs (MOOs) (1990), *Animal Crossing* (2001) and *Second Life* (2003), allowed users not only to communicate with others in an invoked space but also to play, build or customise convocational environments. With broadband communications and PCs, the location of the magical circle became more complex. Popular games such as *Counter-Strike* (2000), *World of Warcraft* (2004), multiplayer *Minecraft* (2011) and *Fortnite* (2017) invoked multiplayer convocations that are not simply games but communication environments.

However, not all convocations are play spaces. Designs for convocations are constructed metaphorically to communicate to users the system's spatial architectures and repertoires of actions. The first generally available convocations were 'bulletin boards' or 'message boards', popular in community public access networks from the 1970s and in commercial dial-up services like America Online (AOL) from the mid-1980s. This metaphor suggested that the convocation was a public space for posting notices that might interest community members. The Usenet, established on the internet in 1980, became one of the largest platforms of this type, circulating peoples' articles, posts and conversations in topic clusters called newsgroups. This was not a site for journalistic news but a collection of thousands of convocational groups for threaded discussions, with names like sci. virtual.worlds, alt.atheism and sci.crypt. At a technical level, it did not require a single central server as all the messages were duplicated on every news server through a synchronisation process that stored messages and forwarded them.

Bulletin boards and Usenet groups were often imagined as kinds of community service, and the community became a common way of imagining convocations overall. This was popularised in Howard Rheingold's (1993) book *Virtual Communities: Homesteading on the Electronic Frontier*, which invokes a particularly American conception of community, homesteads and frontiers. He draws on another set of mythologies of the early internet and renowned figures such as Doug Engelbart, to whom he attributes a vision for online communities. Many advocates of virtual communities see online connectivity in the spirit of Tönnies's (2017 [1887]) concept of community – *Gemeinschaft* – which he distinguishes from society, or *Gesellschaft*. According to this view, virtual communities are characterised by relationships of kinship, spirit and consensual association that transcend the individual. More than links to uniformly identified network connections, communities have multidimensional investments in complex connections between individuals and groups. However, the community metaphor both underplayed the importance of embodied ongoing relationships in physical communities and undersold the specificities of the invocational platforms that helped constitute convocations. For example, the cultural form of message boards has been incrementally refined in platforms such as Reddit. Reddit's success arguably comes from its many community-moderated topic-based convocations called subreddits and a crowd-sourced ranking feature that allows users to vote collectively to promote or demote posts.

The research field of virtual ethnography began as a study of the everyday life of convocational online communities, such as in Christine Hine's (2000) early work on Usenet and the popular massively multiplayer online role-playing game *Everquest*. She would later extend her work to study how communities never existed purely online, identifying several communities brought together through different means and platforms: gifting objects through Freecycle; collaborating on biological taxonomies; or sharing fan interactions around the TV program *Antiques Roadshow* (Hine, 2015). In these cases, convocations enabled forms of connection that would otherwise be impossible. As Hine argues, a diversity of social relations can involve a mix of interactions in physical places and multiple platforms. Rather than following a logic of replacement or simulation (virtual communities), the convocation has its sociotechnical dynamics that play out across all three levels of invocation.

Another common hope for convocations is that they might become virtual public spheres – spaces for the free exchange of ideas and the formation of public opinion, such as the one that Jürgen Habermas famously analysed in its formation among the bourgeoisie in eighteenth-century Europe. In discussing the politics of the internet, Zizi Papacharrisi (2002) distinguishes between a 'virtual space', which enhances discussion, and a 'virtual sphere', which 'enhances democracy' (p. 11), concluding that 'the internet may actually enhance the public sphere, but it does so in a way that is not comparable to our past experiences of public discourse' (p. 18). Like the 'community' concept, the instrumental concept of the public sphere carries too much baggage to transfer convincingly into the invocational domain.

Once the telegraph was used to communicate stock prices in 1863, the social practices of stock markets became invocatory events. Subscribers used 'tickers' that produced a stream of stock codes and prices extracted from the point of the transaction and circulated through the network. A few years later in 1872, Western Union allowed 'wire transfers' to send money from one telegraph office to another,using passwords and code books for security. These specialised financial convocations for market information and transferring money were further refined with invocational media.

From the early 1990s, businesses embraced the internet as a platform for marketplaces – instrumental and ritualised forms of sociality. A retail platform must evoke trust and create a desire in visitors to invoke purchases. E-commerce sites almost universally adopted the same ritualised workflow with a spatial, procedural and psychological logic: view highlighted products on the front page; browse, search and compare products; view the product more closely; add items to a shopping basket; click on a prominent 'buy' button to commit to the purchase; enter payment information; and finalise the purchase. This invocational theatre of commodity exchange evoked consumer desires through mobilising networks.

Networks are another way of imagining complex relationships, as discussed in Chapter 3. For sociologists Lee Rainie and Barry Wellman (2012), digital media have provided alternative ways to connect with others. Rather than being formed through the face-to-face interactions that characterise community, networks are formed through establishing connections, including many people (or nodes) known only peripherally – 'weak ties'. This brings into play new social-relationship patterns of 'networked individualism'.

When 'social networking' sites emerged in the mid-2000s with convocational architectures connecting networks of friends or followers, they quickly became one of the dominant forms of online sociality. From the point of view of each user, the platform was an egocentric convocation of networked individualism more than a community, as users shared connections only with a selected network rather than a collective based on common interests or a history of mutual interaction. Launched in 2003, Myspace became hugely popular first as a platform for musical subcultures and band self-promotion. Introduced a year later, Facebook was initially available only to university students. Inverting an earlier internet norm that users should use pseudonyms, Facebook required people to use their true names. This was the first of several changes introduced unilaterally that ultimately drove traffic and advertising, such as the News Feed (2006), the Like button (2009), the Timeline (2011) and the Graph API (2012), each of which intensified certain forms of convocation. The News Feed aggregated a user's friends' updates and other activities onto a single page, thus requiring fewer clicks to discover salient events. The Like button allowed users to react publicly to others' events with a single invocationary act. The Timeline, visible to users and their friends, introduced another form of aggregation in a modified personal profile page that framed Facebook events alongside life events, presenting an integrated personal narrative. The Graph API allowed developers to invoke large volumes of user data such as profile information, friend lists and activity history.

During the 2010s, the prominence of social networking receded, and the focus moved towards the social consumption and production of evocative media. Consumption of services such as YouTube, Instagram and TikTok became increasingly recreational and communicative, promoting interpersonal relationships with those the user knows and parasocial relationships with people the user does not know personally. In the space of the convocation there can be little distinction between the two.

Another related complication with convocations is the presence of non-human participants: non-playing characters, AIs and other manifestations. This became a feature of the medium: the co-authorship or even authorship of evocations through the machine's agency. Computers complicated the question of whether a message should be attributable to a human in the manner imagined by Turing's (1950) famous imitation game. As Heidegger observed, even for

Invocational Machines and Assemblages 189

the nineteenth-century invocatory device, the typewriter, writing's mechanical homogenising of physical writing alienated it from the distinctive hand of the author. For invocational media, attributions of human authorship or other forms of agency needed to be secured through various forms of programming and encryption that validated communicative actors. Spoofing is quite easy until layers of security are imposed. With artificial intelligence systems such as voice assistants or ChatGPT, however, the computer complicates this further by invoking apparently natural speech or writing that has not first passed through a human brain.

The next chapter deals in more detail with the other component in invocational assemblage: the human user. The nature of the relationship between users and invocational machines is inherently cyborgian and often posthuman. As this chapter has shown, invocational assemblages are produced through machines of command, connection, memory, encoding, time, decision, evocation, force and convocation in a manner that is always interwoven. Individuals simultaneously create and are created by media. The computer forms the user as much as the user commands the computer.

Invoking users

Great! Great! Perfect! Perfect! Perfect! Perfect! Great! Miss. Miss. Miss.

A crowd encircles Sam, who is stomping his feet on the dance floor, building up a sweat. The chants of 'Perfect!' come not from the mystified passers-by who have stopped to watch but appear as animated text flashing on the screen of the classic arcade video game, Konami's *Dance Dance Revolution*. The game rates how well Sam is dancing by electronically measuring each footfall to the millisecond. The game is in an arcade in the middle of the city, but Sam is indifferent to the world around him and stares intently at a relentless stream of arrows flowing from the bottom of the screen. He must match the arrows by stepping on four footpads, marked with matching arrows. Each time he misses the beat, he loses points and shortens the duration of his game.

Meanwhile, across town in my office, a cursor flashes at the top of my word processor's blank page. It patiently waits for me to start typing. It is the most intense point in my field of action. It marks a gap where my words are about to appear. The flashing cursor hails me as a prospective user and a writer. Perhaps the call of the cursor interpellates me as a subject (Althusser, 1971), inviting me to act, as discussed in Chapter 1. Microsoft Word quietly asks me to type. In fact, I have been hailed continually since I started up the computer and the glowing apple appeared on the screen. What else can I do but start typing?

As my fingers start typing, the cursor slides across the page, a vanguard ahead of my emerging words, a compact but powerful on-screen avatar giving birth to word after word, sentence after sentence. Its flow marks my presence and activity, increasing the word count, increasing the file size, recording my thoughts. As long as my inspiration comes, it is alive. I pause again. The cursor flashes. It waits in untiring subservience. I resume writing, and once again it is the centre of my power over this emerging text. It gives me agency but only within prescribed limits of its modes, feature set and hardware. My desires and intentions are constrained and directed through the narrow space that the cursor cuts into the computer-invoked world.

When an invocational machine addresses users, it doesn't necessarily speak as an authority like a schoolteacher or drill sergeant. The cursor doesn't demand obedience so much as make an offer. It addresses me individually, because I personalised the system myself. The cursor is not telling me something but indicating that it is listening for my command. It doesn't demand that I write but gently nudges me, offering to support my work. *Dance Dance Revolution* doesn't command Sam to dance. It's not like my primary school teachers who circled around me and my eight-year-old classmates and told us to dance the Pride of Erin. Instead, it offers him constant depersonalised feedback – praise and warnings. It asks only for a willing body and another token.

As users, we have special hailing powers – powers of invocation. Sam's skilful feet build up an impressive high score. My dancing fingers summon words onto the screen, and the word processor replies with a word count and spelling corrections. I have other powers, too. When I demand a printed document, it rolls out of my inkjet printer. I switch to my web browser and call up a reference on Google Scholar. I check Facebook, which prompts me to wish a friend happy birthday. In magical and technological senses, the computer is the *medium* through which we call into presence new daemons: charmed dance floors, writing environments, databases, social media platforms. Each of these daemons has its own logics, habits and economics and its own relationships with potential and actual users.

Different invocational devices address users in different ways. Computer systems inside institutions speak with a voice of authority, monitoring subjects and making them accountable. For those working with machines until the 1980s, avocations tended to be external to the machine itself, requiring hours of training and consulting arcane manuals and documentation. The early minicomputers and microcomputers offered direct invocational powers to private individuals but remained limited in power. As PCs became commonplace, at least three generations of human–computer interaction approaches moved avocation from an engineering problem to a design problem to a question of understanding sociotechnical situatedness. Until the 1980s, human factors tended to constitute users as rational actors attributed with characteristics (human memory, senses and bodily capacities) and prone to error. In the 1990s, users were more often imagined as part of the design of practices of interaction. In the 2000s, users tended to be seen as engaging in situated sociocultural practices in a range of contexts (Baumer & Brubaker, 2017). But by the 2010s, users were increasingly constituted as consumers targeted not only as part of a market segment but also as 'dividuals' (Deleuze, 1992, p. 5) whose tastes and desires were measured, analysed and influenced by the avocations offered to them.

Invocational media are responsible for subjection, subjectification and subjectivation (Reckinger, Wille, Boesen & Schnür, 2015). Machines of subjection impose power over the subject from outside, as seen in Foucault's (1991) work on panopticism. In this case, power disciplines subjects to behave in a certain manner according to totalising legal, moral or political edicts. Technology used by police or tax departments imposes coercive power over subjects. People subjected to these kinds of power tend to internalise the forces to which they are subjected, engendering a process of subjectification as they come to identify with the structures that oppress them.

Machines of subjectivation, on the other hand, emerge with subjects in the process of formation – as desires, pleasures and identities. With these machines, people adopt their own personal style by drawing from available cultural resources. Whereas subjection gives subjectified subjects little choice, subjectivation is all about openness to becoming (Deleuze & Hand, 1988). In many ways subjectivation is more powerful than subjectification but sometimes equally normative. Foucault (1992) sees subjectivation as consisting in processes by which subjects make ethical and aesthetic choices. Dorrestijn (2012) observes that technology is very much implicated in the formation of subjects:

> The decisive point is that behavioural constraints by technologies should not be seen as replacing moral law, but as part of the hybrid character of the self that one can problematize and actively shape. Technical mediations should thus be understood under the aspect of the ethical substance and not of the subjection mode. Ethics is then not about obeying, subjecting to technology, but about concern for the influences of technology and the wish to give style to our hybrid form of existence. (p. 236)

The subjection/subjectivation binary maps roughly onto the diagrams of invocational media. When people are *made invocable* or are *invoked* they are often exposed to subjection. When a bank calls up your credit history or the border patrol calls up your visa status, you are at risk of being subjected to power. On the other hand, when people can *perform invocations*, they may experience subjectivation. They have power, but they may be constrained because their actions are largely determined by algorithms, invocable domains and modes not of their own making. For example, iMovie software provides templates that allow users to make 'trailers', asking them to insert their own clips into a storyboard to make movie trailers in a chosen genre. This enables creative practice but constrains it, making cookie-cutter trailers that appear very similar. Creative practices may also be influenced by the norms of globally distributed peers, such as performances on TikTok or Instagram.

As explored in Chapter 3, the history of invocational media has been characterised by an oscillation between utopian and dystopian conceptions of the ethics and politics of computing. The giant brains that fascinated people from the 1940s became agents of oppressive and alienating power. State and corporate computing from the 1950s imposed rigid practices of surveillance and control. Advocates of microcomputers in the 1970s and the internet in the 1990s promised social liberation (Nelson, 1974; Barlow, 1994). By the mid-2010s, surveillance capitalists on broadband networks recentralised power by monitoring user subjects not with state power or employment but consumption. Facebook captured and analysed users' social behaviours. Google profiled users by search terms, physical location and voice. Users of search and social media were increasingly asked to trade off their own identities to vectoralists in return for conditional access to the means of invocation.

In many cases, invocational media have involved trading off autonomy for convenience and connectivity. During the 1990s, widespread uptake of mobile phones brought invocatory power and invocability to the roaming body. Mobile devices became constant companions, mediating everyday voice and text encounters with others and aiding in the microcoordination of space and time (Ling & Lai, 2016). At the same time, they made users traceable through cell triangulation and call records. From the mid-2000s, smartphones with GPS and apps extended the infrastructure of surveillance to locations even more precisely defined. Extending invocational powers to virtually all places and times also promoted the spillover of work into all other spaces. Norms about preserving autonomy and protecting privacy shifted gradually towards creating what David Lyon (2017) refers to as a surveillance culture, in which being constantly visible becomes casually accepted.

In this chapter, I explore in more depth the roles of avocations and vocations in producing users. I distinguish the different modes of power associated with avocations that assign privileges, perform surveillance and evoke allures. The remainder of the chapter looks at the roles of hardware, software, avatars, modes and contracts in constituting users. Throughout, I explore the historical

Invoking Users 195

differences in how users have been constituted in the ages characterised by different monoliths of domination such as IBM, Microsoft, Google and Meta.

Invocations, avocations and vocations

The cursor and the dance floor daemons call Sam and me away from our regular paths. I am not a programmer and Sam is not a professional dancer, but we are called to partly defined identities inscribed into our invocational devices. Like any invocational assemblage, *Dance Dance Revolution* and Microsoft Word have their own conventions and standard rules for operating, which we learn and internalise. While some systems require substantial training for users, the ideal 'user-friendly' system is 'intuitive' – it supposedly requires no tuition. It is immediately apparent. It speaks for itself. This supposed quality of 'speaking for itself' in software and hardware reflects the effective operation of avocations, for better or worse. These empower user subjects but also coerce and subjectify them.

Every invocation that a user makes is anticipated, or prehended, by many avocations, as discussed in Chapter 1. Every call to the machine by a user answers a chorus of quiet callings to them. Every key on a keyboard is an avocation. Each software feature is an avocation. They appear in all platforms on which invocations are made and in the vectors along which they are articulated. Avocation is related to vocation: a special aptitude and sense of destiny for a specific role in life. Vocation was first a theological concept – a sense that someone was called by God to perform religious work, but it has been secularised to refer to an individual's sense that they are being called to a profession. Vocation mediates between individual and collective wills. For Weber (1946), secular vocations are significant as forces of predestination in modern professions. At the same time, people in professional or political roles can invoke their vocation as a form of symbolic power that legitimates their speech and actions. Their authority may be invested in their position or in their own personal qualities of charisma (Weber, 1946).

In its usual sense, an avocation is a hobby or a distraction from one's central path rather than a final calling. It may be a minor form of vocation, but it can reflect an activity more core to one's identity. Weber (1946) uses the term in the essay 'Politics as a Vocation' to distinguish those whose entire vocation is politics from those who occasionally engage in it. Avocations don't replace vocations but begin softly calling subjects towards certain identities and practices.

In the theory of invocational media, I have adapted the term 'avocation' to refer to the semiotic, psychological, affective and technical forces that guide users in performing invocations. They divert users from the path they would otherwise take to solve a problem. For example, faced with an arithmetical problem, I might submit the problem as invocations to a calculator or a spreadsheet rather than resorting to mental arithmetic or using a pen and paper. Rather than visiting a friend, I might call them, compose a Facebook message or launch Discord. We make pragmatic judgements about the most appropriate forms of connection or convocation based on the situation and available media options. The success of invocational platforms is built on their attractive avocational offerings. I will speak of the capacity of systems and interfaces to avoke subjects.

Visible 'affordances' are a subset of avocations: controls for which 'the method of operating it would be apparent – to most people in the culture for which it is intended – by merely looking at it' (Raskin, 2000, p. 63). Affordances call directly to users and provide constraints that guide and limit their possible actions (Norman, 2013). In each case, the platform establishes a sociotechnical situation within which participants adhere more or less to the conventions of the environment. They gradually adopt the identity of the platform's implied users: programmers, authors, photographers, vloggers, players, spectators and so on.

While avocations are broader than affordances, they are specific to invocational media, encompassing all the cultural and psychological resources that influence the formation of invocations and evocations. They include advertising, documentation, personal and professional advice, hardware components (mice and keyboards), tutorials, help systems, software environments and individual user interface elements and command sets. Many software applications assemble a whole set of avocational features that require subjects to undergo pedagogical transformation to become users within a broader vocation. For example, a desktop publishing application like Adobe InDesign gathers and integrates a set of avocations for the vocations of the graphic designer or the publisher. The avocations offered by financial packages like MoneyGuidePro or eMoney Pro complement training and serve to produce financial advisers. Where individual features (find and replace; cut and paste) are generic avocations, some applications support the practices of a whole profession. Since the 1980s, many fields have been transformed or even established by invocational systems. Developers of avocations borrowed and translated the terminology and practices of their target vocations. After a period of negotiation, the work of photographers, graphic designers and film editors came to be performed predominantly as invocations, rather than through the more heterogeneous mechanical, chemical and photographic processes previously associated with those forms of work. Weather forecasting, theoretical physics, policing and any number of other vocations have materially changed through an accumulation of avocations. While some of these have clearly measurably improved these practices, they have also qualitatively transformed them.

Just as there are three levels of invocation, there are three levels of avocation:

- Third-level avocations invoke conceptual tropes, ideological meanings and institutional affiliations that encompass identities appropriate to certain professions. For example, the avocations of police crime mapping and crime analysis adopted categories of victims, incidents, suspects, crimes and so on, materially transformed policing practices (Manning, 2008).
- Second-level avocations configure user experiences appropriate to those identities and required competencies: a spreadsheet offers graphing features to help a businessperson perform visual rhetoric in a sales pitch; the game *Fortnite* encourages players to buy skins to adopt their own distinctive appearance to avoid marking themselves as 'noobs'; video editors customise their workspace in Adobe Premiere Pro to suit their own style and workflow.
- First-level avocations in programming languages such as Java, Python and C++ offer different communities concepts and features suited to different applications. As discussed in Chapter 3, even lower-level avocations address specific kinds of subjects, such as business programmers with COBOL and scientists with FORTRAN. Even hardware speaks to those who build or repair it: these components can be repaired, while these must simply be replaced.

The game that Sam was playing is at the far end of the scale of fixed user avocation – special-purpose machines. It offers a limited range of functions and specialised dedicated input and output devices. Of course, it is a machine for play, and the social force of its avocations belongs to the domain of leisure and consumption. The PC is a more general-purpose machine with customisable user avocations, even if different systems may be geared towards simple network connectivity, business use, media production or playing games. The smartphone's avocations are established through an extensive repertoire of apps, each of which invokes a special-purpose avocational environment that works with the phone's sensors, effectors and operating system to support specific domains of practice: manipulating and sharing images, checking the weather, posting and reading social media messages and so on.

The design of avocations and algorithms is socially situated. Media innovations rarely emerge fully formed, despite the myth of the genius programmer and despite the need for secrecy in developing new products. Large companies typically dedicate significant resources to in-house user testing (or play testing for games). Companies often access communities of users by releasing 'beta' versions to a select group who test it in return for access to pre-release software. In the 1990s, the internet dramatically accelerated the circuit between production and consumption, allowing people to download software and access online services easily. This allowed companies to rapidly adopt and change strategies based on how users were using their technologies. In the 2010s, software companies adopted the practice of software as a service, requiring users to invoke permissions every time they used it.

The development of streaming media is a good example of the co-production of technological resources, the enrolment of existing cultural practices and identities and the emergence of software genres and avocations. Before streaming media, users downloaded files from servers that could only be opened on the host computer once downloading was complete. Streaming allows users to access media as it is downloading so that the content is available immediately, on demand. This technical innovation made possible new genres of online media services, serving existing audiences and creating new audiences. It is not surprising that this technological development was taken up first in cultural practices of intense sensation, affect and sociality: in fields such as sport spectatorship, porn and video games. The earliest widely used streaming platform was developed by Seattle-based Progressive Networks (later RealNetworks), which oversaw the first audio livestream in September 1995: a baseball game between the Seattle Mariners and the New York Yankees (Levy, 2020). Not long after, adult entertainer Danni Ashe developed her own video streaming and online payment technologies, which attracted thousands of subscribers (McCullough, 2015). In the 1990s, the infrastructure for creating media streams was expensive, the standards were primitive and the audiovisual quality was poor. Livestreamed porn performances with live text chat interaction preceded the wider uptake of videoconferencing and streaming media and set the benchmark for their wider use.

It was not until the broadband era of the mid-2000s that other distinctive genres of games livestreaming emerged. As with many cultural forms, they emerged quite organically. In March 2007, budding tech entrepreneur Justin Kan attracted media attention by streaming his life from a webcam on his head. In October of the same year, his company Justin.tv launched a website that allowed people to broadcast video online to as many people as they could reach, while banning porn, copyright violations and defamation. By 2011, the most popular use of this medium was game streaming, so the founders launched a service called *twitch.tv*, dedicated to this genre. The livestreaming invocational assemblage combined the cultures of videogaming, broadband internet, Twitch software, the performances of players and the attention of spectators. Spectators watched gameplay juxtaposed with players' facial reactions and speech. These practices encouraged parasocial interaction and participatory culture as observed by Woodcock and Johnson (2019):

> Twitch affords new ways to mediate affective performance, allowing the audience to connect with facial expressions, voice, and immediate surroundings. Streamers' physical reactions are thus embedded visually within the virtual experiences generating those reactions – winning or losing, discovering something new in a game, and so forth. (p. 816)

Woodcock and Johnson interviewed professional livestreamers and found that many said they began their practice as a kind of play, but this gradually became a form of work. In this transition from avocation to vocation, streamers became more conscious of the quality of their performances – playing a social role and securing parasocial intimacy resembling friendship that made it easier to solicit donations from viewers. In this assemblage, which favours hypermediated virtuosic performances, there is a complex exchange of avocations, evocations and invocations.

While avocations may seem merely instrumental, large tech companies and governments conceive them strategically. Vectoralists build avocations attractive for users but at the same time monitor, regulate and monetise their activities. Facebook admits to tracking mouse movements and collecting a large amount of information about the user's hardware and software configurations. The state, too, establishes avocations for its subjects: software for managing and assessing tax, speed cameras for traffic regulation, machine-readable passports for international travel and so on.

While not all invocational assemblages are developed with sophisticated subjectifying machinery, some common strategies exist. The design of avocations commonly addresses users in three different (but often intermixed) ways:

- *Privileging avocations* grant access to physical and invoked spaces by strategically addressing only those with a given authority. Users are tactically admitted or excluded based on the performance of a method of invoking an identity: a swipe card, a recognisable face, fingerprint, a username and password or many other identity markers. The login process interpellates the invoking subject, whether that is a citizen or a police officer, a customer or a CEO. In some systems, privileging avocations position the user with power over surveilled or attracted users, as discussed later. Privileging systems do not offer unconditional power – they also often feature strategies that make the privileged subject responsible for their actions.
- *Surveillant avocations* extract involuntary invocations to make the observed subject measured and accountable. Where most invocational systems reward user activity with satisfying evocations, surveillant avocations are often inscrutable and alienating. They give nothing back. Particularly when the mechanisms of surveillance are visible, such as a security camera, they serve as a subjectifying veiled threat of possible examination. These disciplinary arrangements are asymmetrical and subjectifying in physical and software architectures. Therefore most people comply with surveillant avocations without resistance, argues David Lyon (2017), because of 'familiarity, fear and fun' (p. 829). These forms of surveillance are familiar, domesticated and taken for granted. What characterises surveillant avocations is the asymmetry between a surveilled space and a secret interiority. Yet Lyon (2017) observes that many internet activities are fun but involve subjecting oneself to surveillance: installing smart speakers, using social media, livestreaming and so on.
- *Attracting avocations* encourage ingress for user groups and identities by inviting them to invoke in the interests of pleasure, play or consumption. These avocations are no less strategic than the forms described earlier. Internet advertisers often measure which versions of ads attract more hits. Differences in avocations come increasingly to be evaluated statistically and designed aesthetically. Online writing has become increasingly tactical, with popular sites using so-called clickbait that manipulates readers into performing invocations.

These three forms of avocation are symptoms of broader trends in contemporary societies to move from discipline to control and from subjection to subjectivation.

Some privileging avocations secure power over dominated subjects in the manner of disciplinary regimes, as analysed by Michel Foucault in *Discipline and Punish* (1991). Foucault's archaeological approach traced the emergence of disciplinary regimes in the nineteenth and early twentieth centuries. These regimes put in place strategies that controlled masses of individuals by ordering them in space. Prisoners were confined and subject to surveillance. Factory workers' movements were measured, and they were moulded into a shape by their position on an assembly line. Over their lives, disciplined subjects moved from one form of confinement to the next – families, schools, factories, prisons and hospitals. These architectures divided those who were privileged from those who were subject to normalised examination.

Many invocational systems incorporate disciplinary avocations as forms of subjection: limited user accounts, individual profiles, activity monitoring, security management, keystroke logging and so on. Alongside physical architecture, privileged invocations are articulated algorithmically within information architectures. For example, software called *InterGuard* monitors employees' productivity, protects companies against insider threats, audits compliance and filters the web (Klein, 2019). This application relies not on physical but on avocational confinement, which limits, measures and traces the invocations of employees. Privileged subjects can also exercise power over users of attracting avocations such as gambling, shopping and social media.

Users of privileging and attracting avocations are creatures of Deleuze's control society (1990b) and Guattari's (1996) processes of subjectivation. These users are different from the disciplined subjects of surveillant avocations of subjection. Control societies are characterised by rapidly shifting softer manipulations, a service economy and moves towards metaproduction mediated by computers:

> In control societies . . . the key thing is no longer a signature or number, but a code: codes are passwords, whereas disciplinary societies are ruled (when it comes to integration or resistance) by precepts . . . [in control societies] [w]e're no longer dealing with a duality of mass and individual. Individuals become 'dividuals', and masses become samples, data, markets, or 'banks'. (Deleuze, 1990b, p. 180)

Instead of confinement or lines of visibility, Deleuze argues that control society operates by 'continuous modulation' (p. 179), but I would argue it is by continuous avocation. In control societies, businesses offer incentives and

202 *Invocational Media*

bonuses and encourage staff to identify with the company as a rival to other companies. Hence users are empowered by a capacity to invoke, conditioned by the dynamics of avocation – which defines what is invocable and how. Avocations can present barriers but also grooves that strategically guide users. The so-called gig economy is a well-developed control society apparatus mediated through avocations.

Invocation as a socially situated practice

While invoking is usually an individual act, invocations are embedded in sociality. It is worth comparing invocation with natural language. Social semioticians argue that language is always a social, not just an individual phenomenon – an 'inter-organism' phenomenon as well as an 'intra-organism' phenomenon (Halliday, 1978, p. 10). Language competency emerges from lived experience in a social world. What you say or write seizes shared resources circulating within communities of speakers internalised by the speaker. Meanings and language acts come from everyday habits that allow people to form utterances that make sense to others (which can be formally codified as vocabulary and grammar). The performance of any utterance is situated in an immediate pragmatic social situation that is defined and transformed through language. According to Voloshinov, an utterance is never an isolated event but exists in a frame of dialogism:

> Any utterance, no matter how weighty and complete in and of itself, is only a moment in the continuous process of verbal communication. But that continuous verbal communication is, in turn, itself only a moment in the continuous, all-inclusive, generative process of a given social collective. (Voloshinov, 1985, p. 62)

When a user invokes an event, we might ask how an invocation participates in these generative processes of social collectives. Like language, the act of performing an invocation draws on shared semiotic and performative resources. However, these resources are not like language, which is largely a mental phenomenon, but both mental and technical, through avocations and invocations that give access to invocable domains: input devices, commands, data, calculations and output devices. Where users of natural language consciously select and order words to perform utterances, users of a computer language or a visual interface select from and arrange avocational primitives to perform invocations. Users first direct these commands not to a human but to a technical apparatus – no longer an inter-organism relation but an inter-actant relation. The invocation transforms the current state of the machine – an intra-device phenomenon. However, these transformations also impact the social collective by mediating invocationary acts.

We might return our attention to the voice assistant, an invocational medium that mimics the dynamics of human conversation. The device operates as a quasi-social actor that everyday users can address in natural language. The only avocational guidance provided with the device is that users must follow a simple protocol: say 'Hey, Google' and ask a question or make a command. This resembles the convention of turn-taking in everyday conversation, while playfully asking users to frame all utterances in this defined format. This socially constituted rule helps for the most part to secure valid invocations.

For this analysis I will return to Austin's (1975) speech act theory, which provides the basis for analysing invocationary acts. Remember from Chapter 2 that Austin explained the dynamics of speech acts by distinguishing between three elements: the locutionary, the illocutionary and the perlocutionary. The act of speaking a grammatically sensible speech act, such as 'What is the capital of Iraq?', is the locutionary act. The illocutionary act is what is performed *in saying* this question. In this case, it is the intersubjective force that obliges the person addressed to respond in some way. If the listener responds, this is the perlocutionary act that occurs as a consequence, even if this is 'I don't know'.

The invocationary act works differently when the computing infrastructure uses machine learning models (1) to interpret the locutionary act using speech-to-text conversion; (2) to interpret the illocutionary act using AI statistical models; and (3) to summon the answer 'Baghdad' from a database using machine learning to select the most probable appropriate response. The assistant then (4) responds in a synthesised voice to perform the perlocutionary act, fulfilling the social obligation.

So, what can we say about speech acts that have taken place? We can use Searle's (1976) classification of five kinds of human speech acts, namely:

- *directives*, which attempt to influence another actor's future actions, for example, a question;
- *representatives*, which represent something as true, for example, an answer;
- *commissives*, which make a commitment to take a future action, for example, the making of a promise;
- *expressives*, which communicate a psychological state; and

204 *Invocational Media*

- *declarations*, which do something in the act of saying them, for example, when a couple agree to a marriage proposition or when a judge passes sentence on a convicted criminal.

In the earlier example, my invocation is a question – a kind of directive speech act. The assistant's response is an answer – a representative speech act that identifies Baghdad as Iraq's capital. Rather than a person remembering that answer, the interaction has been mediated as an invocationary act.

Taking 300 common smart speaker invocations from lists on *CNET, Lifewire, Android Authority, Tech Ranker, Tom's Guide* and *Lifehacker*, I found that users' invocationary acts are almost all directive speech acts: 98 questions and 166 commands. Non-directive acts were much rarer, with only ten responses that were usually scripted. For example, when I said, 'I am your father' (representative), the assistant made a *Star Wars* reference by answering, 'I'm sorry, I'm not Luke' (representative), then 'This is kind of awkward' (expressive). When I said, 'It's my birthday' (representative), it gave the expressive response, localised for Australia: 'G'day and happy birthday. I hope you have a cracker.' When I performed an expressive act by saying 'That's disgusting', the assistant responded with another expressive: 'I didn't mean to gross you out, sorry.' I even performed a declaration by saying 'I am Chris', which prompted the assistant to say 'You'd like me to call you Chris. Is that right? I'll call you Chris from now on' (a commissive). I then asked, 'Who am I?', and the assistant used speaker recognition to identify me uniquely: 'Your name is Chris.' This response was based on an implicit representative in the unique voiceprint of my voice. If the assistant could not recognise an invocation, it responded with an error such as 'I'm sorry, I don't understand' – indicating that my speech act had failed and expressing a faux psychological state of incomprehension (expressive).

Where user invocations were almost always directives, the smart speaker speech acts were mostly representatives providing facts. However, responses can take many other forms (see Table 6). They can make promises, ask the user to do things, make declarations and express emotions.

With some reverse engineering, I identified the operations in play with several invocationary acts (see Table 7). Many invocationary acts search internal or external databases or look up data from an online service, such as the weather forecast. Others perform mathematical calculations. Many play media, such as music from a streaming service or a radio station. Some invoke scripted responses or generate random responses. Some create more complex

Invoking Users 205

Table 6 Language Acts Performed by Smart Speakers

Speaker's Invocation	Smart Speaker Speech Act	Speech Act Type
What is the capital of Tanzania?	'Dodoma is the capital of Tanzania.'	Representative
Set a timer for five minutes	'Alright. Five Minutes. And that's starting now.'	Commissive
Play the trivia game	'Welcome to "Are you feeling lucky" . . . I'm the host of this silly show . . . How many are playing this time?'	Directive
(at the beginning of the quiz and at the end of the quiz)	'Player One. I'll call you "dingo"' . . . 'And now for your score. Not bad at all. You got four right.'	Declaration
Do you love me?	'Love. I knew the way I felt about you had a name.'	Expressive

interactions such as tutorials or games. Some commands control devices like smart lights or thermostats.

It is from variations on this repertoire of invocationary acts that users are able to get an impression of intelligence or even companionship. Exchanges of invocationary speech acts with voice assistants mimic the dynamics of conversation. Of course, the speakers must be close enough to hear each other and must respond quickly enough to sustain an interaction – 200 milliseconds is the average gap between conversational turns (Enfield, 2017). With Google's Continued Conversation feature (Gebhart, 2018) it became possible for users to respond to the smart speaker's turn within eight seconds without saying 'Hey Google'. The interactivity with smart speakers changes when using voice assistants in a social context, where the voice assistant is used tactically within a social interaction (such as to settle a dispute over facts). In mediating invocationary acts, voice assistants have become a distinctive media form whose implications are only now becoming apparent. But unlike everyday conversations, invocations are implicitly supplications to corporations with monopolies of invocation, as suggested by the need to invoke the company's name to start an invocation.

As the voice assistant reveals, then, natural language and invocational media are not equivalent but distinct and complementary. Invocations move through their own layers, which remain independent from them – invocationary acts. When there are data transfer or system errors these are inter-actant failures, which are not the same as human misunderstandings. However, there are many invocations that succeed or fail socially in convocationary language acts.

206   *Invocational Media*

Table 7 Classification of Voice Assistant Invocationary Acts

Invocation (User's Locutionary Act)	Evocation (Machine's Locutionary Act)	Invocationary Act	Classification
What is the capital of Iraq?	Baghdad is the capital of Iraq. (representative)	Searches Google database for answers	Search
What is the weather?	Currently in Newtown it is 24 and cloudy. (representative; commissive)	Looks up information from an established authority	Lookup
Play 'Lust for life' by Iggy Pop.	Sure. Lust for life by Iggy Pop. Playing on Spotify. (commissive) [Plays song]	Looks up song in media database and starts streaming	Media
What is spelunking?	According to Wikipedia, caving, also known as spelunking in the United States . . . (representative)	Looks up Wikipedia article	Third-party search
I'm talking nonsense.	My apologies. I don't understand.	Gives error message	Error
Roll a dice.	[sound effect] It's a five. (declarative)	Chooses a random number	Random
Are you Skynet?	No way. I like people. Skynet hates people. I rest my case. (expressive)	Responds with a response scripted for a defined invocation	Scripted response (often randomly selected from multiple answers)
How do you make devilled eggs?	OK, I've got a recipe from Food Network. (representative) Would you like to hear the ingredients or skip to the instructions? (directive)	Accesses recipe information and steps through ingredients and method. Users must invoke each step.	Interaction (tutorial)
Turn on the light.	Declarative: Turning on the kitchen light. [physical act: the light turns on]	Turns on smart home lights	Device
Set a timer for ten minutes.	Got it. Ten minutes, starting now. (commissive)	Sets timer. [Ten minutes later a chime sound effect plays]	Clock

Computers constitute many other 'natural language' situations in convocations – which would otherwise not be possible or practical in the same way: emails, online discussions, social media and live chat (see Chapter 4). Invocationary acts of choosing Facebook reactions, clicking 'buy' on an e-commerce site or performing a search engine search are just as efficacious within the flow of social activity as natural language events are.

But there remain other important differences between natural language and invocations in their practical and political status. Many avocations are proprietary – copyrighted or patented as commercial intellectual property and licensed by terms of service. Unlike natural language, avocations, invocations, algorithms and the hardware that supports them are owned and protected by technology companies. They are communicative resources and private property at the same time. However, invocations have extended well beyond speech and writing, to automated production of algorithms, images, simulations, multimodal symbolic activities and generative AI. Invocational media have become a dominant and familiar form of popular culture. I will argue that this ease of use is no accident. Since the 1970s an array of strategies has been deployed to inform and form subjects who are comfortable becoming users.

Usergenesis

It was not always so comfortable to become a user. Computer literacy is both a form of subjection and subjectivation, even for digital natives. In learning to invoke, users respond to and internalise the conventions established through avocations. In this way, invocational media come to function as machines that generate users. This process of usergenesis involves entire assemblages – users, machines, and social situations around it. It includes official and unofficial regimes of training, reference materials, advertising, apprenticeships, architectural changes and so on. Usergenesis is apparent at several levels in relation to the invocational assemblage itself.

Guattari's work on the machinic processes of subjectivation helps draw out the significance of usergenesis (Guattari, 1995a). He critiques and extends Freudian and Lacanian concepts of the psyche by emphasising a multiplicity of forces that create the self. The psyche cannot be reduced to a single conscious/ unconscious opposition. The forces that produce subjectivity are not only in the self but also connected with collectives. These collectives are machines of all sizes, from tiny to global. They tend to emerge from affective as well as logical, social and political connections. Particularly crucial are 'refrains', a term Guattari borrows from music but extends to all manner of regularities and rhythms, repetitions and continuities. This approach privileges events over objects and processes over essences:

> [T]he refrain is not based on elements of form, material, or ordinary signification, but on the detachment of an existential 'motif' (or leitmotiv) which installs itself like an 'attractor' within a sensible and significational chaos. The different components conserve their heterogeneity, but are nevertheless captured by a refrain which couples them to the existential Territory of my self. (Guattari, 1995a, p. 17)

In processes of usergenesis, then, users do not robotically follow the scripts written as computer programs. Avocations are offers to prospective users regarding the resources from which they can generate invocations. Users' invocations are not simply technical events but refrains that draw on the user's desires and intentions, affects and obligations. Invocations make connections with other users and with worlds outside, but users always need to express their desires in terms established through avocations.

Therefore, I must accept and learn the invocational dialect of the application I am using. If I want to add page numbers to the bottom of every page of this document in Microsoft Word, I can invoke the automatic page numbering avocation. The programmers chose to include this avocation because page numbering is a cultural convention in document production. This avocation will save me the work of adding numbers manually. However, it requires me to negotiate the 'Header and Footer' avocations, calling me away from my task of writing and forcing me to try to understand the avocational structures of document sections, tabs, page layouts, obscure keystrokes and page number formats. If I want to change the style or order of page numbering (e.g. switching from Roman to Arabic numerals), I need to understand the Section avocation. Over time, my writing practices, and those of others bound by a virtual monopoly, become bound irrevocably to it. I can't write the same way without it.

Even within an apparently simple invocational relationship such as writing a document on a word processor, there are several different levels in play – bodily, linguistic, political and psychological – each of which is affected by the mediation of the invocational medium. Picture me again writing this document. Here I am,

Invoking Users   209

a user in-the-world, sitting at a desk, typing and waving a mouse around. There I am again, a reader–writer working with several symbol systems including English, macOS and Microsoft Word. And that's me playing the employee, author, husband, father, citizen, customer and probably many other roles. Here I am once more, thinking about this, supposedly as a rational thinking subject or a bundle of subconscious urges ruled by desire and Oedipal dramas. In each case, the presence of the invocational media complicates the picture. It is not a question of how they change the user or how users change them but how invocational assemblages emerge from invocational refrains between users and avocations.

I will pursue this a little further by analysing four distinctive dimensions of user avocation:

1. *Material interfaces* like keyboards and screens nudge the user to take up certain physical positions in relation to the machine, whether that means sitting in an office chair or framing a selfie with a smartphone. User invocation is always embodied.
2. *Invoking languages* are the linguistic and quasi-linguistic formations and standards that constitute the virtual language system (*langue*) with which users perform (*parole*). These define the power and constraints of statements that users can make in different platforms and environments.
3. *User avatars* stand in for the user in invoked environments. It is the central node that marks the attention and agency of the user at any moment. An avatar can be as simple as a cursor in a text editor or a pointer in a graphical user interface, but in a video game, it can allow the player to play a character.
4. *User modes* determine the immediate forms of invocationary action that are available to the user or agent. In some cases, modes protect the authorised speaking positions of the user with logins, passwords, fingerprints, Face ID and other strategies for securing the identity of the user.

Material interfaces

All uses of invocational media at some point involve an interplay between computer hardware and human bodies. The human fills a gap between computer output and input – evocation, avocation and invocation. The configuration of a computer, games console, VR kit or smartphone requires that users literally take up certain positions in relation to the machine. Like many technologies, computers were engineered to suit the capacities of human bodies as normatively defined in the discipline of 'human factors'. The PC mouse fits users' hands. The screen displays images for a users' eyes, refreshing 30 to 360 times each second. The keyboard is the width of two hands, with pads for users' fingers. Users internalise the QWERTY key positions developed in the nineteenth century, until typing is second nature. Many users find their own ways of using – including people with disabilities who develop uses of technology not necessarily anticipated by designers (Goggin & Newell, 2007). Sometimes, though, hardware and software designs serve to systematically exclude certain potential users, leading to social movements for universal accessibility. In this and other ways, there is a politics of material interfaces.

The modern conventions for interactive computing are not only designs for machines but also designs for humans. A key legendary figure in this project is Doug Engelbart, mentioned earlier, whose life's work was a technological vision for the computer *augmentation* of humans and institutions. In his work at the Stanford Research Institute, he insisted that augmentation offered 'huge potential gains for mankind' (Engelbart, 1988, p. 188):

> Metaphorically, I see the augmented organisation or institution of the future as changing, not as an organism merely to be a bigger and faster snail, but to achieve such new levels of sensory capability, speed, power, and coordination as to become a new species – a cat. (Engelbart, 1988, p. 188)

Faced with exploding complexity after the Second World War, Engelbart believed that 'mankind [*sic*]' was 'in trouble', and he hoped to find ways of '[b]oosting mankind's ability to deal with complex, urgent problems' (p. 189). Engelbart said that the vision came to him in a flash of inspiration:

> Ahah – graphic vision surges forth of me sitting at a large CRT console, working in ways that are rapidly evolving in front of my eyes. (p. 189)

As much as Engelbart framed this as a humanistic vision, in practice it was grounded in militarism. Not only was it funded by the Department of Defense's Advanced Research Projects Agency (DARPA), but it also drew from Engelbart's personal experience as a radar operator during the war. We can read radar as an undulatory medium for transmitting radio pulses to extract involuntary

Invoking Users 211

invocations from enemy aircraft. The operator could observe traces of these aircraft as on-screen blips that appeared in the sweep of the radar trace. This experience inspired a vision for an invocational screen-based world view.

After more than six years of work, the dream of an embodied invocational environment had taken physical form in the oN-Line System (NLS). In the famous 'mother of all demos', Engelbart presented the NLS to an audience in San Francisco in 1968 (Salamanca, 2009). This was the public debut for the mouse, hypertext, the graphical interface and videoconferencing, and it would seed a conceptual framework that would inform the creation of the user in companies such as Xerox, Apple and Microsoft for decades. During one moment in the demonstration, the computer text and images were directly superimposed over the user's face. Here was not only a vision of the computer of the future but also a vision of the cyborg human. While the human was ostensibly at the centre, in command, simply augmented by the machine, this image told a different story. The dynamic text and images ran over the user's face. The human face mingled with the invoked face of the machine. The augmented human was not simply empowered by this relationship but transformed by it (Bardini, 2000).

The NLS signalled the death and rebirth of invocation. The system translated embodied actions of a user into invocations and presented the world back to the user as evocations from output devices. In a form of stage magic, users were placed at the cybernetic centre of vision, tactility and action, establishing second-level invocatory action in which humans and machines worked together (Salamanca, 2009). Invocational systems became *present* for users once they evoked embodied results in real time. There is an experiential threshold above which evocations return fast enough to feed back seamlessly. Above this speed, the flow of invocations can give a feeling of open-ended possibility. Action and awareness merge in invocationary action.

If the NLS became the mythical machine for high-end, high-concept graphical user interfaces in the late 1960s, in the early 1970s the Altair 8800 became the mythical machine for affordable commodity hardware, helping create the identities of hackers and computer fans. Computers began attracting passionate advocates, none more effusive than Ted Nelson (1974), whose double-sided book *Computer Lib/Dream Machines* promised that the computer would be 'a completely general device, whose method of operation may be changed, for handling symbols in any way' (Nelson, 1974, p. 10). Nelson presented a patchwork of physically cut-and-pasted insights, musings and ravings about the emerging computer culture. Nelson's call to action invoked the identity of the 'computer fan' (Nelson, 1974, p. 2) which played out in gatherings such as computer clubs and in publications such as Stewart Brand's *Whole Earth Catalog.* The computer fan identity existed in somewhat deferential relation to those who worked 'close to the machine' (Kidder, 1981) – the engineers, programmers, hackers or computer whizzes. For fans like Nelson, programming was a powerful but mysterious force that everybody should understand, if not master:

> Everyone should have some brush with computer programming, just to see what it is and isn't. What it is: casting mystical spells in arcane terminology, whose exact details have exact ramifications. What it isn't: talking or typing to the computer in some way that requires intelligence by the machine. What it is: an intricate technical art. What it isn't: science. (Nelson, 1974, p. 15)

Nelson's rhetorical transformation of computer science into art and magic reflected and reinforced indefinable collective desires for invocational power. These devices evoked a sense of mystery and potency that followed the medium well into the twenty-first century. However, in the 1970s, neither the user nor the machine was yet fully formed.

By the 1980s, when teams were making a second generation of microcomputers, they had only begun to develop avocational strategies for creating users from those uninitiated in the 'dark arts'. Grint and Woolgar's (1997) account of efforts to 'configure the user' documents this period well, ethnographically tracing the development process of a new series of 286-based personal computers (known only by the initialism 'DNS') from inception through to release. He watched the dynamic interplays between different sections of the company, all negotiating images of the ideal user:

> In configuring the user, the architects of DNS, its hardware engineers, product engineers, project managers, salespersons, technical support, purchasing, finance and control, legal personnel and the rest are both contributing to a definition of the reader of their text and establishing parameters for readers' actions. Indeed, the whole history of the DNS project can be construed as a struggle to configure (that is define, enable and constrain) the user. (Grint & Woolgar, 1997, pp. 73–4)

Grint and Woolgar found that members of design teams had highly variable conceptions of the user and the problems they had with the system. Technical support staff, who had direct experience with users' problems, were scornful of hardware engineers' poorly conceived designs that generated many of these problems. One of the technical writers said she was surprised at the marketing department's unsophisticated conception of future users. Grint and Woolgar argue that throughout the process the image of the user was highly fluid. Neither the user (who was inexperienced) nor the machine (which was incomplete) was settled or established until quite late in the project. They interpret the entire design process as a struggle to capture, fix and control the reader-user and to define the computer as a distinct and stable object.

Grint and Woolgar compare designers' aspirations for a seamless experience with a writer's task of creating a readerly text. Designers wanted to create the impression that the computer was an object with its own integrity, not just a collection of components. The engineers delayed the usability trials until the machine had a proper physical case. Although they themselves regularly worked with the boxes open, the engineers insisted the box be sealed for end users. The physical case defined the boundaries of the machine as a book's cover distinguishes it from other texts. This was an illustrative example of making the machine into a 'black box' (p. 154), by which much first-level work becomes invisible and enigmatic at the second level.

Grint and Woolgar's (1997) comparison between the user of a computer and the reader of a text marks a change from Nelson's 'computer fan' because it draws computers further into the everyday life of actual users. They argue that like reading, using computers is an active process for each user, and different users can have different readings of the same text. At the same time, their reading paths are guided and constrained by the writers' strategies and embedded assumptions. Grint and Woolgar argue that the success of a text or device is measured by how many different readers find uses for it. However, casting users as readers does not capture the dynamism and diversity of the user–machine relationship in the invocational assemblage. The reader analogy also neglects findings in the same article relating to the multiplicity of 'authors' (engineers, marketers, support staff) involved in making the text or machine.

Even at the level of designing microprocessors, first-level technical decisions are not made entirely for technical reasons. Rather, they reflect market strategies, organisational cultures, images of users, accidents, competitors and a wider climate. For example, the early history of Intel's x86 chip series reflects its sociotechnical construction. The first version of the Intel 8086 processor 'was intended to be short-lived and not have any successors' (Morse, 2017, p. 9) and was developed relatively quickly between 1976 and 1978 in response to the release of an enhanced version of Intel's earlier 8-bit chip, the

8080, by its competitor, Zilog. Intel countered with its own 16-bit chip to head off this competition, while working on a superior new design. A key design consideration for the 8086 was backwards compatibility with the older, 8-bit 8080 chip that would 'lock in their existing customer base' (p. 9). As it turned out, the chip that was supposed to replace the 8086 did not perform well, and the 8086, which was proving popular, became the basis for what would become the dominant computing platform for decades. These almost accidental events created a legacy in architecture and instruction set that constrained and enabled future designers and programmers.

In sum, the relationships between users, competitors, customers, investors and regulators have informed invocational media down to the lowest level of their technical foundations. In the 2000s, ethnographers at Intel, which has a history of in-house qualitative ethnographic research alongside its more quantitatively oriented market research, used their research to create imaginary personas that would inform the design and marketing of processor chips. In one such study (Anderson, Faulkner, Kleinman & Sherman, 2017), researchers spent time with users who created digital content, such as producers of video, 3D modelling, audio, graphic design and social media. The researchers generated user personas such as the 'Tech Whizzes', who enjoyed customising and experimenting with their machines, and distinguished them from 'Minimalists', for whom the technical details were less important. They also found that content creators were very different from gamers in the demands they would place on hardware. They argued that these personas helped direct priorities and promotional strategies within Intel and even for equipment manufacturers outside the company. Many people across the company took up in their work the personas that this research group had created. Elsewhere, Intel has drawn on user research to prioritise power efficiency to improve the battery life of portable devices and at another point recognised the demand for accelerating start-up processes in personal computers.

Even if programmers are influenced by users, we must recognise that programmers themselves are also users. They too call upon on the dead labour of engineers, designers and philosophers inscribed into invocational machines. Their tools anticipate and structure the ways they work. They call upon production in the globally dispersed supply chain. All social groups have increasingly come to call upon the world as black-boxed invocable domains dominated by big tech corporations from the United States, Taiwan and China. In these ways, invocations are alienated and alienating, which is why so much work is put

Invoking Users

into designing them not to seem to be that way. Invocational practices mediate complex relationships of entrustment and consignment to other invocable layers. Delegations pass as invocational resonations through heterogeneous connections between psychological, social, conceptual, software and hardware levels, or layers. Because each layer is separated, black-boxed and addressable from other levels, it is possible for designers to replace and rearrange components indefinitely. From the level of the hardware and up, introducing new concepts, swapping a hard drive, updating an operating system or changing the user will change the system but keep it functioning. Over time all the components can be upgraded or replaced, so it is constantly becoming a different system yet remaining somewhat the same.

The strategy of layering invocational machines had paradoxical effects. It supported more refined divisions of human labour in the IT industries. It supported the establishment of new vocations (such as the games developer) while eliminating others (such as CD-ROM multimedia producer). It fostered new skills while outmoding others. It sometimes dispersed power but often recentralised it. Over time, the work of adding new layered elements tended towards specialisation and institutionalisation. Human roles associated with layers were formalised as vocations in themselves (developing different hardware components, applications, operating systems, protocols or compilers). Computer science gradually differentiated into specialised subfields. A report by the ACM Task Force on the Core of Computer Science (1989) defined nine subareas that the authors thought defined the field: algorithms and data structures; programming languages; architecture; numerical and symbolic calculation; operating systems; software methodology and engineering; database and information retrieval systems; artificial intelligence and robotics; and human–computer communication. These subdisciplines formalised the tasks involved in creating and managing invocational assemblages. It is notable that in the computing paradigm, human–computer communication is the last of the listed disciplines.

Invocational systems tend to add more features as they mature, often reducing the precision of their invocations. Users of word processors must accept the avocational decisions of Microsoft or another software company, because for practical purposes a writer has few choices (any more than there is the option of building one's own car). Powerful features that first appeared as magic become ritualised as invocational religious standards that foster the habits and identity of the system's users. Some standards are set by official standards organisations like the International Organisation for Standardisation (ISO), but more often they emerge through patents and the force of 'installed base'. If enough people come to rely on the stability provided by proprietary layers, they become the *de facto* standard – the 'reference platform' or just the 'environment'.

There is a characteristic form of social and economic power in controlling the means of invocation, and corporations have found many ways to exploit it, including contracts, patents, hardware dongles, standards, network verification and other practices. On the other hand, governments have regulated the media and practices of invocations since the beginning of computing. From as early as the 1930s, IBM attracted the attention of the US Department of Justice Antitrust Division for its monopolistic practices with leasing (rather than selling) tabulating machines. For example, the Division challenged IBM's practice of requiring customers to use IBM's proprietary punch cards – the material mediator of invocations for these invocatory devices (Diaz, 2019). In the 1990s, Microsoft chose to give away their web browser for free with their Windows operating system and made it difficult for users to install other browsers. The Antitrust Division challenged this as a monopolistic practice. In 1998, Microsoft was deemed to have violated the Sherman Antitrust Act and was ordered to break up its company. On appeal, though, the case was settled, with Microsoft agreeing to share interfaces with other companies, thereby avoiding the break-up (Gavil & First, 2014). In 2000, Amazon was controversially granted a software patent covering one-click ordering: a feature that would allow a website to offer a button that would complete a transaction with a single invocationary act. Critics argued this patent should never have been granted because, among other things, it was too obvious. In each of these cases, struggles over control of avocations spanned financial, technical, legal and social relations.

Despite legal and activist challenges, invocational media have a tendency towards monopoly in which avocational systems achieve a totalising, interpellating force. Users become invested in the operating systems, programming languages and applications that speak to them, and these avocations constitute complete invoked environments suited to particular social institutions, vocations and competencies.

Invoking languages

Avocations of programming languages have tended to reflect different philosophies, address different communities and produce different users. For example, the structure and syntax of the programming language FORTRAN (FORmula TRANslation), which looks like equations, avoked scientists for whom mathematics was part of their habitus. This language was the first to allow comments to be inserted into the code, so scientists could make some sense of the source code as a text before compiling it. As mentioned earlier, COBOL (COmmon Business Oriented Language) is a more verbose language suited to handling large quantities of business data with relatively simple algorithms. Its standards strictly separate data from procedures and require clear statements of authorship (see upcoming section on user modes). BASIC, by contrast, is a less structured language designed to be easy to learn and rewarding for users (Walter, 1993; Appleby, 1991; Biermann, 1997). The Logo language developed by Seymour Papert and others was claimed to be a humanistic project to draw computers into classrooms in a more creative manner than drill-and-practice instructional paradigms (Papert, 1980). Papert's pedagogical vision was unapologetically a strategy to produce users in a certain image:

> [C]omputers can be carriers of powerful ideas and of the seeds of cultural change . . . they can help people form new relationships with knowledge that cut across the traditional lines separating humanities from sciences and knowledge of the self from both of those. (Papert, 1980, p. 4)

Conventional views of users shifted after the 1980s, when commoditised computers became easy-to-use 'information appliances' rather than devices for all to program. Where the term 'hacker' once meant an inquisitive and independent-thinking programmer, it came to mean an antisocial outcast bent on wreaking havoc on legitimate system users. At the same time 'power users' gained more respect. With visual programming tools, using became more like coding. Faster hardware and more 'mature' software gave users capacities to perform more and more work on their desktop machines. The most dramatic shifts came when software companies began realising that their task was not only to design the machine but also to design the user.

The first edition of Ben Shneiderman's (1986) book *Designing the User Interface* sits in the middle of the transition in user design that refined user agency and identity. He starts by summarising much of the scientific empirical work on user interfaces from ergonomics, cognitive science and computer science. Much of this earlier research concentrated on quantitative measures of able-bodied human capacities. It measured perceptual abilities, human 'central processes' and 'factors affecting perceptual motor performance' (p. 22). It took measures of short-term and long-term memory, problem-solving, decision-making and time perception (p. 22). It defined the tolerances within which the engineers were working with human components of the system.

As the book progresses, though, Shneiderman develops more qualitative 'theories, principles and guidelines' (p. 41) of designing for users. He emphasises principles of consistency, informative feedback, easy reversal of actions and reducing short-term memory load (pp. 61–2). Among Shneiderman's most celebrated contributions in this edition of the book is the principle of 'direct manipulation' (pp. 180–223), which he says creates 'the really pleased user' (p. 180):

> The central ideas seem to be the visibility of the objects and actions of interest, rapid reversible incremental actions, and replacement of complex command language syntax by direct manipulation of the object of interest. (Shneiderman, 1986, p. 180)

Direct manipulation is one of the distinctive features of the graphical interfaces pioneered by Engelbart in the 1960s, Xerox in the 1970s and Apple in the 1980s that became standard for computers by the mid-1990s. This directness is, of course, only possible by a radical move towards something indirect: the creation of a 'user illusion'. Graphical user interfaces, often developed using object-oriented coding languages, allow users to perform invocationary actions rather than composing invocations. Commands are mediated through gestures and menu selections. Interaction with smart devices would later become even more direct with touchscreens and gestural interfaces.

From the late 1980s, a global mass market for commoditised general-purpose hardware and 'shrink-wrapped' software grew, and their avocations fostered new forms of dependency on graphical user interfaces. What was known as 'human factors' research came more be called 'human–computer interaction design' (HCI) or 'usability research'. Rather than studying human or machine capabilities independently, it concentrated on emergent dynamics between the two in situated events (Suchman, 2007). Research also moved towards more interdisciplinary approaches. Interfaces became sites of struggle and collaboration between art and science (Bickford, 1997).

Into the twenty-first century, the personal computer receded from being the principal mediator of invocations to become just one product category among many invocational devices. After the release of the iPhone in 2007 and the iPad in 2010, not to mention many generations of games platforms before these, desktop computers came under challenge as the primary means of invocation. By 2011, smartphones had outstripped desktop machines in unit sales (Menn, 2011). Internet publishers took a 'mobile first' strategy as smartphones became the dominant mode of accessing online content. At the same time, invocational media took on a multitude of other forms such as home games consoles, mobile games platforms, smart TVs, VR and AR systems, smart home devices, the internet of things, toys, wearables, robots and so on. Despite this fragmentation into platforms dedicated to different cultural practices, all these devices mobilised the invocational abstract machine in some way. Many connected with other devices to exchange invocational events: smartphones, smart televisions, robots and PCs.

With the proliferation of this range of devices, invocational media moved away from the model of the general-purpose computer towards more consumer-oriented dedicated media technologies. These traded hackability for usability, openness for closedness and 'critical modernism for post-modern populism' (Burgess, 2012, p. 30). That is, designers targeted their avocations at an untutored general user rather than at programmers or even power users. In doing so they made first-level invocations even more inaccessible and channelled them towards the limited imagined practical needs of the user at the second level of invocation. While hackers learned to 'jailbreak' the phone to access the lower level, for all other users the experience was heavily designed. The emergence of apps was a form of openness; they nevertheless gelled with this heavily designed experience. Apps proved profitable for corporations, generative for developers and useful for user communities. As special-purpose pieces of software providing small but tailored sets of avocations, they could serve categories of users that were much more niche.

Many apps that proved popular articulate a rich invocation of cultural practices and milieux and user experience. As mentioned earlier, invocations are articulations in two senses (Hall, 1986). First, they must be clearly articulated and properly expressed. Second, like an articulated vehicle or road train, they are comprised of one or more units joined at a pivot point. The invocational articulation joins independent elements together:

> An articulation is thus the form of the connection that can make a unity of two different elements, under certain conditions. It is a linkage which is not necessary, determined, absolute and essential for all time. (Hall, 1986, p. 53)

An invocation performs an algorithmic articulation that joins together not only hardware and software but also physical space, ideology, social connections and individual affect and psychology. Its enactment constitutes a singular assemblage: it holds things together as an instrumentality, environment, game or narrative. Software is usually distinguished by the functionality it can invoke. It is defined by features that make it powerful and attractive with avocations that call it to particular communities and vocations.

Invocations also comprise environments: physical, logical, imaginary and conceptual. They are always materially situated, even when distributed through networks and 'clouds'. They are logically and mathematically coherent informational and electronic events. Some constitute spatial simulations that map onto real spaces or model imagined spaces. Users often synchronously imagine invoked events with more or less cohesive 'mental maps' and concepts that allow them to form invocations, anticipate their effects and respond to their consequences.

Video games have the greatest variety of all invocational assemblages. They are usually associated with leisure and entertainment uses and judged by their aesthetic values and affective impact at the second level of invocation. Yet their innovation and complexity at the technical level can easily be underestimated. Games are often spatial, logical, rule-bound and performative. They must also be assessed in terms of their conceptual and ideological dimensions and their status as a major industry.

Another way in which invocations are held together is in narratives. These are not written or recited like a classic narrative text. Rather, they are algorithmically mediated emergent accounts that attach to invocational events: a traveller's story of a journey informed by Google Maps; an influencer's story of an image's production, distribution and consumption through Instagram. The attraction of richer narrative elements in social media was captured when Snapchat introduced the 'Stories' feature in 2013 – time-limited multimedia narrative sequences, which were soon copied in other forms in other social media. In 2017, TikTok was released in the West, encouraging playful invocations of attraction. These were invocational short stories told quickly and casually rather than fully developed.

The Pokémon GO app, which became a global fad in 2016, invoked algorithmic singularity, cultural resonance, gameplay and everyday spatiality in combining location-based gaming with augmented reality. The world of the game is coextensive with physical space, while invoking a parallel world inhabited by monsters. These not only appealed to fans of Nintendo's earlier Pokémon trading cards, games, anime and movies but also introduced the Pokémon characters to a new audience. The basic gameplay mechanic is to locate monsters on a map, walk to their locations and to capture them by throwing a 'Poké Ball' at

Invoking Users

them. The Pokémon GO app articulates bodily movements in physical space (measured by the GPS and displayed in an abstracted version of Google Maps); a database of geographically defined sites; a mini game in which users swipe the touchscreen to throw Poké Balls at monsters; and the phone's accelerometer and gyroscope for aiming within the augmented reality space. This approach of attracting players to an invocationally charmed physical place is an example of 'ambient play', which means 'augmenting the atmosphere of a pre-existing place by creating a spectrum of experiences of co-presence' (Apperley & Moore, 2019). The game therefore exploits existing meanings of body and place and juxtaposes them with the game world. It motivates the player to develop skill in the mini game, collect as many monsters as possible and learn how to fight with other monsters. Even after the game's moment as a global sensation had passed, its popularity in a subculture was sustained, particularly with the addition of community features.

Instagram is another app that developed generative machines of convocation, avocation, invocation and evocation. When the app was released, it was one among many camera smartphone apps but was distinguished by its evocatively named filters, such as Moon, Lark and Reyes. However, it began articulating algorithmic flows of action from the consumption of the images of others, establishing the norms and conventions of the platform. At some point the user moves on from image capture to editing, annotating and exhibiting in other people's timelines and stories and (if desired) opens it to public comment. This circuit of consumption, production, consumption and evaluation by others manages the exchange of personal-visual identities (O'Donnell, 2018).

Despite its algorithmic predestination, Instagram supports a multiplicity of different modes of use. In the Feed, Instagram (n.d.) orders the photos and videos based on an AI assessment of the '[l]ikelihood you'll be interested in the content' as well as the date the post was submitted and the '[p]revious interactions with the person posting'. Interactions vary in scale from private connections among small groups to broadcasts to hundreds of millions of followers – the Instafamous. As Marwick (2015) has argued, some Instagram users have adopted the strategies of large brands in attracting attention to build online popularity. These strategies aim to 'create affective bonds between audience and microcelebrity subject' (Marwick, 2015, p. 148). A brand summons a known identity formation from the chaos of indecision through the construction of names, images, identities and narratives. This articulation of name, identity, reputation, follower status and narrative is held together with attractors that increase the likelihood that a particular property might be invoked. The Instafamous find their own ways of constructing a cohesive and attractive persona while also maintaining the impression of authenticity. The follower role is a parasocial relationship that is actualised in a technical relationship in Instagram's information architecture.

Another method that invokes coding within Instagram is the hashtag, which establishes an invocable domain that clusters posts and images according to their tags. Users can tag their images to mark them as belonging to a given collectively defined set, allowing other users to gather, enjoy and evaluate disparate images from otherwise heterogeneous spaces. A hashtag can be a discursive marker of identity, affect, taste, opinion, style, trope or whatever. It brings emergent order to massive datasets through a practice of collaborative auto-curation. It performs a mode of vernacular collective classification or 'folksonomy'. This provides an alternative way of summoning or ordering posts. Through offering multiple algorithmic orderings of posts, Instagram supports a range of habits and preferences for invoking from the same enormous and constantly updated dataset.

Users and avatars

Avatars are entities that function as the grammatical subject and performative persona within invoked environments. While the commonly cited derivation for the term 'avatar' is from Sanskrit for the incarnation of a deity in the physical world, avatars do not necessarily appear as a body in an invoked space. Rather, avatars magically become part of the user who performs invocations. They can take a range of forms and configurations but are typically animated when a user's body manipulates hardware devices to form invocational cybernetic feedback relations within an invoked environment. However, we must remember that the user–avatar relation has already been substantially constituted by avocations: instructions on how to use the system; affordances of the hardware; a cognitive understanding of the user–avatar relation in software; and often an affective identification with the avatar. Sometimes avatars appear as simple sprites or as photorealistic 3D-modelled bodies that can be moved in naturalistic ways. At other times they are only implied by a point of view, such as in 'god games', or they are coextensive with the user's spoken voice, such as with a voice assistant. In other cases, they are simply names, numbers or placeholders. Avatars

Invoking Users 223

of all kinds perform as a special category of invoked–invoking actor in the chains of human and non-human actors in invocational systems.

The archetypical instance of user avatar is the cursor, which marks the text insertion point, as introduced at the start of the chapter. First used in command-line interfaces such as DOS and UNIX, it also features in word processors and text editing software. The term 'cursor' is of Latin origin. It means 'runner' or 'running messenger', but it was most familiar to mathematicians from the cursor in mechanical slide rules: a mobile runner that could be moved up and down to determine the results of a calculation. The computer cursor became the indicator that marks the active node in the user–avatar pair that the user directs and controls. The cursor functions as an agent with powers to perform the specified set of tasks established by user modes. The trained user, paired with a cursor and pointer, perform as a cyborg assemblage, jumping across the screen, and transforming its textual landscape. The graphical user interface transforms the relationships between users, avatars, screen space and invocations by introducing a pointing device and transforming the screen into a game-like space of possibilities for invocationary action. The pointer and mouse supplement the cursor–keyboard assemblage by capturing the movement of the user's body in invocationary action.

Some of the most evocative avatars are those found in video games, which often invoke archetypes and stereotypes in the collective imaginary to inspire the design of heroes, companions, enemies and the environments they inhabit. Within popular genres of science fiction, warfare, sport and fantasy, video games involve role-playing – so the avatar sometimes becomes a character with depth, identity and special forms of agency. Some games allow a high degree of customisation of a character's race, appearance and abilities. In the process, users also become players, developing a sense of identification with the avatar.

Of course, avatars are defined not only by their appearance, skin or character but also by commingling of the bodies of players and avatars. The bat and ball in the game *Pong* were among the most basic images ever to appear on a television screen, but their interactive mobile agency within the play field animated them and their players as part-subjects in a convocational space. The simple shapes of spaceships in *Space War, Space Invaders* and *Asteroids* captured a cultural imaginary of radar screens and science-fiction laser battles. Players developed a sense of embodied identification with an avatar confronted with inevitable death, which temporarily severed the player–avatar connection. *Second Life* allowed players to customise their avatar's appearance, physical proximity to other avatars, personal property and forms of communication. Researchers have found, perhaps not surprisingly, that players behave quite differently depending on the avatar they are playing in a game world – what Yee, Bailenson and Ducheneaut (2009) refer to as the 'Proteus effect'. In one experiment, they found that after playing as a taller character in a game, players became more assertive in real-world social interactions than those who had been playing with a shorter avatar. Therefore, the design of the ways that characters carry themselves in a game can be carried into everyday life. Many games genres are defined by how players and avatars are paired as agents in an invoked game universe: first-person shooters typically reveal only part of the avatar's body, while third-person game avatars are controlled like a puppet.

In many convocations, though, the persona that players are expected to perform is themselves. In this case, when the avatar's character aligns with the user's identity, an assault on the avatar can be an affront to the player and their sense of self (Graber & Graber, 2010). Even somebody engaged in identity play is considered to have some accountability for their actions. Therefore, many of the processes of subjectification in invocational media are enforced within the system, particularly through the management of user modes.

User modes and control

Users' capacities to perform invocationary action at any given moment are governed by modes. Modes establish how input invocations are performed – they establish the user–avatar's agency and authority to engage physically and symbolically with invocable domains. In general computer discourse, the term 'mode' refers to a 'particular method of operation for a hardware or software device' (Chandor & Williamson, 1985, p. 304). User modes define the user's repertoire of invocations at any moment. A familiar example of a mode is the choice between 'insert' and 'replace' mode in word processing. Insert mode adds new characters at the insertion point, pushing any text to its right further across. Replace mode overtypes text to the right of the cursor. The same physical action by the user has a different effect on the text depending on which mode is operational.

The environment of a modern personal computer offers a range of modes based on the user's choice of application and modes within applications. One of Apple

Computer's early 'human interface principles' for the Macintosh was to create an impression of 'modelessness' (Apple, 1992, p. 12). For example, a graphics program provides a palette of 'tools', 'brushes' and menu choices. Each performs different transformations on the image. One tool creates lines of variable width and shape, another makes selections of portions of the image, another adds or erases parts of the image and so on. Because these modes correspond with 'real-life' modes, like the difference between using a paint brush and an air brush, they seem to enable rather than restrict the operations of a user. But each is a mode that has been carefully designed as a material metaphor and made apparently natural. Many applications integrate and combine an appropriate set of modes for a vocation, including its social relations.

Users' agency is often regulated by differentiating between modes. For example, games often make a distinction between a mode for playing the game and a mode that pauses the game to allow the player to take a break from the action and customise settings. In these modes the meanings and actions of the buttons or keys change, and the spatiality, mood and temporality are quite different, even though they both relate to the game. Of course, software developers have one mode for coding and another for compiling and executing programs: a distinction that is like the difference in science between the lab and the clinic or the desk and the field.

Modes also establish the identity and authority of a user-subject to perform certain invocationary acts. In a networked word processor like Google Docs, the creator of a document can limit other users to modes for viewing or suggesting changes or can give them full edit access. Assigning modes is a way in which control is asserted. In the same way that regions of space such as private property and public space are subject to different rights and expectations of legitimate behaviour, modes are deterritorialised, automated ways of exerting control over avocations and invocable domains.

Control sometimes undermines the liberal notions of human rights based on the subject's inviolability. It changes what a subject is. Katherine Hayles (1999) observes that until sometime after the Second World War, the primary questions about the human related to where the subject was physically placed. She traces a cultural and technological transition towards new regimes that privilege pattern and noise over absence and presence (p. 29). For example, in what she calls the 'posthuman' condition, the measure of a bank customer becomes the pattern of the password or PIN, rather than their bodily presence in a bank branch. The word processor document exists as invisible patterns in archiving devices, which can be physically located anywhere or in multiple places, rather than on physical pages with print on them. These posthuman politics are based not only on the pattern/noise opposition but also on a politics of user modes. Beyond Lessig's (2006) maxim that code is law, I would argue that modes are law enforcement.

Modes simultaneously differentiate and aggregate users. Many systems restrict certain modes to groups of users by requiring authentication of privileging avocations. Depending on the system, users authenticate themselves with a username and password, a 'tap-and-go' card or part of their body. These identification mechanisms are equivalent to signatures on a contract but have invocationary force through the operations of modes. The virtual signature can then be attached to any invocation that the user performs, along with an automatic time and date stamp. Their identity is invoked with any changes they make according to their modes.

Enabled and constrained by modes, users perform with a limited invocational vocabulary and spatial confines to fulfil their immediate desires and needs. Avocational user modes are implicit in every function in any genre of software. In fact, software genres can be defined by their sets of user modes. Banking computers support the user modes and workflows of the customer or account holder on one side and administrators, technicians and other bank staff on the other. Word processors, graphics applications and design applications constitute different user modes for authors, designers, editors and readers. Microsoft Word itself has modes (or views) for different relations to documents: Draft, Print Layout and Outline views. The Track Changes mode allows editors to make changes that can later be approved or rejected. Each of these modes implies an imagined or virtual type of user who will play the role of author, editor or customer.

According to Deleuze and Guattari (1987) apparatuses of capture have two poles: a system of privileges and a mechanism of modes. Modes make major politics into micropolitics. Privileges usually reflect hierarchies within the institution in which the system is installed. Each user (operator) is assigned a category which gives them privileges to read, write, erase or add new data or programs. Systems of privileges are enforced by restricting which modes are available. Each user is captured and positioned inside an array of virtual forces. The categories of privileged users are enacted by defining what a user can do within a system.

System administrators and developers usually have a higher and special level of 'privileges' because they are responsible for the overall functioning of the systems. They tend to follow the dynamics and logics of the invocational assemblages as much as fulfilling the requests of those who commission the development. They know the system inside out and have special rights because of this. Arthur Kroker (1994) refers to this group as the 'virtual class'. As beneficiaries of these special invocational powers, the virtual class agitates to further its own interests. But it tends to present the expansion of invocational systems as though it was inherently in the common good (Kroker, 1994). For Wark (2004), these are the hackers, who can act with impunity in a sandbox or in the interests of vectoralists to whom they are indentured.

In other cases, user privileges reflect the stations in institutional hierarchies. A university's central computer gives students, administrative staff, academic staff and senior staff privileges to access the system appropriate to their responsibilities. Each can see or change only specified parts of the total data set. Students can change their own contact details, but only certain staff can assign grades. Mechanisms that identify operators are essential to any systems that track other individuals as objects. Student records are only valid when the systems have ensured that every change is authorised. Data integrity is critical. Any forceful invocational statement must be legitimated by the identity of the operator who made the change.

The rights assigned to each operator (and to other subjects as data entities) seem at first simply to manifest agreements founded on Enlightenment political theory and articulated in contract law. Locke helped establish the modern principle that authority should derive not from inherited right but through operations of reason (Locke, 1988 [1689]). In invocational systems, users (re-)establish contractual relationships with the entity that controls the system. However, the reasoned relations between parties to contracts become manifest as Boolean variables and ultimately as switched signals in integrated circuits. Invocations blindly allow changes only if modes are in operation. This blindness and the blinding speeds at which invocations operate start to expose the contradictions and limitations of liberal subjectivity. How can users remain stable at the centre when processes follow invocational dynamics?

For some users, the instability of invocational identity is unsettling and threatening. In a world where identity is invoked, users must become pragmatic about the identity of others. Rather than constantly seeking proof of some stable foundation for every person or institution with whom they deal, users must evaluate the thresholds of proof that are appropriate to each invocational transaction. Users also become expert at presenting their own invocable identities: customising their own avatars. These tactical interventions resist the strategic programs of avocational modes, tweaking the parameters of systems of control.

As becoming a user became a global social norm, the processes of creating users have become increasingly invisible. Just as the market regulations that governed private property after the sixteenth century became generally accepted as the natural order, constraining modes in invoked environments simply became a normal part of everyday life. The apparent fluidity of identity on the internet during the transitional period of the 1990s gradually crystallised when users were increasingly expected to perform as themselves. Users developed invocational literacies and cultural conventions that relied on the operation of dominant invoked platforms. Users came to perceive the world differently, without really thinking about it. Invocational media seemed to bring everything closer by making everything invocable, but the same move also produces unfathomable distances.

Conclusions

By this stage, I have established that the concept of invocational media offers an alternative to a traditional view that computers fit primarily into histories of mathematics, logic and abstraction. In contrast to this conventional conceptualisation, invocational media, as I have presented them, are grounded in sociotechnical histories in everyday practices, the imagination, mythology, social relations, language and materiality. Before its appropriation in computing discourse, the term 'invocation' elicited a range of meanings. It might be summarised as the use of a voice to seek immediate magical assistance, calling to an outside agent for guidance, artistic inspiration, authority, information or spectacle. In computer programming and computer operation, an invocation became an event by which a human or non-human agent used instructions and addresses to call on invocable domains – black-boxed resources or routines to initiate and automate summoned events. Depending on the invocable domains, such events can be on any scale, performing all manner of symbolic and material transformations. Taken broadly, it is accurate to say that most operations of digital computers are invocations, whether that is to perform a simple calculation, to invoke an evocative image to a screen, to invoke someone's criminal record or to invoke a simulation of a nuclear explosion. In this book, I have extended these meanings to build an array of terms for reconceptualising computers as invocational media.

At one level, invocational media belong to a history of invocatory devices – switches, buttons and levers. But invocational media are a special phylum of switches – with memories and other invocable domains – creating what I have called the 'invocational interval'. Where a simple switch can mark a user's single and immediate decision, the circuits within this interval can interleave commands with memories to produce many more finely differentiated and delayed decisions. Invocation is a cultural form, or abstract machine, marked by this combination of command, memory and decision.

Projects for creating invocational media, then, come not only from a capacity for abstraction but also from a desire for machines that hear, mediate and

230   *Invocational Media*

respond to commands. This desire is not entirely rational. To make a command, users must imagine and articulate what they want. Freud argued that in civilised societies, technology displaced primitive magic. It offered a means of answering desires in the subconscious (Freud, 1950, 1995 [1930]). So when invocational media appeared, they were somewhat familiar to Western cultures because they fit these primitive archetypes of magic, offering to call up events at the whim of the invoker (be they a mathematician, hacker, business executive, scientist, artist or consumer). The invocation came to mediate intensive performative powers to generate interpersonal, affective and material events that aligned with individual and collective desires. They create convocational social spaces that afford communication at a distance.

The details of these seductive and quasi-magical powers sometimes exceed the awareness and control of the invoker. As the myth of the Muses suggests, invocations must be articulated carefully and precisely, because their consequences will not necessarily be exactly what the supplicant had in mind. Performing an internet search finds an intersection between the user's own expressed desires and a sublime corpus of indexed texts beyond consciousness. Algorithmically selected results reveal and make tangible intersubjective patterns and collective meanings that to some extent fulfil the desires of the invoker. At the same time, the invoker has performed involuntary invocations that supply them with targeted advertising, based on a profile and search history.

The most significant thing delegated to invocational media is delegation itself. Detailed commands can be stored up and distributed indefinitely, often with minimal human intervention. Some systems operate in real-time, invoking environments that mediate perception and action through networks that are not only technical. Delegation is as much about having already persuaded or coerced resources as it is about articulating instructions clearly. As Kittler says, '[u]niversal discrete machines settle the old question – how to make people die for others' (1997, p. 118).

The main project of this book has been to build a concept that captures the distinctiveness of invocational media assemblages. Mediated invocations have become naturalised as simultaneously technical, cultural and operations of unmarked power. Invocational media mediate these events. In refusing to separate technology from language, culture or society, I am arguing that technical, psychological, conceptual and social factors have non-trivial consequences. So, while invocational media may answer existing cultural desires, they also have unanticipated consequences, which emerge from their sociotechnical

Conclusions 231

characteristics. As actor–network theory suggests, invocations are mediated through complex networks of human and non-human actors. Using the concept of invocation, then, I have traced connections between the technical level of microelectronics, the experiential level of computers in use, the intersubjective level of the cultural imaginary and the political level of social institutions and power. Along the way, the book has made connections between a wide range of literatures: from technical manuals to political manifestos. With the breadth of this sweep, there remains plenty of scope for further work that might deal in more depth with these levels and domains.

If our era is defined by the invocation, it is because this genetic element has infused itself into everyday practices and social institutions. Invocations work at multiple scales in networked combination with billions of others to mediate complex and sometimes contradictory processes that are social, aesthetic, political, economic or any combination of these. This approach of conceptualising complexity as something emergent has something in common with Latour's call to 'follow the actors' and their 'programs' (Latour, 1991) and with de Landa's 'non-linear histories' (de Landa, 1997). While the genetic element of invocation in digital electronics emerged as early as the 1940s, it is undeniable that the complete designs for contemporary invocational assemblages were not available from the beginning. Rather, development proceeded in complex and iterative ways, often in multiple directions simultaneously, and always being itself subject to the dynamics of iterative invocations (computer-aided software engineering, computer-aided design, computer-aided manufacturing). Small differences in initial conditions could have produced quite different outcomes in what invocational media have become. Today's PCs are not the optimal design of all possible computers but a result of cumulative, non-linear invocational processes.

Drawing on the concept of invocational media can also help ask ethical and political questions about technological choices and programs. Modes of convocation create any number of mediatised formations and social situations that establish positions for speakers and listeners. Each mode can be evaluated according to how avocational structures position different classes of user. Avocational structures can be assessed by their user modes, which determine what and how a user can invoke at any moment. This approach can incorporate the familiar concept of privacy but go beyond it towards more subtle readings of usergenesis – the processes by which user subjectivities are generated.

The concept of invocational media offers a way out of some long-standing controversies. Artificial intelligence, virtual reality and artificial life are three contentious fields based on claims about the capacity of computers to reproduce 'real-world' phenomena. Invocational theory resolves this by concluding that these fields are better conceived as invoked intelligence, invoked reality and invoked life. The distinctions between human and machine intelligence, between reality and VR, and between life and artificial life do not have to be absolute. At one level, they are like stage magic, while at another level they model and reveal new things about human thought and experience and the genesis of life. These technologies will never reproduce the phenomena they claim to model, but the work they do in trying to invoke these things will have real effects. Of course, this observation won't stop these debates, but it will offer those who are tired of them a way to move on to more interesting questions.

This may be the end of this book, but in many ways, it is only the beginning of the concept of invocation. This work is not a complete program or theoretical model but an intervention into the discourse around new media forms. If it is taken up by other writers, it will be transformed into something else again. The concept itself could function as a genetic element in future work in media and cultural theory. The technological lineage that I have dubbed 'invocational media' will undoubtedly continue to be a powerful component in cultural, economic and social practices into the foreseeable future. With massively parallel computing, the emergence of quantum computing and the 2020s explosion in large language models for artificial intelligence the development of AR and VR, the mechanisms for invocation are clearly changing, but in many ways, they only extend invocational relationships to reality.

References

Aarseth, E. (1997). *Cybertext. Perspectives on ergodic literature*. Baltimore and London: John Hopkins University Press.

Aarseth, E. (2001). Computer game studies, year one. *Game Studies, 1*(1). http://gamestudies.org/0101/editorial.html

Abbate J. (1999). *Inventing the internet*. Cambridge, MA: MIT Press.

Abbate, J. (2010). The pleasure paradox: Bridging the gap between popular images of computing and women's historical experiences. In T. J. Misa (Ed.), *Gender codes: Why women are leaving computing* (pp. 211–27). Hoboken: Wiley.

Agre, P. E. (1994–2001). *Red Rock Eater* electronic mail list. Archival website: http://dlis.gseis.ucla.edu/people/pagre/rre.html. Accessed 22 April 2022.

Agre, P. E. (1997). *Computation and human experience*. Cambridge: Cambridge University Press.

Al-Kadit, I. A. (1992). Origins of cryptology: The Arab contributions. *Cryptologia, 16*(2), 97–126. https://doi.org/10.1080/0161-119291866801

Althusser, L. (1971). *Lenin and philosophy and other essays*. London: Unwin.

Anderson, K., Faulkner, S., Kleinman, L. & Sherman, J. (2017). Creating a creators' market: How ethnography gave Intel a new perspective on digital content creators. *Ethnographic Praxis in Industry Conference Proceedings, 2017*(1), 425–43. https://doi.org/10.1111/1559-8918.2017.01162

Anderson, Laurie (1982). O Superman [Song]. On *Big Science*. Nonesuch Records.

Anton, C. (2016). On the roots of media ecology: A micro-history and philosophical clarification. *Philosophies, 1*(2), 126–32. https://doi.org/10.3390/philosophies1020126

Antonelli, W. & Haasch, P. (2020). A Couple Held a Wedding in "Animal Crossing" after Coronavirus Forced them to Cancel their Real-World Ceremony. *Insider*, 25 March 2020. Available at: https://www.insider.com/animal-crossing-wedding-coronavirus-social-distancing-2020-3. Accessed 22 April 2022.

Apperley, T. & Moore, K. (2019). Haptic ambience: Ambient play, the haptic effect and co-presence in Pokémon GO. *Convergence, 25*(1), 6–17.

Apple Computer, Inc. (1992). *Macintosh human interface guidelines*. Reading: Addison-Wesley Publishing Company.

Apple Computer, Inc. (1994). *Inside Macintosh: Imaging with QuickDraw*. Cupertino: Apple Computer Inc.

Appleby, D. (1991). *Programming languages. Paradigm and practice*. New York: McGraw-Hill.

Aspray, W. (1990). *John von Neumann and the origins of modern computing*, Cambridge, MA: MIT Press.

Aspray, W. and Burks, A. (Eds) (1987). *Papers of John von Neumann on computers and computer theory*. Cambridge, MA and London: MIT Press.

Aupers, S. D. (2011). Technopagans: Online magic and the mysterious manifestation of cyberspace. In A. Molendijk, P. Post & J. Kroesen (Eds), *Sacred Places in Modern Western Culture* (pp. 321–6). Leuven: Peeters.

Austin, J. L. (1975). *How to do things with words*. Oxford: Clarendon Press.

Barabási, A.-L. (2002). *Linked: The new science of networks*. Cambridge, MA: Perseus.

Barbrook, R. (2000). Cyber-communism: How the Americans are superseding capitalism in cyberspace. *Science as culture*, *9*(1), 5–40.

Barbrook, R. with Cameron, A. (2014). *The internet revolution: From dot-com capitalism to cybernetic communism*. Amsterdam: Institute of Network Cultures. https://networkcultures.org/blog/publication/no-10-the-internet-revolution-from-dot-com-capitalism-to-cybernetic-communism-by-richard-barbrook-with-andy-cameron/

Bardini, T. (2000). *Bootstrapping, Douglas Engelbart, coevolution, and the origins of personal computing*. Stanford: Stanford University Press.

Barglow, R. (1994). *The crisis of the self in the age of information*. New York: Routledge.

Barlow, J. P. (1990). Being in nothingness. John Perry Barlow Library, Electronic Frontier Foundation. https://www.eff.org/pages/being-nothingness

Barlow, J. P. (1994). Jack in, young pioneer!. *Keynote essay for the 1994 Computerworld College Edition*, Electronic Frontier Foundation website. https://www.eff.org/pages/jack-young-pioneer. Accessed February 2022.

Barlow, J. P. (2015 [1990]). Virtual reality and the pioneers of cyberspace. Being and nothingness. *Wired*. https://www.wired.com/2015/04/virtual-reality-and-the-pioneers-of-cyberspace/

Barney, D. (2000). *Prometheus wired. The hope for democracy in the age of network technology*. Sydney: UNSW Press.

Barthes, R. (1982). *Camera lucida: Reflections on photography*. New York: Hill and Wang.

Bashe, C. J. (1982). The SSEC in historical perspective. *Annals of the History of Computing*, *4*(4), 296–312.

Bataille, G. (2018). On the ambiguity of pleasure and play. *Theory, Culture and Society*, *35*(4–5), 233–50.

Baudrillard, J. (1996). *The system of objects*. London and New York: Verso.

Baumer, E. P. S. & Brubaker, J. R. (2017). Post-userism. *Proceedings of the 2017 CHI Conference on Human Factors in Computing Systems. Denver Colorado USA May 6–11, 2017*, 6291–303.

Bauwens, M., Kostakis, V. & Pazaitis, A. (2019). *Peer to peer: The commons manifesto*. London: University of Westminster Press.

Beck, J. & Bishop, R. (2016). *Cold war legacies: Systems, theory, aesthetics*. Edinburgh: Edinburgh University Press.

References 235

Begley, P. (2021). Food delivery driver's death wasn't recognised by Uber Eats and his family are still fighting for the insurance. *ABC News*, 25 June 2021. https://www.abc.net.au/news/2021-06-25/background-briefing-uber-eats-delivery-drivers-death/100239920. Accessed 3 February 2022.

Bell, A. G. (1876). Researches in telephony. *Proceedings of the American Academy of Arts and Sciences, XII.* https://doi.org/10.2307/25138430

Benedikt, M. (1992). *Cyberspace. First steps.* Cambridge, MA: MIT Press.

Beniger, J. R. (1986). *The control revolution. Technological and economic origins of the information society.* Cambridge, MA: Harvard University Press.

Bergson, H. (1998 [1911]). *Creative evolution.* Toronto and London: General Publishing Co.

Berkeley, E. C. (1949). *Giant brains; or, Machines that think.* Hoboken, NJ: Wiley.

Berners-Lee, T., Cailliau, R., Groff, J.-F. and Pollermann, B. (1992). World-Wide Web: The information universe. *Electronic Networking, 2*(1), 52–8.

Bezaitis, M. and Robinson, R. E. (2017). Valuable to values: How "user research" ought to change. In A. J. Clarke (Ed.), *Design anthropology: Object cultures in transition* (pp. 53–68). London: Bloomsbury.

Bickford, P. (1997). *Interface design: The art of developing easy-to-use software.* Boston: AP Professional.

Biermann, A. W. (1997 [1990]). *Great ideas in computer science.* Cambridge, MA and London: MIT Press.

Blackwell, A. F. (2015). 'HCI as an inter-discipline'. *Proceedings of the 2015 CHI Conference on Human Factors in Computing Systems, 18*, 503–12. https://doi.org/10.1145/2702613.2732505

Blom, J. N. & Hansen, K. R. (2015). Click bait: Forward-reference as lure in online news headlines. *Journal of Pragmatics, 76*, 87–100.

Bogost, I. (2007). *Persuasive games: The expressive power of videogames.* Cambridge, MA: MIT Press.

Bogost, I. (2015). The cathedral of computation. *The Atlantic*, 19 January 2015. https://www.theatlantic.com/technology/archive/2015/01/the-cathedral-of-computation/384300/

Bollmer, G. (2018). *Theorising digital cultures.* London: Sage.

Bolter, J. D. (1991). *Writing space. The computer, hypertext, and the history of writing.* Hillsdale: Lawrence Erlbaum Associates.

Bolter, J. D. and Grusin, R. (1999). *Remediation. Understanding new media.* Cambridge, MA and London: MIT Press.

Bolton, W. F. (1984). *The language of 1984.* Oxford: Basil Blackwell.

Boole, G. (2005 [1854]). *An investigation of the laws of thought.* Project Gutenberg. https://www.gutenberg.org/files/15114/15114-pdf.pdf

Boole, G. (2017). *An investigation of the laws of thought on which are founded the mathematical theories of logic and probabilities.* Project Gutenberg. https://www.gutenberg.org/files/15114/15114-pdf.pdf

Borges, J. L. (1985). *Fictions; edited and with an introduction by Anthony Kerrigan.* London: J. Calder.

Borning, A., Friedman, B. & Logler, N. (2020). The "invisible" materiality of information technology. *Communications of the ACM, 63*(6), 57–64.

Borschke, M. (2017). *This is not a remix: Piracy, authenticity and popular music.* New York: Bloomsbury.

Bourdieu, P. (1991). *Language and symbolic power.* Cambridge: Polity.

Brahnam, S., Karanikas, M. & Weaver, M. (2011). (Un)dressing the interface: Exposing the foundational HCI metaphor "computer is woman." *Interacting with Computers, 23*(5), 401–12.

Bratton, B. H. (2015). *The stack. On software and sovereignty.* Cambridge, MA: MIT Press.

Broderik, D. (1997). *The spike: How our lives are being transformed by rapidly advancing technologies.* Kew: Reed.

Brooks, R. A. (1991). Intelligence without representation. *Artificial Intelligence, 47*(1–3), 139–59. https://doi.org/10.1016/0004-3702(91)90053-M

Browne, S. (2015). *Dark matters: On the surveillance of blackness.* Durham: Duke University Press.

Bruce-Briggs, B. (1988). *The shield of faith.* New York: Touchstone.

Budiansky, S. (2006). Colossus, codebreaking, and the digital age. In B. J. Copeland (Ed.), *Colossus: The secrets of Bletchley Park's codebreaking computers* (pp. 52–63). Oxford: Oxford University Press.

Burgess, J. (2012). The iPhone moment, the Apple brand, and the creative consumer: From "Hackability and Usability" to cultural generativity. In L. Hjorth, J. Burgess and I. Richardson, *Studying mobile media: Cultural technologies, mobile communication and the iPhone.* Milton Park: Taylor & Francis.

Butler, S. (1863). Darwin among the machines. [To the Editor of the Press, Christchurch, New Zealand, 13 June 1863.] https://nzetc.victoria.ac.nz/tm/scholarly/tei-ButFir-t1-g1-t1-g1-t4-body.html

Cain, S. (2023). "This song sucks": Nick Cave responds to ChatGPT song written in style of Nick Cave. *The Guardian*, Online. https://www.theguardian.com/music/2023/jan/17/this-song-sucks-nick-cave-responds-to-chatgpt-song-written-in-style-of-nick-cave. Accessed 9 February 2023.

Carter, M., Gibbs, M. & Wadley, G. (2013, September). Death and dying in DayZ. In *Proceedings of The 9th Australasian Conference on Interactive Entertainment: Matters of Life and Death* (pp. 1–6). New York: Association of Computing Machinery.

Casemajor, N. (2015). Digital materialisms: Frameworks for digital media studies. *Westminster Papers in Culture and Communication, 10*(1), 4–17. https://doi.org/10.16997/wpcc.209

Castells, M. (1996). *The rise of the network society.* Cambridge, MA: Blackwell.

Castells, M. (1997). *The power of identity: The information age – Economy, society and culture.* Cambridge, MA: Blackwell.

Castells, M. (2000). *End of millennium* (2nd edn). Cambridge, MA: Blackwell.

Ceruzzi, P. (1983). *The prehistory of the digital computer, from relays to the stored program concept, 1935–1945*. Westport: Greenwood Press.

Ceruzzi, P. (1986). An unforeseen revolution: Computers and expectations, 1935–1985. In J. Corn (Ed.), *Imagining tomorrow. History, technology and the American future*. Cambridge, MA: MIT Press.

Ceruzzi, P. (1998). *A history of modern computing*. Cambridge, MA and London: MIT Press.

Chambers, I. (1990). A miniature history of the Walkman. *New Formations: A Journal of Culture/Theory/Politics, 11*, 1–4.

Chandor, A., & Williamson, R. (1985). *The Penguin dictionary of computers* (3rd edn). Harmondsworth, Middlesex: Penguin Books.

Chenery, S. & Gordon, V. (2020). Sam Neill's "cheering-up" business. *ABC News*. https://www.abc.net.au/news/2020-04-27/sam-neill-cheering-up-business-during -coronavirus/12147500?nw=0. Accessed 22 April 2022.

Chesher, C. (1994). Colonising virtual reality. *Cultronix, 1*(1). http://xroads.virginia .edu/~DRBR/chesher.

Chesher, C. (1997). The ontology of digital domains. In D. Holmes, *Virtual politics* (pp. 79–92). London: Sage.

Chesher, C. (1998). Digitising the beat: Police databases and incorporeal transformations. *Convergence*, Summer, 72–81.

Chesher, C. (2009). Binding time in digital civilisations: Re-evaluating Innis after new media. *Global Media Journal: Australian Edition*. http://www.hca.westernsydney .edu.au/gmjau/archive/v3_2009_1/pdf/Chris_Chesher.pdf. Accessed 27 April 2022.

Chun, W. H. K. (2011). *Programmed visions: Software and memory*. Cambridge, MA: MIT Press.

Claburn, T. (2007). Google restores Katrina's scars to Google Earth. *InformationWeek*, 2 April 2007. https://web.archive.org/web/20090819110834/http://www .informationweek.com/news/internet/search/showArticle.jhtml?articleID =198701867. Accessed 22 April 2022.

Coeckelbergh, M. (2019). *Moved by machines: Performance metaphors and philosophy of technology*. New York: Routledge. https://doi.org/10.4324/9780429283130

Conley, V. A. (1999). Whither the virtual: Slavoj Žižek and cyberfeminism. *Angelica. Journal of the Theoretical Humanities, 4*(2), 129–36.

Cooley, M. (1980). *Architect or bee? The human/technology relationship*. Sydney: TransNational Co-Operative Ltd.

Copeland, B. J. (Ed.) (2006). *Colossus: The secrets of Bletchley Park's codebreaking computers*. Oxford: Oxford University Press.

Cosgrove, D. (1994). Contested global visions: One-World, Whole-Earth, and the Apollo space photographs. *Annals of the Association of American Geographers, 84*(2), 270–94.

Couldry, N. & Mejias, U. A. (2019). *The costs of connection: How data is colonizing human life and appropriating it for capitalism*. Stanford, CA: Stanford University Press.

Cowan, P. (2014, August 15). NSW Police, courts to exchange warrants within minutes. *IT News*. https://www.itnews.com.au/news/nsw-police-courts-to-exchange-warrants -within-minutes-391077

Cox, G. & McLean, A. (2013). *Speaking code: Coding as aesthetic and political expression*. Cambridge, MA: MIT Press.

Crary, J. (2022). *Scorched earth: Beyond the digital age to a post-capitalist world*. London: Verso (e-book).

Crogan, P. (2011). *Gameplay mode: War, simulation and technoculture*. Minneapolis: University of Minnesota Press.

Crutcher, M. & Zook, M. (2009). Placemarks and waterlines: Racialized cyberscapes in post-Katrina Google Earth. *Geoforum, 40*(4), 523–34.

Curran, J., Fenton, N. & Freedman, D. (2016). *Misunderstanding the internet*. New York: Routledge.

D'Amour, E., Heller, K. Moldovan, D. et al. (2020). Underspecification presents challenges for credibility in modern machine learning. arXiv preprint arXiv:2011.03395.

Danks, D. and London, A. J. (2017). Algorithmic bias in autonomous systems. *IJCAI, 17*, 4691–7.

DARPA (n.d.). DARPA tiles together a vision of mosaic warfare. Defense Advanced Projects Agency Website. https://www.darpa.mil/work-with-us/darpa-tiles-together -a-vision-of-mosiac-warfare. Accessed 22 June 2020.

Dasgupta, S. (2014). *It began with Babbage: The genesis of Computer Science*. Oxford: Oxford University Press.

Davies, S. (1992). *Big Brother: Australia's growing web of surveillance*. Sydney: Simon and Schuster.

Davis, E. (1998). *Techgnosis. Myth, magic and mysticism in the age of information*. New York: Harmony Books.

De Landa, M. (1991). *War in the age of intelligent machines*. New York: Swerve Editions.

De Landa, M. (1997). *A thousand years of non-linear history*. New York: Swerve Editions.

De Mol, L. & Bullynck, M. (2018). Making the history of computing. The history of computing in the history of technology and the history of mathematics. *Revue de Synthèse*, Springer Verlag/Lavoisier.

Debord, G. (2002). *The society of the spectacle*. Canberra: Hobgoblin Press.

Debord, G. & Knabb, K. (Trans) (2014). *The society of the spectacle*. Berkeley: Bureau of Public Secrets.

References

Deleuze, G. (1986). *Cinema 1: The movement image*. Minneapolis: University of Minnesota Press.

Deleuze, G. (1989). *Cinema 2: The time image*. Minneapolis: University of Minnesota Press.

Deleuze, G. (1990a). *Negotiations*. New York: Columbia University Press.

Deleuze, G. (1990b). Postscript on control societies. In Deleuze, Gilles (1990a), pp. 177–82.

Deleuze, G. (1992). Postscript on the societies of control. *October, 59*(Winter), 3–7.

Deleuze, G. and Guattari, F. (1983). *Anti-oedipus*. Minneapolis: University of Minnesota Press.

Deleuze, G. and Guattari, F. (1987). *A thousand plateaus*. Minneapolis: University of Minnesota Press.

Deleuze, G. and Guattari, F. (1994). *What is philosophy?*. London and New York: Verso.

Deleuze, G. & Hand, S. (1988). *Foucault*. Minneapolis: University of Minnesota Press.

Derrida, J. (1996). *Archive fever: A Freudian impression*. Chicago: University of Chicago Press.

Derrida, J. (1997). *Of grammatology*. Baltimore: John Hopkins University Press.

Dery, M. (Ed.) (1994). *Flame wars. The discourse of cyberspace*. Durham: Duke University Press.

Dery, M. (1996). *Escape velocity. Cyberculture at the end of the century*. London: Hodder & Stoughton.

Deutsch, K. W. (1954). Game theory and politics: Some problems of application. *The Canadian Journal of Economics and Political Science, 20*(1), 76–83.

Diaz, G. (2019). *Software rights: How patent law transformed software development in America*. New Haven: Yale University Press.

Digital Equipment Corporation (1969). *FOCAL Promotional Booklet*. Reproduced on Department of Computer Science, University of Iowa website. http://www.cs.uiowa.edu/~jones/pdp8/focal/. Accessed February 2000.

Dooley, J. F. (2013). *A brief history of cryptology and cryptographic algorithms*. Cham: Springer.

Dorrestijn, S. (2012). Technical mediation and subjectivation: Tracing and extending Foucault's philosophy of technology. *Philosophy and Technology, 25*(2), 221–41.

Dourish, P. (2004). *Where the action is. The foundations of embodied interaction*. Cambridge, MA: MIT Press.

Dourish, P. (2016). Algorithms and their others: Algorithmic culture in context. *Big Data & Society, 3*(2), 1–11.

Dreyfus, H. (1972). *What computers can't do. A critique of artificial reason*. New Yrok: Harper & Rowe.

Dunn, J. C. (2020). Critical rhetoric in the age of the (first) reality TV President: A critique of freedom and domination. *International Journal of Communication, 14*(0), 813–30.

During, S. (2002). *Modern enchantments: The cultural power of secular magic.* Cambridge, MA: Harvard University Press.

Edwards, P. N. (1996). *The closed world: Computers and the politics of discourse in cold war America.* Cambridge, MA: MIT Press.

Eggers, D. (2014). *The circle.* Harlow, England: Penguin Books.

Eisenhower, D. (1961). President Dwight D. Eisenhower's farewell address. https://www.archives.gov/milestone-documents/president-dwight-d-eisenhowers-farewell-address

Elliott, J. R. & Pais, J. (2006). Race, class, and Hurricane Katrina: Social differences in human responses to disaster. *Social Science Research, 35,* 295–321.

Emmeche, C. and Sampson, S. (Trans) (1994). *The garden in the machine.* Princeton: Princeton University Press.

Enfield, N. (2017). *How we talk. The inner workings of conversation.* New York: Basic Books.

Engelbart, D. (1988). The augmented language workshop. In Adele Goldberg (Ed.), *A history of personal workstations.* New York: ACM Press.

Exarchos, M. (2019). Sample magic: (Conjuring) phonographic ghosts and meta-illusions in contemporary hip-hop production. *Popular Music, 38*(1), 33–53. https://doi.org/10.1017/S0261143018000685

Feenberg, A. (2002). *Transforming technology: A critical theory revisited.* New York: Oxford University Press.

Finn, E. (2017). *What algorithms want: Imagination in the age of computing.* Cambridge, MA: MIT Press.

Foucault, M. (1963). *The birth of the clinic: An archaeology of medical perception.* New York: Random House.

Foucault, M. (1991 [1975]). *Discipline and punish.* London: Penguin.

Foucault, M. (1992 [1969]). *The archaeology of knowledge.* London: Routledge.

Foucault, M. and Gordon, C. (Eds) (1980). *Power/knowledge. Selected interviews and other writings.* New York: Pantheon Books.

Frasca, G. (1999). Ludology meets narratology: Similitude and differences between (video)games and narrative. https://ludology.typepad.com/weblog/articles/ludology.htm. Accessed 30 April 2022.

Freud, S. (1950). *Totem and Taboo.* London: Routledge.

Freud, S. (1995 [1920]). Beyond the pleasure principle. In S. Freud and P. Gay (Ed.), *The Freud reader* (pp. 594–626). London: Random House.

Freud, S. (1995 [1930]). Civilisation and its discontents. In S. Freud and P. Gay (Ed.), *The Freud reader* (pp. 722–72). London: Random House.

Freud, S. (1995). *The Freud reader* (P. Gay, Ed.). London: Random House.

Fuchs, C. (2015). Dallas Smythe and digital labor. In R. Maxwell (Ed.), *Routledge companion to labor and media* (pp. 51–62). New York Routledge.

Fuchs, C. (2019). *Rereading Marx in the age of digital capitalism.* London: Pluto Press.

References

241

Gabbard, D. & Saltman, K. J. (2011). *Education as enforcement: The militarization and corporatization of schools* (Second edn). New York: Routledge.

Galič, M., Timan, T. & Koops, B. J. (2017). Bentham, Deleuze and beyond: An overview of surveillance theories from the panopticon to participation. *Philosophy and Technology, 30*(1), 9–37. https://doi.org/10.1007/s13347-016-0219-1.

Galliers, R. D. (2022). Review: *LEO remembered – By the people who worked on the world's first business computer,* Second edition. Edited by Hilary Caminer and Lisa-Jane McGerty. *Information Systems Journal, 33*(2), 218.

Galloway, A. R. (2004). *Protocol. How control exists after decentralization.* Cambridge, MA: MIT Press.

Galloway, P. (2020). Online gaming is getting a big boost from the coronavirus pandemic — And experts say it's just the beginning. *ABC News* (Website), 9 April 2020. https://www.abc.net.au/news/2020-04-09/online-gaming-hits-huge-numbers -during-coronavirus-pandemic/12135714

Gauntlett, D. (2011). *Making is connecting: The social meaning of creativity, from DIY and knitting to YouTube and Web 2.0.* Cambridge: Polity.

Gavil, A. I. & First, H. (2014). *The Microsoft antitrust cases: Competition policy for the twenty-first century.* Cambridge, MA: The MIT Press.

Gazzard, A. (2016). *Now the chips are down: The BBC Micro.* Cambridge, MA: MIT Press.

Gebhart G. (2018). Google Home's new continued conversation setting keeps the mic hot for a smoother chat. *C-net,* 21 June 2018. Available at: https://www.cnet.com/ news/google-home-continued-conversation-setting-keeps-the-mic-hot/

Geraci, M. (2020). Algorithmic management: Liability-free method to manage Workers' performance?. *Revista de la Facultad de Jurisprudencia (RFJ), 7,* 244–70.

Gibson, W. (1984). *Neuromancer.* New York: Ace.

Gibson, W. (1987). *Count zero.* London: Grafton.

Gibson, W. (1989). *Mona Lisa overdrive.* London: Grafton.

Goggin, G. (2006). *Cell phone culture: Mobile technology in everyday life.* London: Routledge.

Goggin, G. & Newell, C. (2007). The business of digital disability. *The Information Society, 23*(3), 159–68.

Goldstine, H. H. (1993). *The computer from Pascal to Von Neumann.* Princeton: Princeton University Press.

Golumbia, D. (2009). *The cultural logic of computation.* Cambridge, MA: Harvard University Press.

Goodchild, P. (1985). *J. Robert Oppenheimer: Shatterer of worlds.* New York: Fromm International.

Google (2020). Google. About Google, our culture & company news. Website. Available at: https://about.google/

Gore, A. (1993). Remarks by the Vice President at the National Press Club Newsmaker Luncheon, National Press Club, Washington DC, 21 December 1993. https://www.ibiblio.org/nii/goremarks.html

Graber, M. A. & Graber, A. D. (2010). Get your paws off my pixels: Personal identity and avatars as self. *Journal of Medical Internet Research*, *12*(3).

Graham, M. (2011). Time machines and virtual portals: The spatialities of the digital divide. *Progress in Development Studies*, *11*(3), 211–27.

Grier, D. A. (2005). *When computers were human*. Princeton: Princeton University Press.

Grint, K. & Woolgar, S. (1997). *The machine at work: Technology, work and organization*. Cambridge: Polity Press.

Grossberg, L. (1996). On postmodernism and articulation. An interview with Stuart Hall. In D. Morley & K. H. Chen, *Stuart Hall: Critical dialogues in cultural studies* (pp. 131–50). London: Routledge.

Guattari, F. (1995a). *Chaosmosis. An ethico-political paradigm*. Sydney: Power Publications.

Guattari, F. (1995b). On machines. *Journal of philosophy and the visual arts*, *6*, 8–12.

Guattari, F. (1996). Subjectivities: For better and for worse. In Guattari and Gonesko (Eds.). *The Guattari reader* (pp. 193–203). Cambridge, MA: Blackwell.

Guillory, J. (2010). Genesis of the media concept, *Critical inquiry*, *36*(2), 321–62.

Gunning, D. & Aha, D. W. (2019). DARPA's explainable artificial intelligence program. *AI Magazine*, *40*(2), 44–58.

Gürer, D. (2002). Women in computing history. *ACM SIGCSE Bulletin*, *34*(2), 116–20.

Gurney, K. (1997). *An introduction to neural networks*. London: University College of London Press.

Guy, J. (2020). Barcelona opera house reopens with performance to 2,292 plants. *CNN* (Website), 24 June 2020. https://edition.cnn.com/style/article/barcelona-opera-plants-scli-intl/index.html. Accessed 30 June 2020.

Haigh, T., Priestley, M., Rope, C., Aspray, W. Jr and Misa, T. J. (2016). *ENIAC in action: Making and remaking the modern computer*. Cambridge, MA: MIT Press.

Hall, S. (1973). *Encoding and decoding in the television discourse*. Discussion paper. University of Birmingham, Birmingham.

Hall, S. (1986). On postmodernism and articulation: An interview with Lawrence Grossberg. *Journal of Communication Inquiry*, *10*(2), 45–60.

Halliday, M. (1978). *Language as social semiotic: The social interpretation of language and meaning*. London: Edward Arnold.

Han, L. C. (2006). New strategies for an old medium: The weekly radio addresses of Reagan and Clinton. *Congress and the Presidency*, *33*(1), 25–45. https://doi.org/10.1080/07343460609507687

Hanke, J. (2007). About the New Orleans imagery in Google Maps and Earth. *The official Google Blog*, 2 April 2007. Available at: https://googleblog.blogspot.com/2007/04/about-new-orleans-imagery-in-google.html

References

Hankins, T. L. & Silverman, R. J. (1995). *Instruments and the imagination*. Princeton: Princeton University Press.

Haraway, D. (1991). A cyborg manifesto. In *Simian, cyborgs and women: Reinvention of nature* (pp. 149–81). New York: Routledge.

Hardie, P. (2019). Ancient and modern theories of epic. In C. Reitz & S. Finkmann, *Structures of epic poetry. Volume 1: Foundations* (pp. 25–50). Berlin: De Gruyter.

Harkins, P. (2015). Following the instruments, designers, and users: The case of the Fairlight CMI. *Journal on the Art of Record Production, 10*(2). https://www.arpjournal.com/asarpwp/following-the-instruments-designers-and-users-the-case-of-the-fairlight-cmi/

Havelock, E. A. (1963). *Preface to Plato*, Cambridge, MA: Harvard University Press.

Hayles, N. K. (1999). *How we became posthuman. Virtual bodies in cybernetics, literature and informatics*. Chicago and London: University of Chicago Press.

Heidegger, M. (1977a). The question concerning technology. In Martin Heidegger, *The question concerning technology and other essays* (pp. 3–35). New York: Harper.

Heidegger, M. (1977b). The age of the world picture. In Martin Heidegger, *The question concerning technology, and other essays* (pp. 115–54). New York: Harper.

Heikkiläm M. (2022, September 16). This artist is dominating AI-generated art. And he's not happy about it. *MIT Technology Review*. https://www.technologyreview.com/2022/09/16/1059598/this-artist-is-dominating-ai-generated-art-and-hes-not-happy-about-it/

Heim, M. (1993). *The metaphysics of virtual reality*. New York and Oxford: Oxford University Press.

Hine, C. (2000). *Virtual ethnography*. London: SAGE.

Hine, C. (2015). *Ethnography for the internet: Embedded, embodied and everyday*. London: Taylor & Francis Group.

Hjarvard, S. (2018). In C. Thimm, M. Anastasiadis & J. Einspänner-Pflock (Eds), *Media Logic(s) Revisited: Modelling the Interplay between Media Institutions, Media Technology and Societal Change* (pp. 63–84). London: Palgrave MacMillan.

Hjelmslev, L. and Uldall, H. J. (1957). *Outline of glossematics*. Copenhagen: Nordisk Sprog-og Kultirforlag.

Homer (2009). *The odyssey*. MIT Classics (website) http://classics.mit.edu/Homer/odyssey.1.i.html

Hong, R. (2021). Probing interfaces: New games, Spacewar!, and the gamification of complexity. *International journal of communication* [Online], March 2021.

Hong, S. H. (2015). When life mattered: The politics of the real in video games' reappropriation of history, myth, and ritual. *Games and Culture, 10*(1), 35–56.

Huizinga, J. (1949). *Homo ludens: A study of the play-element in culture*. London: Routledge & K. Paul.

Ihde, D. (1993). *Postphenomenology. Essays in the postmodern context*. Evanston: Northwestern University Press.

Innis, H. A. (1951). *The bias of communication*. Toronto: University of Toronto Press.

Innis, H. A. (1986). *Empire and communications*. Oxford: Oxford University Press.

Instagram (n.d.). How does Instagram determine the order of posts in my feed? https://help.instagram.com/1066482030107872

Intersoft Consulting (2022). *General Data Protection Regulation*. https://gdpr-info.eu/. Accessed January 2022.

Jagoda, P. (2018). On difficulty in video games: Mechanics, interpretation, affect. *Critical Inquiry 45*(1), 199–233.

Jenkins, H., Ford, S. and Green, J. (2013). *Spreadable media*. New York: New York University Press.

Jindra, M. (1994). Star Trek fandom as a religious phenomenon. *Sociology of Religion*, *55*(1), 27–51.

Jones, M. L. (2016). *Reckoning with matter: Calculating machines, innovation, and thinking about thinking from Pascal to Babbage*. Chicago: University of Chicago Press.

Kaplan, S. (2009). Josh Harris and QUIET: We live in public. *Steven Kaplan's blog*. https://post.thing.net/node/2800

Katsiaficas, G. (2006). *The subversion of politics: European autonomous social movements and the decolonization of everyday life*. Chico: AK Press.

Kay, A. and Goldberg, A. (2000 [1977]). Personal dynamic media. In R. Packer and K. Jordan (Eds), *Multimedia: From Wagner to virtual reality* (pp. 173–84). New York: W. W. Norton.

Kempf, K. (1961). *Electronic computers within the ordnance corps* (historical monograph). Aberdeen Proving Ground: US Army November, reproduced on The U. S. Army Research Laboratory website. http://ftp.arl.mil/~mike/comphist/61ordnance/chap1.html. Accessed March 2023.

Kidder, T. (1981). *Soul of a new machine*. Boston: Little, Brown and Company.

Kim, E. E. and Toole, B. A. (1999). Ada and the first computer. *Scientific American*, *280*(5), 76–81.

Kitchin, R. and Dodge, M. (2011). *Code/Space: Software in everyday life*. Cambridge, MA and London: MIT Press.

Kittler, F. (1990). *Discourse networks 1800/1900*. Stanford: Stanford University Press.

Kittler, F. (1997). There is no software. *ctheory*, 10–18. https://journals.uvic.ca/index.php/ctheory/article/view/14655/5522.

Kittler, F. (1999 [1986]). *Gramophone, film, typewriter*. Stanford: Stanford University Press.

Kittler, F. and Johnson, J. (Ed.) (1997). *Literature, media, information systems*. Netherlands: G+B Arts.

Klein, E. (2019). Five tools for user activity monitoring. *Logz.io*. https://logz.io/blog/user-activity-monitoring-tools/

Krajewsky, M. (2018). *The server: A media history from the present to the Baroque*. New Haven: Yale University Press.

References

245

Kroker, A. and Weinstein, M. A. (1994). *Data trash: The theory of the virtual class.* New York: St Martin's Press.

Krzysztofek, M. (2021). *GDPR: Personal data protection in the European Union.* Alphen aan den Rijn: Wolters Kluwer Law International.

Lakoff, G. and Johnson, M. (1980). *Metaphors we live by.* Chicago: University of Chicago Press.

Langton, C. G. (1996). Artificial life. In M. A. Boden, *The philosophy of artificial life* (pp. 39–94). Oxford: Oxford University Press.

Latour, B. (1987). *Science in action.* Cambridge, MA: Harvard University Press.

Latour, B. (1991). Technology is society made durable. In J. Law, *A sociology of monsters. Essays on power, technology and domination* (pp. 103–31). London: Routledge.

Latour, B. (1993). *We have never been modern.* Cambridge, MA: Harvard University Press.

Latour, B. (2005). *Reassembling the social. An introduction to actor-network theory.* Oxford: Oxford University Press.

Latour, B. & Woolgar, S. (1979). *Laboratory life: The social construction of scientific facts.* Beverly Hills: Sage Publications.

Laurel, B. & Mountford, S. J. (Eds) (1989). *The art of human computer interface design.* New York: Addison-Wesley.

Lee, E., Lee, J., Moon, J. & Sung, Y. (2015). Pictures speak louder than words: Motivations for using Instagram. *Cyberpsychology, Behaviour and Social Networking, 18*(9), 552–6.

Leeder, M. (2017). *The modern supernatural and the beginnings of cinema.* London: Palgrave Macmillan.

Lessig, L. (2006). *Code: Version 2.0* (2nd edn). New York: Basic Books.

Levinson, P. (1997). *The soft edge. A natural history and future of the information revolution.* London: Routledge.

Levinson, P. (2001). *Digital McLuhan: A guide to the information millennium.* New York: Routledge.

Levinson, P. (2015). *McLuhan in an age of social media.* Seattle: Connected editions.

Levy, S. (1994). *Insanely great. The life and times of Macintosh, the computer that changed everything.* New York: Viking.

Levy, S. (2011). *In the plex: How Google thinks, works, and shapes our lives.* New York: Simon & Schuster.

Levy, S. (2014 [1984]). A spreadsheet way of knowledge. *Wired.* https://www.wired.com/2014/10/a-spreadsheet-way-of-knowledge/. Accessed 22 April 2022.

Levy, S. (2020). *Facebook: The inside story.* New York: Blue Rider.

Light, J. S. (1999). When computers were women. *Technology and Culture, 40*(3), 455–83.

Ling, R. & Lai, C. H. (2016). Microcoordination 2.0: Social coordination in the age of smartphones and messaging apps. *Journal of Communication, 66*(5), 834–56.

Linzmayer, O. W. (1994). *The Mac bathroom reader*. Alemeda: Sybex.

Locke, J. (1988). *Two treatises of government*. Cambridge: Cambridge University Press.

Lovink, G. (2016, September). On the social media ideology. *E-flux journal #75*.

Lundby, K. (Ed.) (2013). *Mediatization of communication*. Berlin: De Gruyter.

Lyon, D. (2014). Surveillance, Snowden, and Big Data: Capacities, consequences, critique. *Big Data and Society, 1*(2), 1–13.

Lyon, D. (2017). Surveillance culture: Engagement, exposure, and ethics in digital modernity. *International Journal of Communication, 11*, 824–42.

Lyon, D. (2018). *The culture of surveillance. Watching as a way of life*. Cambridge: Polity.

Mackenzie, A. (2006). *Cutting code. Software and sociality*. New York: Peter Lang.

Mackenzie, A, Sutton D. & Patton, P. (1996). Phantoms of individuality: Technology and our right to privacy. *Polemic, 7*(1), 20–5.

Macrae, N. (1999 [1992]). *John von Neumann: The scientific genius who pioneered the modern computer, game theory, nuclear deterrence, and much more*. Providence: American Mathematical Society.

Madhani, A. and Colvin, J. (2021). *A farewell to @realDonaldTrump, gone after 57,000 tweets*. Associated Press. https://apnews.com/article/twitter-donald-trump-ban-cea450b1f12f4ceb8984972a120018d5

Maher, J. (2012). *The future was here: The Commodore Amiga*. Cambridge, MA: MIT Press.

Mahoney, M. S. (2011). *The histories of computing*, ed. with an introduction by Thomas Haigh. Cambridge, MA: Harvard University Press.

Mangee, N. (2021). *How novelty and narratives drive the stock market: Black swans, anomal spirits and scapegoats*. London: Cambridge University Press.

Manning, P. K. (2008). *The technology of policing: Crime mapping, information technology, and the rationality of crime control*. New York: New York University Press.

Manovich, L. (1999). Database as symbolic form. *Convergence, 5*(2), 80–99.

Manovich, L. (2002). *The language of new media*. Cambridge, MA: MIT Press.

Manovich, L. (2013). *Software takes command: Extending the language of new media*. New York: Bloomsbury.

Manovich, L. (2018). *AI Aesthetics*. Moscow: Strelka Press. Kindle Edition.

Marchand, P. (1989). *Marshall McLuhan. The medium and the messenger*. New York: Tichnor and Fields.

Marino, M. C. (2020). *Critical code studies*. Cambridge, MA: MIT Press.

Martin, C. D. (1995). ENIAC: Press conference that shook the world. *IEEE Technology and Society Magazine, 14*(4 (Winter 1995/1996)), 3–10.

Marvin, C. (1988). *When old technologies were new: Thinking about electric communication in the late nineteenth century*. New York: Oxford University Press.

Marwick, Alice E. (2015). Instafame: Luxury selfies in the attention economy. *Public Culture*, *21*(1), 137–60.

Marx, K. (1973 [1939]). *Grundrisse: Foundations of the Critique of Political Economy.* London: Penguin Classics.

Marx, K. (2015 [1867]). *Capital: A critique of political economy, Volume I.* Moscow: Progress Publishers. Reproduced on *Marx/Engels Internet Archive*, http://www.marxists.org/archive/marx/works/1867-c1/index.htm. Accessed 21 January 2022.

Marx, K. and Engels, F. (2000 [1848]). *The Manifesto of the Communist Party.* Moscow: Progress Publishers. Reproduced on *Marx/Engels Internet Archive*. http://www.anu.edu.au/polsci/marx/classics/manifesto.html. Accessed 21 January 2022.

Mathers, P. (Trans) (1949). *The Book of the thousand nights and one night.* London: Routledge & Kegan.

McCarthy, J., Minsky, M. L., Rochester, N. & Shannon, C. E. (2006). A proposal for the Dartmouth Summer Research Project on Artificial Intelligence, 31 August 1955. *AI Magazine*, *27*(4). Available at: https://doi.org/10.1609/aimag.v27i4.1904

McCullough, B. (2015). Chapter 6 – A history of internet porn. *Internet history podcast* (transcript). http://www.internethistorypodcast.com/2015/01/history-of-internet-porn/. Accessed 11 January 2022.

McGeachie, J. S. (1973). Multiple terminals under user program control in a time-sharing environment. *Communications of the ACM*, *16*(10), 587–90. https://doi.org/10.1145/362375.362376

McKelvey, F. (2018). *Internet daemons: Digital communications possessed.* Minneapolis: University of Minnesota Press.

McLuhan, E. and Zingrone, F. (Eds) (1995). *The essential McLuhan.* New York: Routledge.

McLuhan, M. (1962). *The Gutenberg galaxy.* Toronto: University of Toronto Press.

McLuhan, M. (1964). *Understanding media. The extensions of man.* London and New York: Ark.

McLuhan, M. (1967). *The medium is the massage.* San Francisco: Hard wired.

McLuhan, M., Carson, D. & Mo Cohen, M. (2007). *The book of probes.* Berkeley: Gingko Press.

McPherson, J. C., Hamilton, F. E. & Seeber, R. R. Jr (1982 [1948]). A large-scale, general purpose digital calculator – the SSEC', reproduced in *Annals of the History of Computing*, *4*(4), 313–26.

Menn, J. (2011). 'Smartphone shipments surpass PCs'. *Financial Times*, 8 February 2011. Retrieved from Factiva 1 May 2022.

Merriner, A. (2017). Aural abjections and dancing dystopias: Sonic signifiers in video game horror. Masters thesis, University of Oregon, Eugene, Oregon, USA. Retrieved from: https://scholarsbank.uoregon.edu/xmlui/bitstream/handle/1794/22733/Merriner_oregon_0171N_11940.pdf?sequence=1&isAllowed=y. Accessed 1 May 2022.

Meyers, J. (1985). Nineteen eighty-four: A novel of the 1930s. In Gertrude Clarke Whittal Poetry and Literature Fund, *George Orwell and nineteen eighty-four. The man and the book, a Conference at the Library of Congress, April 30 and May 1, 1984*, 79–93.

Meyrowitz, J. (1985). *No sense of place. The impact of electronic media on social behaviour.* New York and Oxford: Oxford University Press.

Middeljans, A. (2010). "Weavers of Speech": Telephone operators as defiant domestics in American literature and culture. *Journal of Modern Literature, 33*, 38–63.

Minton, W. W. (1962, January). Invocation and catalogue in Hesiod and Homer. In *Transactions and Proceedings of the American Philological Association* (Vol. 93, pp. 188–212). Baltimore: Johns Hopkins University Press, American Philological Association.

Mitcham, C. (1994). *Thinking through technology: The path between engineering and philosophy.* Chicago: University of Chicago Press.

Mollick, E. (2006). Establishing Moore's Law. *IEEE Computer Society, 28*(3), 62–75.

Montfort, N. & Bogost, I. (2009). *Racing the beam: The Atari video computer system.* Cambridge, MA: MIT Press.

Montfort, N., Bogost, I., Douglass, J., Reas, C., Mateas, M., Marino, M. C., Sample, M., Bell, J., Vawter, N. & Baudoin, P. (2012). *10 Print Chr$(205.5+Rnd(1));: Goto 10.* Cambridge, MA: The MIT Press.

Moreno, J. L. (1934). *Who shall survive? A new approach to the problem of human interrelations.* Washington D.C.: Nervous and Mental Disease Publishing Company.

Morse, S. P. (2017). The Intel 8086 chip and the future of microprocessor design. *Computer, 50*(4), 8–9.

Mumford, L. (1967). *Technics and civilization.* New York: Harcourt, Brace and World.

Murray, A. S. (1954). *Manual of mythology.* New York: Tudor.

Murray, A. T. (1945). *Homer. The odyssey.* Cambridge, MA: Harvard University Press.

Murray, J. H. (1997). *Hamlet on the holodeck. The future of narrative in cyberspace.* New York: Free Press.

Murray, J. H. (2005). The last word on ludology vs narratology in game studies. *DIGRA.* Vancouver BC. https://www.researchgate.net/publication/251172237_The_Last _Word_on_Ludology_v_Narratology_in_Game_Studies. Accessed 1 May 2022.

Murray, P. (1983). Invocation to the Muses. In T. Winnifrith & P. Murrray, *Greece old and new.* London: Macmillan.

Myhrvold, N. (1999). John von Neumann: Computing's Cold Warrior. *Time, 153*(12) website. http://content.time.com/time/magazine/article/0,9171,21839,00.html. Accessed 30 April 2022.

Nahin, P. J. (2017). *The logician and the engineer: How George Boole and Claude Shannon created the information age.* Princeton: Princeton University Press.

Nail, T. (2017). What is an assemblage? *Sub-Stance, 46*(1), 21–37. https://doi.org/10 .3368/ss.46.1.21

Naiman, A. (1988). *The Macintosh Bible*. Berkeley: Goldstein and Blair.

Natale, S. (2012). A short history of superimposition: From spirit photography to early cinema. *Early Popular Visual Culture, 10*(2), 125–45.

Natale, S. (2019). If software is narrative: Joseph Weizenbaum, artificial intelligence and the biographies of ELIZA. *New Media & Society, 21*(3), 712–28. https://doi.org/10.1177/1461444818804980

Nelson, T. H. (1974). *Computer lib: You can and must understand computers now/Dream machines*. Chicago: Hugo's Book Service.

Nelson, T. H. (1990). The right way to think about software design. In B. Laurel and S. J. Mountford (Eds), *The art of human computer interface design*. New York: Addison-Wesley.

Noble, D. F. (1997). *The religion of technology: The divinity of man and the spirit of invention*. New York: Knopf.

Norman, D. (2013). *The design of everyday things*. New York: Basic Books.

O'Donnell, N. H. (2018). Storied lives on Instagram: Factors associated with the need for personal-visual identity. *Visual Communication Quarterly, 25*(3), 131–42. https://doi.org/10.1080/15551393.2018.1490186

Ong, W. (1982). *Orality and literacy: The technologizing of the word*. London and New York: Methuen.

Ott, B. L. (2017). The age of Twitter: Donald J. Trump and the politics of debasement. *Critical Studies in Media Communication, 34*(1), 59–68.

Packer, J. & Reeves, J. (2020). *Killer apps: War, media, machine*. Durham: Duke University Press.

Papert, S. (1980). *Mindstorms: Children, computers and powerful things*. New York: Basic Books.

Papacharissi, Z. (2002). The virtual sphere: The internet as a public sphere. *New Media & Society, 4*(1), 9–27.

Pariser, E. (2011). *The filter bubble: How the new personalised web is changing what we read and how we think*. New York: Penguin.

Park, S. (2017). *Digital capital*. London: Palgrave MacMillan.

Pasquale, F. (2015). *The black box society. The secret algorithms that control money and information*. Cambridge, MA: Harvard University Press.

Peirce, C. S. (1955). *Philosophical writings of Peirce*. New York: Dover.

Penrose, R. (1989). *The emperor's new mind: Concerning computers, minds, and the laws of physics*. Oxford: Oxford University Press.

Penrose, R. (1994). *Shadows of the Mind: A Search for the Missing Science of Consciousness*. Oxford: Oxford University Press.

Perron, B. (2012). *Silent Hill: The terror engine*. Annarbor: University of Michigan Press.

Pinch, T. & Bijker, W. E. (2012). The social construction of facts and artifacts: Or how the sociology of science and the sociology of technology might benefit each other. In

W. E. Bijker, T. P. Hughes & T. Pinch, *The social construction of technological systems: New directions in the sociology and history of technology* (pp. 17–50). Cambridge, MA: MIT Press.

Plato (1974). *The Republic*. London: Penguin.

Poole, S. (2000). *Trigger happy: The inner life of video games*. London: Fourth Estate.

Poster, M. (1990). *The mode of information. Poststructuralism and social context*. Cambridge: Polity.

Powerhouse Collection (n.d.). PDP-8 computer. https://api.maas.museum/object /373038. Accessed 27 April 2022.

Proudfoot, D. & Copeland, J. (2019). Turing and the first electronic brains: What the papers said. In M. Sprevak & M. Colombo, *The Routledge handbook of the computational mind* (pp. 23–37). London: Routledge.

Rainie, H. & Wellman, B. (2012). *Networked: The new social operating system*. Cambridge, MA: MIT Press.

Randell, B. (1973). *The origins of digital computers*. Selected papers. (Third edn). Berlin: Springer-Verlag.

Raskin, J. (2000). *The humane interface: New directions for designing interactive systems*. Boston: Addison Wesley.

Reckinger, R., Wille, C., Boesen, E. & Schnür, G. (Eds) (2015). Subjectifications and subjectivations. In C. Wille, R. Reckinger, S. Kmec and M. Hesse (Eds), *Spaces and identities in border regions* (pp. 241–51). Bielefeld: Transcript.

Rex, A. F. and Leff, H. S. (2003). *Maxwell's demon 2: Entropy, classical and quantum information, computing*. Bristol: Institute of Physics Publishing.

Rheingold, H. (1991). *Virtual reality*. London: Mandarin.

Rheingold, H. (1993). *The virtual community: Homesteading on the electronic frontier*. Reading: Addison-Wesley.

Rheingold, H. (2000 [1985]). *Tools for thought*. Cambridge, MA: MIT Press.

Rockmore, T. (1995). Heidegger on technology and democracy. In Andrew Feenberg and Alastair Hannay (Eds), *Technology and the politics of knowledge*. Bloomington: Indiana University Press.

Roosth, S. (2017). *How life got made*. Chicago: University of Chicago Press.

Salamanca, C. (2009). The mother of all demos. *Digital Arts and Culture*, 12–15 December 2009.

Schama, S. (1997). *The Embarrassment of riches: An interpretation of Dutch culture in the Golden Age*. New York: Vintage Books.

Schiffer, M. B. (2003). *Draw the lightning down: Benjamin Franklin and electrical technology in the Age of Enlightenment*. Berkeley: University of California Press.

Schindler, C. (2019). The invocation of the Muses and the plea for inspiration. In C. Reitz & S. Finkmann, *Structures of epic poetry. Volume I: Foundations* (pp. 489–529). Berlin: De Gruyter.

Schindler, W. (1984). *Voice and crisis. Invocation in Milton's poetry*. Hamden: Archon Books.

Schloss, J. (2014). *Making beats: The art of sample-based hip-hop*. Middletown: Wesleyan University Press.

Schmidhuber, J. (2006). Colossus was the first electronic digital computer. *Nature, 441*(4). (Letter to the editor).

Schmitt, W. F. (1988). The UNIVAC short code. *Annals of the History of Computing, 10*(1), 7–18.

Sconce, J. (2000). *Haunted media: Electronic presence from telegraphy to television*. Durham: Duke University Press.

Searle, J. R. (1969). *Speech acts: An essay in the philosophy of language*. London: Cambridge University Press.

Searle, J. R. (1976). A classification of illocutionary acts. *Language in Society, 5*(1), 1–23.

Searle, J. R. (1980). Minds, brains, and programs. *The Behavioural and Brain Sciences, 3*, 417–57.

Serres, M. (1995). *Angels. A modern myth*. New York: Flamarion.

Shallis, M. (1984). *The silicon idol. The micro revolution and its social implications*. Oxford: Oxford University Press.

Shannon, C. E. (1938). A symbolic analysis of relay and switching circuits'. *Electrical Engineering, 57*(12), 713–23.

Shannon, C. E. (1948). A mathematical theory of communication. *Bell System Technical Journal, 27*(3), 379–423.

Sheldon, S. (1965). The lady in the bottle. *I Dream of Jeannie* [Television broadcast], 18 September 1965. https://www.dailymotion.com/video/x6u4jbk. Accessed 30 April 2022.

Sherman, B. & Judkins, P. (1992). *Glimpses of heaven, visions of hell. Virtual reality and its implications*. London: Hodder & Stoughton.

Shneiderman, B. (1986). *Designing the user interface: Strategies for effective human-computer interaction*. Reading: Addison Wesley.

Shurkin, J. (1996 [1984]). *Engines of the mind*. New York: Norton.

Silk, L. (1980). Economic scene; The candidates' money policies. *New York Times*, 31 October 1980, 2. Accessed on *Factiva*.

Simondon, G. (2017 [1958]). *On the mode of existence of technical objects*. Minneapolis: Univocal Publishing.

Slater, R. (1987). *Portraits in silicon*. Cambridge, MA: MIT Press.

Sloan, J. W. (1997). The Reagan presidency, growing inequality, and the American dream. *Policy Studies Journal, 25*(3), 371–86.

Smith, A. (2012). *Totally wired. The rise and fall of Josh Harris and the great dotcom swindle*. New York: Black Cat.

Smith, A. (2019). We're in the business of programming people's lives. *Wired*, 15 March 2019. https://www.wired.com/story/josh-harris-social-media-totally-wired-excerpt/

Stahl, W. A. (1999). *God and the chip. Religion and the culture of technology*. Waterloo: Wilfrid Laurier University Press.

Starwave and Jim Henson Interactive (1996). *The Muppet CD-ROM: Muppets Inside.* Seattle: Starwave.

Stokel-Walker, C. (2021). *TikTok Boom: China's dynamite app and the superpower race for social media.* London: Canbury Press.

Suchman, L. A. (1994). Do categories have politics? The language/action perspective reconsidered. *Computer Supported Cooperative Work, 2,* 177–90.

Suchman, L. A. (2007). *Human-machine configurations. Plans and situated actions* (2nd edn). Cambridge, MA: Cambridge University Press.

Suisman, D. (2009). *Selling sounds: The commercial revolution in American music.* Cambridge, MA: Harvard University Press. https://doi.org/10.4159/9780674054684

Swade, D. (1991). *Charles Babbage and his calculating machines.* London: Science Museum.

Szilard, L. (1964). On the decrease of entropy in a thermodynamic system by the intervention of intelligent beings. *Behavioral Science, 9*(4), 301–10.

Talbott, Stephen L. (1995). *The future does not compute. Transcending the machines in our midst.* Sebastopol: O'Reilly and Associates.

Tedre, M. (2015). *The science of computing. Shaping a discipline.* London: Chapman & Hall.

Thatcher, J., O'Sullivan, D. & Mahmoudi, D. (2016). Data colonialism through accumulation by dispossession: New metaphors for daily data. *Environment and Planning D: Society and Space, 34*(6), 990–1006.

Tönnies, F. (2017). *Community and society.* New York: Routledge.

Towns, A. R. (2022). *On black media philosophy.* Oakland: University of California Press.

Tsatsou, P. (2014). *Internet studies: past, present and future directions* (1st edn). Farnham: Ashgate Publishing Ltd.

Turing, A M. (1950). Computing machinery and intelligence. *Mind, 51,* 433–60, reprinted in J. L. Britton, D. C. Ince and P. T. Saunders (Eds) (1992). *Collected works of A.M. Turing.* Amsterdam and New York: Elsevier.

Ubisoft (2018). *Assassin's Creed: Odyssey.* (Computer game)

Ullman, E. (1997). *Close to the machine: Technophilia and its discontents.* London: Faber.

Van den Boomen. (1990). *Transcoding the digital: How metaphors matter in new media.* Amsterdam: Institute of Network Cultures.

Vanderveken, D. (1990). *Meaning and speech acts. Volume 1. Principles of language use.* Cambridge: Cambridge University Press.

Veal, A. J. (2019). *Whatever happened to the leisure society?* London: Routledge.

Virilio, P. (1993). The third interval: A critical transition. In Verena A. Conley (Ed.), *Rethinking technologies.* Minneapolis: University of Minnesota Press.

Vitores, A. & Gil-Juárez, A. (2016). The trouble with 'women in computing'": A critical examination of the deployment of research on the gender gap in computer science. *Journal of Gender Studies, 25*(6), 666–80.

Voloshinov, V. N. (1985). Verbal interaction. In R. E. Innis (Ed.), *Semiotics. An introductory anthology* (pp. 47–65). Bloomington: Indiana University Press.

References

Von Neumann, J. (1944). *Theory of games and economic behaviour*. New York: John Wiley and Sons.

Von Neumann, J. (1958). *The computer and the brain*. New Haven: Yale University Press.

Von Neumann, J., Tucker, A. W. (Ed.) and Luce, R. D. (Trans) (1959). On the theory of games of strategy. In *Contributions to the Theory of Games* (Volume IV, *Annals of Mathematics Studies*, 40, pp. 13–42). Princeton: Princeton University Press. Originally published [1928] as 'Zur theorie der gesellschaftsspiele, mathematische annalen 100', 295–320.

Vonnegut, K. (2000). *Player Piano*. New York: Rosetta Books.

Wagner, W. P. (2017). Trends in expert system development: A longitudinal content analysis of over thirty years of expert system case studies. *Expert Systems with Applications*, 76, 85–96. https://doi.org/10.1016/j.eswa.2017.01.028

Walter, R. (1993). *The Secret guide to computers* (18th edn). Boston: self-published.

Wark, M. (1994). *Virtual geography*. Bloomington: Indiana University Press.

Wark, M. (2004). *A hacker manifesto*. Cambridge, MA: Harvard University Press.

Warren, T. (2020). Zoom grows to 300 million meeting participants despite security backlash. *The verge*, 23 April. Available at: https://www.theverge.com/2020/4/23/21232401/zoom-300-million-users-growth-coronavirus-pandemic-security-privacy-concerns-response

Watts, D. (2003). (ebook). *Six degrees: The science of a connected age*. New York and London: W.W. Norton.

Weber, M., Mills, C. W. (Ed.) & Gerth, H. H. (Ed.) (1946). *From Max Weber*. New York: Oxford University Press.

Wendling, A. E. (2009). *Karl Marx on technology and alienation*. London: Palgrave Macmillan.

Wendte, A. (2016). *Magical mechanics: The player piano in the age of digital reproduction*. Thesis: University of Texas. Available at: https://repositories.lib.utexas.edu/handle/2152/40979

Wertheim, M. (1999). *The pearly gates of cyberspace: A history of space from Dante to the internet*. New York: W.W. Norton.

Williams, R. (1965 [1961]). *The long revolution*. London: Penguin.

Williams, R. (1990 [1975]). *Television: Technology and cultural form*. London: Fontana.

Williams, R. & Edge, D. (1996). The social shaping of technology. *Research Policy*, 25(6), 865–99.

Winkler, D. F. (1997). *Searching the skies: The legacy of the United States cold war defense radar program*, on United States Air Force Air Combat Command website, last modified June 1997. http://www.fas.org/nuke/guide/usa/airdef/searching_the_skies.htm. Accessed January 2001.

Winner, L. (1977). *Autonomous technology. Technics-out-of control as a theme in political thought*. Cambridge, MA: MIT Press.

Winograd, T. and Flores, F. (1986). *Understanding computers and cognition*. Norwood: Ablex Publishing.

Woodcock, J. & Johnson, M. R. (2017). Gamification: What it is, and how to fight it. *Sociological Review*, *66*(3), 542–58. https://doi.org/10.1177/0038026117728620

Woodcock, J. & Johnson, M. R. (2019). The affective labor and performance of live streaming on Twitch.tv. *Television and New Media*, *20*(8), 813–23. https://doi.org/10.1177/1527476419851077

Woolgar, S. (1991). Configuring the user: The case of usability trials. In J. Law, *A Sociology of monsters. Essays on power, technology and domination* (pp. 57–99). London: Routledge.

World Bank (2022a). Individuals using the internet. The World Bank. Available at: https://data.worldbank.org/indicator/IT.NET.USER.ZS

World Bank (2022b). Mobile cellular subscriptions. The World Bank. Available at: https://data.worldbank.org/indicator/IT.CEL.SETS

Yee, N., Bailenson, J. N. & Ducheneaut, N. (2009). The Proteus Effect: Implications of transformed digital self-representation on online and offline behavior. *Communication Research*, *36*(2), 285–312.

Zappavigna, M. (2015). Searchable talk: The linguistic functions of hashtags. *Social Semiotics*, *25*(3), 274–91. doi:10.1080/10350330.2014.996948.

Žižek, S. (1998). Cyberspace, or how to traverse the fantasy in the age of the retreat of the Big Other. *Public Culture*, *10*(3), 483–513.

Žižek, S. (2008). *The plague of fantasies*. London: Verso.

Zuboff, S. (2019). *The age of surveillance capitalism*. London: Profile Books.

Zuckerberg, M. (2021). Meta (Facebook) Connect 2021 Metaverse Event Transcript. Available at: https://www.rev.com/blog/transcripts/meta-facebook-connect-2021-metaverse-event-transcript. Accessed 16 January 2022.

Index

3D models 129, 150
3D networked space 116, 117
1984 (Orwell) 96, 109

Aarseth, E. 119
abstract machine 3, 35, 80–2, 136, 137, 142, 156, 229
ACM Task Force on the Core of Computer Science 215
active defence systems 100, 101
actor-network theory 63–4, 231
Adobe Animate 152–3
Adobe Illustrator 149, 151
Adobe InDesign 196
Adobe Premiere Pro 197
advertisements 105, 106, 110–11
advertising 3, 13, 51, 53, 70, 84, 91, 94, 109, 126, 127, 145, 160, 161, 176, 177
aerial photographs 125, 126
aesthetic styles 33
affordances 196
Afghanistan war (2000s) 102
ALGOL 24
algorithmic logic unit (ALU) 61
algorithms 34, 48, 49, 51, 58, 61, 62, 70, 82, 118, 119, 130, 139, 140, 142, 149, 155, 159, 161, 164–5, 198
  biased 174
  speech-to-text 43
  text-to-speech 53
Allen, J. 129
Altair 88
Altair 8800 108, 211
Althusser, L. 40, 67–9, 81
amateur media 146
Amazon 58, 63, 168, 177, 216
American Standard Code for Information Interchange (ASCII) standard 60, 73, 111
America Online (AOL) 117, 185
analogue broadcasts 44

Analytic Engine 97
Anderson, Laurie 18, 113
Android Authority 204
Animal Crossing (2001) 185
Animal Crossing: New Horizons (2020) 128
animal spirits 34
animism 74
anthropomorphic metaphors 93
anthropomorphism 5
Antiques Roadshow (TV show) 186
any-instant-whatever approach 153, 154
Apache 67
APIs 50
Apple 88, 111, 113, 117, 181, 218, 224
Apple II 88
Apprentice, The (TV show) 129
apps 219
Architect or Bee? (Cooley) 65
archival machines 138–9, 156–61
  limits of invocability 160–1
Archive Fever (Derrida) 157
articulations 58
artificial intelligence (AI) 1, 6, 7, 13, 29, 42, 49, 57, 91, 93, 94, 96, 98, 115, 129–32, 159, 160, 173, 188, 189, 231, 232
  connectionist 173
  symbolic 6, 173
artificial life 172, 231, 232
artificial nervous system 173
artworks 42
Ashe, Danni 198
Assassin's Creed: Odyssey (2018) 49
associated milieu 84–7, 91, 100, 108, 133
asynchronous convocational spaces 52
Atari VCS games platform 26
atomic bomb 99, 100
AT&T 110
audio tapes 139, 156, 157
augmented reality 176
auratic performances 12

256 *Index*

Austin, J. L. 54, 55, 57, 203
authentic identities 51
Autodesk 115
auto-invocations 76
automated music 18
automated player pianos 17–18
autonomists 66, 71
avatars 209, 222–4
avocations 27–30, 40, 51, 58, 61, 69, 70,
    72, 76, 124, 146–7, 162, 195–202
    attracting 200, 201
    continuous 201
    disciplinary 201
    dynamics 201
    first-level 197
    privileging 200, 201
    second-level 197
    surveillant 200
    third-level 197

Babbage, Charles 20, 86, 97, 131
Bailenson, J. N. 224
Barabási, A.-L. 89, 123, 124
Barbrook, R. 66, 71
Barglow, R. 72, 75, 76, 79
Barlow, J. P. 115, 116
Barnes, Gladeon M. 20
Barthes, R. 18
BASIC language 163, 217
Bataille, G. 78, 79
Baudrillard, J. 106
Bauwens, M. 67, 70
BBC micro 88
'becoming user' 67
behavioural surplus 53
being-in-the-world 6, 59, 60
Bell, Alexander Graham 19
Benedikt, M. 116, 117
Bergson, H. 150, 151, 153–6
Berners-Lee, T. 117
Big Brother 14, 77, 96–9, 108
big data 23, 98–9, 159
Big Other 76–9
Big tech platforms 132
Bijker, W. E. 85
binary code 8
biometrics 226
bitstreams 133, 149, 153, 154
Black Lives Matter 128

Bletchley Park 86, 92
Bogost, I. 26, 34, 165
Bolter, J. D. 21, 111
bomba 162
bombe 162
Boole, George 170
Boolean algebra 170
Borges, Jorge Luis 126
Bourdieu, Pierre 55
Brahnam, S. 13
Bratton, B. H. 9
bricolage 33
British Institution of Radio Engineers 93
broadband infrastructures 127
Brodie, Bernard 101
bulletin boards 50, 117, 185–6
Burks, Arthur 93
Bush, Kate 18
Bush, Vannevar 20, 44
Butler, Samuel 96

C++ 24, 197
Cailliau, R. 117
calculative logics 47
capitalism 40, 64–8, 72, 79, 166, 167,
    175, 177
capitalist ideology 68, 70
Cartesian geometrical principle 152
Castells, Manuel 66, 122, 123, 167
Cave, Nick 174
CD-ROM game 118
CD-ROM multimedia 29, 88, 112–14
central processing unit (CPU) 4, 5, 8, 12,
    23, 61, 140, 156, 165, 169–75
CERN research centre 117
Chaosmosis (Guattari) 80
chatbot designers 94
chatbots 132
Chat Generative Pre-Trained Transformer
    (ChatGPT) 47, 49, 91, 131–2, 47,
    174–5, 189
Chinese government 118
Christianity 69
Chun, W. H. K. 9, 164
cinema 14, 21, 84, 116, 120, 127,
    152–4, 156
Cinema 1: The movement image
    (Deleuze) 14
cinematic apparatus 154

Index

cinematic image 154
cinematographic illusion 151, 154
Circle, The (Eggers) 121–2
Civilisation and Its Discontents
(Freud) 74
clickbait 73, 127, 200
Clipper chip 118
'Clippy' 181
cloud computing 102, 140
CNET 204
codebreakers 86, 92
coded abstractions 25
code machines (software) 139–40,
161–5
codespaces 52
coding languages 162
Cold War 73, 87, 99
colonialism 103, 116
Colorado State Fair awards 129
Colossus 86, 92, 162
command and capture machines 138,
142–7, 149–56, 168
change sample 154–6
code and action, intellect and
intuition 150–4
input modes 147, 149–50
invocational work and
pleasure 145–7
machines of surveillance and
creativity 143–5
command-line interfaces 1, 111, 223
commodification 1, 5, 13, 40, 44, 101,
111, 177
Commodore 64 microcomputer 163
Commodore Amiga 88
COmmon Business Oriented Language
(COBOL) 24, 163, 197, 217
communism 100
composition 42, 44
compression techniques 155
CompuServe 117
computational logic 171
Computer and the Brain, The (Von
Neumann) 93
computerisation 65
computerised defensive system 100
computerised production 65
*Computer Lib/Dream
Machines* 109, 211

computer(s) 73, 77, 97, 106
analogue 8
components 59
desktop 7, 218–19
digital 1, 8
evolution of 85
fan identity 212, 213
generated image 130
graphics 116
as human concept 5–7
institutional 88
interactive digital 81
interactive media 27
literacy 207
masculinity and 20, 21
as medium concepts 44
modern 9
multimedia 112, 115
networks 66, 123
and religion 34
systems 75
technologies 21, 33
visible 87
computer science 29, 41
computer-supported cooperative work
(CSCW) 44
computing 8, 41, 47, 73, 106
concept 2
digital 139
discourse 34
history 20–2, 83, 157
institutional 87
interactive 13
ontologies of 59
problem with 5–10
'Computing Machinery and Intelligence'
(Turing) 94, 131
Conley, A. 77
contemporary computer culture 79
Continued Conversation feature 205
continuous modulation 27, 201
control society 144, 167, 201
convocations 39, 50–3, 122, 139, 141–2,
168, 183–9
Cooley, M. 65
'The Coordinator' 56
copyright 67, 70, 130, 160, 199, 207
coronavirus 127–9
corporate power 64, 115

258   *Index*

Cosgrove, D. 89, 90
Counter-Strike (2000) 185
Count Zero (Gibson) 114, 115
COVID-19 127, 128
   lockdowns 62
   pandemic 90
Crary, J. 71
creative practices 4, 11, 42, 78, 130, 146, 180, 194
'Crisantemi' (Puccini) 128
Crogan, P. 104
Crutcher, M. 125
cryptocurrency fever (2020s) 34
cryptograms 162
cryptography 92, 99, 162
cultural analytics 159
cultural capital 72
cultural forms 22, 43, 47, 84, 113
cultural frustration 75
cultural histories 84
cultural memories 48
cultural objects 159, 160
Cyan, Inc. 118
cybercommunism 66
cyberculture 66
cyberfeminist 77
cyberscapes 125, 126
cyberspace 7, 77, 89, 107, 114–20, 132, 163
Cyberspace: First Steps (Benedikt) 116
cyberspace initiative 115
cyber technologies 66
cyborg human 211

daemons 8
DALL•E 2 91, 130, 174
Dance Dance Revolution (1998) 191, 192, 195
Dark Messiah of Might and Magic (2006) 103
Dartmouth College 93, 185
database query 22, 159
data processing 73, 98
data processor 96–9
Davis, E. 33
Debord, G. 176, 177
decimal system 8
decision-making 8, 140, 161, 169–70
decision theory 172

decoding 33, 139
deep learning 91, 159, 160, 173, 174
de Landa, M. 8, 231
Deleuze, G. 3, 14, 40–3, 55, 72, 73, 78–82, 88, 122, 144, 151, 153, 155, 167, 181, 182, 201, 226
Department of Defense's Advanced Research Projects Agency (DARPA) 102, 210
Derrida, J. 53, 158
Descartes, René 63
Designing the User Interface (Shneiderman) 217
desire 4, 22, 28, 30, 40, 58, 71–5, 78, 105, 159, 193, 208, 229, 230
desiring machines 72, 73, 78–80
Destiny 2 (2017) 51
Digital Arts/Digitally Manipulated Photography prize 129
digital cameras 129, 138, 149, 153
digital capital 72
digital communication 45
digital cultural practices 21–2, 219
digital electronics 18, 231
Digital Equipment Corporation (DEC) 73, 87, 107, 108
digital media 13, 32, 39, 67, 187
digital networks 120
digital ontology 63
digital switching 25, 81
digital video 149, 150
digital voice assistant 1, 47, 53, 157, 173, 189, 203, 205
digitised markets 63
Discipline and Punish (Foucault) 201
Discord 130, 133
Disk Operating System (DOS) 88, 111, 161
Disney 116
Dodge, M. 182
Doom (1993) 89, 114, 118, 181
Dorrestijn, S. 193
dotcom 118, 124
Dourish, P. 165
Dreyfus, H. 6, 94
Drift Hunters (2017) 149
Dr Strangelove (1964) 172
dualist ontology 152
Ducheneaut, N. 224

Index

259

Dunn, J. C. 129
dystopia 83, 87, 96, 98, 115, 122, 194

eBay 25
Eckert-Mauchly Computer
    Corporation 162
e-commerce 187
Eden, Barbara 110
EDVAC 97
Eggers, Dave 121
egocentric convocation 51, 188
Eisenhower, D. 100
electricity 16
electric light 16
electric media 47
electronic battlefield systems 101–3
electronic media 39, 49–51
electronic music 18
Electronic Numerical Integrator and
    Computer (ENIAC) 20, 28, 93,
    99, 108
Electronic Rapid Input Computer
    (ERIC) 106
Electronic Transactions Regulations,
    Australia (2000) 25
ELIZA 73
eMoney Pro 196
Empire Strikes Back, The (1982) 26
Encarta 113
encoding 33, 139
Encyclopedia Britannica 52
Enframing 59, 61, 62
Engelbart, Doug 186, 210, 211, 218
Enigma machine 162
entropy 170
epic narration 49
Eros 73
error correction 45
Euclidean geometrical principle 152
European Union 121, 161
Eventide H910 Harmonizer 18
Everquest (1999–2013) 186
evocational machines 176
evocations 27, 28, 30–1, 57, 70, 73, 139,
    175–83
eWorld 117
Exarchos, M. 181
existentialism 59
extropians 33

Facebook 49, 51, 71, 90, 126–7, 129, 146,
    181, 188, 192, 194, 199
Facebook Live 128
face-to-face relationships 71, 187
faciality 181, 182
Fairlight CMI 18
Feenberg, A. 26, 65
feminisation 13
file compression 45
Final Fantasy XIII (2009) 103
financial crisis (2008) 34, 63
first-level hardware components 23–4
first-level TCP/IP protocol 52, 124, 125
Flores, F. 56, 59
FLOW-MATIC 163
Floyd, George 128
FOCAL language 108
Ford, S. 146
formal languages 9
FORmula TRANslation
    (FORTRAN) 24, 197, 217
Fortnite (2017) 185
Foucault, Michel 143, 193, 201
Fox News 164
Franklin, Benjamin 16
Frasca, G. 119
Freecycle 186
free market 99
Freud, S. 40, 72, 73, 75, 78, 80, 207, 230
Freudianism 78
Funk & Wagnalls Encyclopedia 113

Gabriel, Peter 18, 113
Galloway, A. R. 124, 125
game streaming 127, 199
game theory 171–2
gamification 145
gendered power relation 13
General Data Protection Regulation
    (GDPR) 121, 161
general intellect 66
Generative Pretrained Transformer 3
    (GPT-3) 94
genetic element 155
Ghost in the Machine (1993) 116
giant brains 86, 91–4, 96, 108
Gibson, William 89, 115
gift economy 66
gig economy 168, 201

260 *Index*

God   69
Goffman, E.   49, 50
Goldstine, H. H.   20
Google   49, 62, 71, 76, 90, 118, 125, 126, 132, 158–9, 194, 195, 205
Google Bard   132
Google Docs   225
Google Earth   89–90, 125
Google Maps   125, 126, 220
Google Scholar   192
Gore, Al   118
Government Code and Cypher School (Station X)   92
GPS   57, 126, 133, 194
Gran Teatre del Liceu opera house, Barcelona   128
Graph API   188
graphical user interface (GUI)   29, 88, 111, 112, 114, 117, 209, 211, 218
Green, J.   146
Grint, K.   212, 213
Groff, J.-F.   117
Grundrisse: Foundations of the Critique of Political Economy (Marx)   66
Grusin, R.   21
Guattari, F.   3, 40–3, 55, 72, 73, 78–82, 88, 122, 135, 136, 181, 182, 201, 207, 208, 226
gun and handgun   15

Habermas, Jürgen   187
hackers   69–70, 88, 219
Hall, Stuart   58
'Happy Mac'   181
hard disks   139, 156, 157
hardware   25, 61, 85
hardware components   27, 112
Harris, Josh   120
Hartree, D. R.   93
hashtags   48, 128, 138, 222
Havelock, E. A.   45
Hayles, N. K.   225
Heidegger, M.   39, 59–64, 71, 80, 98, 188
Heim, M.   183
high-tech bureaucracy   107
Hine, C.   186
hip-hop   180, 181
Histories of Computing, The (Mahoney)   20

Hollerith Tabulator   97
Homer   48
Homo Ludens (Huizinga)   185
Hopper, Grace   20
Horizon Worlds   117
How to Do Things with Words (Austin)   54
HTML   117, 124
HTTP   117
Huizinga, Johan   185
human-computer interaction (HCI)   29, 44, 218
human-computer interface   69, 116
human creativity   91, 175
human cultural evolution   45
human intelligence   6, 232
humans as rational actors   5–6
Hunter, Duncan   164
Hurricane Katrina   125–7
hypertext   117

IBM   87, 88, 96, 97, 104, 111, 161, 195, 216
IBM computers   101, 107, 108
   IBM 650   97
   IBM 701   97
ideological state apparatuses (ISAs)   68
I Dream of Jeannie (1960s, sitcom series)   105–7, 109
   'The Used Car Salesman' (episode)   107
id Software   119
Ihde, Don   63
ILLIAC   100
image generators   42, 130–2, 174, 175
imitation game   5, 94, 188
iMovie   194
incorporeal transformations   56
individualisation   84
industrial capitalism   167
Industrial Revolution   115
information spaces   50
information superhighway   118
information systems   56, 57
information technologies   11, 12, 33, 65, 72, 75, 122
Innis, H.   45, 46, 123, 156
input devices   9, 61, 75, 142, 151, 153–6
Instafamous   138, 221, 222

Index

Instagram 49, 71, 90, 128, 137–8, 157, 188, 191, 220–2
instrumental devices 60
instrumental rationalism 73
integrated circuits 101
Intel 110, 213–14
Intel 8086 processor 213, 214
intellectual property 41, 66, 174, 207
inter-actant relation 203, 205
interactive multimedia 112
interactive systems 73
interfaciality 183
InterGuard 201
International Organisation for Standardisation (ISO) 215
internet 8, 50, 66, 70, 71, 75–7, 89, 90, 101, 127, 161, 198
internet bubble 34
Internet Classics Archive 49
internet of things 90
inter-organism 202, 203
interpellations 68, 69, 82
interpersonal relationships 26, 28, 58, 71
intra-organism 202
invocability 160–1
invocable domains 9, 23, 24, 43, 48, 58–64, 71, 82, 119, 120, 124, 126, 139, 144, 145, 155, 160
invocational articulation 58, 219
invocational art practices 42
invocational assemblages 7, 8, 23–5, 27, 28, 31–2, 40, 48, 61, 67, 69, 72, 77, 79, 83, 86, 91, 96, 98, 120, 132, 133, 135, 136, 168
invocational dialects 24, 28
invocational infrastructures 58, 87, 125
invocational interval 155, 165, 173, 229
invocational machinic assemblage 137–42
  archival machines 138–9, 156–60
  code machines 139–40, 161–5
  command, control and capture machines 138, 142–7, 149–56
  machines of calculation and decision 140–1, 169–75
  machines of connection and convocations 141–2, 183–9
  machines of expression and force 141, 175–83
  machines of temporality 140, 165–9

invocational media 22, 29, 74, 132, 229, 230. *See also individual entries*
  control of 64–71
  definition 44–53
  as desiring machines 40, 72, 73, 78
  hazards 32–5
  as machines 3, 80–2
  as machinic heterogenesis 80
  reconceptualising computers as 39–44
invocational mediation 39, 78
invocational mediatisation 30, 34
invocational power 9, 10, 34, 47, 65, 68, 90, 121, 160, 161, 168
invocational relationships 6, 98, 123
invocational rights 121, 161
invocationary action 28, 30, 72, 119, 142–143, 145, 147–149, 211
invocationary acts 39, 49, 53–9, 72, 111, 132, 141, 144, 145, 165, 203, 205
invocation(s) 1–2, 43, 70, 81, 139, 195–202, 230
  concept of 3–4, 8
  contemporary 40
  of decision 8, 140, 161, 169–70
  digital 8, 71
  doubled asymmetrical 96
  electronic 49
  experiential 3
  influence of 13–14
  involuntary 51, 53, 121, 160, 200, 211
  levels of (*see* levels of invocation)
  as magical and religious practices 10–11, 34–5
  means of 64, 70, 194, 216, 218
  mechanical 15, 16
  as mediatised speech acts 39
  modern 13
  monopoly of 126
  pleasurable 71–2
  primary 4, 8, 140, 141, 169
  psychology of 71–9
  secondary 4, 8, 140, 141, 169
  as socially situated practice 202–5, 207
  understanding 10–13
  voluntary 121
  weapon 15

invocatory devices   3, 8, 13–20, 22, 27, 45, 53, 119, 127, 140, 229
invocatory switching   16, 17
invoked intelligence   6, 96, 232
iPad   218
iPhone   126, 218

Jacquard loom   97
Jagoda, P.   179
Java   8, 24, 197
Jenkins, H.   146
Jim Henson Company   113
Jobs, Steve   111
JOHNNIAC   100
Johnson, M. R.   145, 199
Justin.tv   199

Kan, Justin   199
Karanikas, M.   13
Kitchin, R.   182
Kittler, F.   24, 25, 176, 230
Konami   178, 179, 191
Kraftwerk (band)   18
Kroker, A.   227
Kubrick, Stanley   172

labour
    free   51, 145
    gendered division of   20
    precarious   58
    saving consumer products   105, 106
    stored   5
Lacan, J.   78, 79, 207
Lady Gaga   128
Lady Lovelace   131
landscape   126
Langton, C. G.   172
language   40, 48, 54, 55, 59, 202
    acts   54, 55, 57
    performativity   39
Lassie Come Home (1943)   92
Latour, Bruno   63, 64, 85, 102, 103, 183, 231
Lawnmower Man (1992)   116
Lessig, Lawrence   25, 163, 226
levels of invocation   22–32
    avocations   28–30
    first-level, sociotechnical   23–6, 43, 124, 136, 137

outputs and evocations   30–1, 175–83
second-level, experience   26–8, 124, 136
third-level, assemblages and discourses   31–2, 43, 83, 132–3, 136, 170
lever   15
Licklider, J. C. R.   44
Lifehacker   204
lightning   16
Like button   188
Lingo   113
liquid transmitter   19
literacy   46, 47
lived experience   90
live mapping   133
livestreaming   127–9, 198–9
Locke, J.   227
Loebner Prize   94
Logo language   217
London workshop   86
Lord Kelvin (William Thomson) 171
Lovink, G.   67
Lyon, D.   121, 194, 200

McCarthy, John   93
machine, concept of   79–81
machine aesthetic   18
machine intelligence   94, 96, 131, 232
machines of calculation and decision   140–1, 169–75
    intelligence   173–5
machines of connection and convocations   141–2, 183–9
machines of expression and force   141, 175–83
    face in interface   181–3
    interface and affect   180–1
    Silent Hill (1999)   178–80
machines of temporality   140, 165–9
    interconnecting   168–9
    processor clocks   140, 167
    real-time clock   140, 165–7
Macintosh   88, 111, 181, 225
McKelvey, F.   8
McLuhan, M.   16, 43, 45–9, 80
Macromedia Director   113
magical beliefs   74

Index

magical thinking/thought   34, 74, 75, 82, 103

magic and technology   102–5, 107

Mahmoudi, D.   99

Mahoney, M. S.   20

malware   73

Manhattan Project   99, 101

MANIAC   99

Manovich, L.   21, 25, 158, 159

mapping   125–7

Marino, M. C.   163

Marvin, C.   17

Marwick, A. E.   221

Marx, K.   65, 66, 80

mass customisation   40

mass media   176, 177

mass surveillance   118, 122

master view approach   102

matchlock mechanism   15

materiality   42, 44

mathematical information theory   44, 45

mathematical network   123

Maxwell, Clerk   170–1

media assemblages   39

media consumption   28, 88, 127, 159

media determinism   49

media ecology   45, 80, 82, 129, 132

media forms   2, 21, 22, 36, 84, 112, 174, 232

medialogical process   100

media production software   42

media studies   32, 39, 45

media technologies   45

memorisation   47

memory   4, 8, 24, 36, 46, 54, 61, 113, 135, 147, 156–61, 165

memory machines   138–9

Meta   49, 51, 71, 117, 195

metaverse   117

Meyrowitz, J.   39, 49–52, 184

microcomputers   66, 192, 194, 212

microelectronics   59, 231

microprocessors   213

Microsoft   88, 111, 113, 161, 195, 215, 216

Microsoft Office 98   181

Microsoft Word   180, 191, 195, 208, 209, 226

MIDI standard   18

Midjourney AI image generator   91, 129–31

militarism   103

military discipline   104

military-entertainment complex   104

military-industrial complex   99, 100, 102, 104

Minecraft (2011)   128, 185

minicomputers   107, 108, 192

Minimalists   214

MINI minicomputer   108

Minsky, Marvin   93

MIT   73, 104, 185

Mitchell, William   163

mobile map   126

mobile media   140

mobile phones   194

mobile phone subscriptions   127

'Model T'   107

modern bourgeois society   65

modernity   63, 64, 102, 103, 152

modern technology   39

Mona Lisa Overdrive (Gibson)   115

MoneyGuidePro   196

monomedia   112

montage   155

Montford, N.   26, 163

Moore, Gordon   109–10

Moore School of Electrical Engineering, University of Pennsylvania   20, 93

Moore's law   110

Moreno, J. L.   123

Morse, Samuel   16, 20

Morse code   16–17, 185

Mosaic   114

Mosaic 1.0   117

Mosaic Warfare concept   102

motion tweening   153

Mountbatten, Louis   93

multimedia encyclopaedias   113

multi-user dungeons (MUDs)   185

Mumford, L.   166

Muppet CD-ROM, The: Muppets Inside   113

Murray, J. H.   119

Muses   11–12, 48, 70, 173, 230

mutually assured destruction   172

Myspace   188

Myst (1993)   89, 114, 118

narratology *vs.* ludology   119, 120
NASA   97, 106, 107
NASDAQ Composite   122
National Center for Supercomputing
    Applications (NCSA)   117
National Information Infrastructure
    legislative program   118
National Security Agency   23
natural language   56, 94, 118, 202, 203,
    205, 207
natural language processing   94, 173
Neill, Sam   128
Nelson, Ted   109, 211–13
nerve impulses   93
nervous system   93
Netflix   90, 159
Netscape   118
networked individualism   188
networked social movements   66
network(s)   120–5, 187
    flows   89
    imaginary   123
    theory   123
neural nets   91, 94, 173
Neuromancer (Gibson)   114
New Orleans   125
News Feed   126–7, 188
'Nike' missile   100
Noble, D. F.   33
noise   44, 45
nomadic assemblages   3
non-humans   11, 12
non-playing characters   188
Norman, Don   29
No Sense of Place (Meyrowitz)   49
nostalgia   63
NSCA Mosaic   89
nuclear weapons   99, 100
Numan, Gary   18

Oakland Raiders   110
Obama, Barack   129
object-oriented MUDs (MOOs)   185
object-oriented programming   153
    approach   24
    languages   8
Oculus   117
Odyssey (Homer)   48, 49
Oedipal relationship   76, 78

omnipotent thought   74, 75
One Thousand and One Nights   105
One World   89, 90
On Exactitude in Science (Borges)   126
Ong, W.   39, 45–8, 51
online payment sites   128, 198
online services   70, 117, 198
oN-Line System (NLS)   211
ontology   81, 89, 117, 165
ontology of production   80
OpenAI   94, 131
open-ended conversations   94
openness   120–5
open networking   89
Open Systems Interconnection (OSI)
    model   9
Oppenheimer, J. Robert   100
ORACLE   100
oral communication   39, 52
oral cultures   45–8
orality   46–8
oral practices   45
order-words   55–7, 82
Orwell, George   96, 98, 109
'Orwellian'   109
O'Sullivan, D.   99
'O Superman' (song)   18
output devices   61

P2P techniques   67
'Pac-Man'   181
panic stations   99–104
panopticism   143, 144, 193
Papacharrisi, Z.   187
paper tapes   97
Papert, S.   217
Pascal, Blaise   20
Pasquale, F.   165
patent   19, 70, 117, 207
patriarchal power   13
peer-to-peer (P2P) movement   67, 69
Penrose, R.   152
Persian Gulf war (1990s)   102
personal computers (PCs)   89, 115, 161,
    192, 197, 212, 218, 224
phenomenology   59, 82
photographic shutter   18
physical access   50
physical archives   139, 157, 158

Index

physical space 50, 62, 116, 120, 125
piano 17
Pinch, T. 85
plane of composition 42
plane of the material 42
planes of immanence 40, 41, 43, 44, 80, 82
planes of reference 41, 43, 44
Plato 41, 47, 151, 152
Platonism 152
play spaces 185
pleasure principle 72, 74, 78
pocket calculators 47
poiesis 60
Pokémon GO app 220–1
'Politics as a Vocation' (Weber) 195
Pollermann, B. 117
Pong (1972) 185, 223
popular art 33
popular culture 5, 19, 83, 84, 88, 108, 111, 114, 207
popular music 33
porn 198
Portraits in Silicon (Slater) 20
posthuman politics 225–6
Postman, N. 45
post-Marxisms 64–71, 80
power law 89, 120–5
pre-Second World War workshop 86
'principle of democratic rationalisation' 65
'principle of the conservation of hierarchy' 65
print cultures 46, 47
printing press 46
print media 45, 50, 176
privacy 98, 161, 231
processor clocks 140, 167
Programmed Data Processor 1 (PDP-1) 73
Programmed Data Processor 8 (PDP-8) 87–8, 107–9
programming languages 24, 162, 216
programming libraries 33
Progressive Networks (RealNetworks) 198
prompt engineering 130
Proteus effect 224
proto-media technologies 176
psyche 73, 78, 79, 207

psychic relationship 75, 76
psychoanalysis 71–80, 82
psychoanalytic tradition 72, 73, 75
psychodynamics 35, 46, 51, 72, 78
Puccini, Giacomo 128
punch cards 97, 98, 216
punctum 18–19
Puppet Motel 113–14
Python 197

quantum computing 232
'The Question Concerning Technology' (Heidegger) 59
QUIET: We Live in Public (2009) 120
QWERTY key positions 210

Racing the Beam (Montford & Bogost) 26
racism 103
Rainie, Lee 187
Ralph Breaks the Internet (2018) 116
RAND Corporation 100
Randell, B. 20
random-access memory (RAM) 12, 61, 139, 156, 157
rap music 180, 181
raster images 149, 150
Rave Family Block Fest 128
reality principle 74
real-time chat 53
real-time clock 140, 165–7
real-time digital computing 99–104
real-world phenomena 153, 171, 224, 232
Red Dead Redemption 2 (2018) 178
Reddit 52, 186
Reidenberg, Joel 163
Rejewski, Marian 162
repressive state apparatuses (RSAs) 68
Rheingold, Howard 186
Rhine River 60
ritual contact 11, 12
ritual practices 103, 104
robotics 63
robots 29, 97
Rockmore, T. 63
role-playing games 51
Roosevelt , Franklin D. 129
Rutkowski, Greg 131, 174

Saint-Simon 65
sampling 154–5
sampling synthesisers 18
SARS-CoV-2 127
scheduled events 140
science 41, 42, 44, 61, 64, 74, 78, 102, 104, 107
science fiction 44, 73, 103, 114–16
scientific modernism 102, 103
scribal 46
search engine 22, 30, 49, 118, 157
Searle, J. R. 6, 94, 203
secondary orality 39, 48, 51
second law of thermodynamics 170
Second Life (2003) 117, 185, 223–4
Second World War 139, 162, 210, 225
Secure Sockets Layer (SSL) 118, 161
security systems 98, 168
Selective Sequence Electronic Calculator (SSEC) 87, 96–7, 115
Semi-automated Business Research Environment (SABRE) 104
Semi-Automatic Ground Environment (SAGE) 87, 99–104
semiotics 30
shamans 11, 12
Shannon, Claude 44, 45, 93, 170
Sherman Antitrust Act (1998) 216
Shneiderman, Ben 217, 218
Short Code 162
'shrink-wrapped' licensed software 161
Silent Hill (1999) 178–80
Simondon, G. 84
Slater, R. 20
Smalltalk 8
smartphone era 29
smartphones 219
smart voice assistant 49
Snapchat 220
socialism 66
social media 7, 67, 68, 121, 127, 129, 145, 188
  convocations 52
  corporations 53
  groups 52
social networking sites 89, 188
social networks 123
social robots 132, 176
social space/spatiality 49, 52

sociograms 123
sociological approach 122
sociotechnical invocation 3
sociotechnical protocols 124
software 25, 85
  code 139
  components 112
  development 26
  operations 61
source code 9, 163, 164
Soviet nuclear attack 99–101
Spacewar! (1962) 73, 185
speech 53
speech act(s) 25, 39, 57, 203, 205
  human 203–4
  illocutionary component 55, 57, 203
  locutionary component 55–7, 203
  perlocutionary component 55–8, 203
  theory 43, 53–6, 59, 80, 203
speech recognition 94, 173
spirit photographs 18
spoofing 189
Spotify 133, 159
SSDs 139, 156, 157
Stable Diffusion 96
'the Stack' 9
Stahl, W. A. 33
Stalinism 67
'standing-reserve' 39, 59–61, 63, 64, 82, 98
Stanford Research Institute 210
Star Wars (1982) 26
Starwave 113
stereotypes 25–6
stock market crash (1987) 63
stock markets 187
storage devices 61, 139, 157
storytellers 11, 12
streaming media 90–1, 198
structured programming
  code 24
  technique 8
subjectification process 193
subjection process 193, 201, 207
subjectivation process 193, 201, 207
Suchman, L. A. 56, 57
Superbowl (1984 American football game) 110
surveillance applications 23

surveillance culture 121, 194
surveillance practices 121
surveillance technologies 68, 121
switchboard operators 19
symmetrical anthropology 103
synthetic biology 172
System/360 97
Szilard, Leo 171

Tangerine Dream (band) 18
target advertising 47, 51, 53
Techgnosis 33
technical components 135, 136
technical networks 123
technical protocols 124, 125
technological innovations 74, 84
technological-social optimism 67
technology 85
    capitalist 66
    essence of 59–60
    machine 65
    modern 60–3, 73, 74, 81
    non-modern 63
    premodern 63
    relationships with human 76
    and religion 33
technology-magic 115
technopagans 33
techno-spatial metaphors 116
tech sector 99
telegraph 16, 17, 19, 184–5, 187
telegraph operators 17
telephone 19, 184–5
text-to-image generators 130–2, 174
Thanatos 73
Thatcher, J. 99
'Théâtre D'opéra Spatial' (Allen) 129
Theranos scam 35
Thousand Plateaus, A (Deleuze &
    Guattari) 80
ticks 166
TikTok 90, 128, 188, 194, 220
Time 34
Timeline 188
time-sharing systems 108, 185
Tinder 178
Tönnies, F. 186
totalitarianism 98
Totem and Taboo (Freud) 74

Towns, A. R. 46
traditional media 27
Transborder Immigrant Tool 163–4
Transport Layer Security 161
Trichel, Gervaise 100
Trinity 100
Tron (1982) 116
TRS-80 88
Trump, Donald 128
'tulip mania' (1600s) 34
Tunny code 92, 162
Turing, Alan 5, 86, 94, 131, 162, 188
twitch.tv 199
Twitter 90, 128, 129

Uber 57, 58, 168
Uber Driver app 57
Uber Eats 168
UceLi Quartet 128
Ullman, E. 26
Unicode 61
United States 106
UNIVAC 97, 162
University of Illinois 100, 117
University of Pennsylvania 93
UNIX operating system 166
unstructured data 98, 159
unsupervised machine learning 159
US Air Force 76, 87, 99, 100
US Department of Justice Antitrust
    Division 216
Usenet 185–6
user avocation
    invoking languages 209, 216–22
    material interfaces 209–16
    user avatars 209, 222–4
    user modes and control 209, 224–8
user experience design (UXD) 29
user experience research (UXR) 29
usergenesis 207–9, 231
user subjectivity 36
US government 101, 118
US Marine Corps 104
US National Security Agency (NSA) 118
utopia 67, 83, 111, 115, 116, 121,
    158, 194

Vaile, Alfred 16
Vandenberg, Hoyt 101

vectoralists 70
vector graphics programs 149, 151
video games 15, 22, 73, 103, 104, 150, 178, 181, 183, 185, 198, 220, 223
video RAM (VRAM) 61
Vietnam War 102
Virilio, P. 167
virtual class 227
virtual communities 186
Virtual Communities: Homesteading on the Electronic Frontier (Rheingold) 186
virtual ethnography 186
virtual machines 9
virtual public spheres 187
virtual reality (VR) 7, 89, 115, 133, 231, 232
virtual space 89, 112, 116, 120, 125
vocations 15, 28, 29, 36, 146, 194–202, 215, 216, 220
Voloshinov, V. N. 202
Vonnegut, Kurt 18
von Neumann, John 5, 20, 93, 96, 99–100, 171, 172
voudou 115

Wald, Abraham 172
Walker, John 115
Wark, M. 69–71, 88, 227
war machines 88
Washington Redskins 110
Watson computer system 108
Watts, D. 89, 123
weapons systems 32, 68, 100, 103
Weaver, M. 13
Web 2.0 50, 89, 124
Web3 67
Weber, M. 195
Wellman, B. 187
Wertheim, M. 107
Western culture 152, 230
Western rationalist tradition 170

Western Union 187
What Is Philosophy? (Deleuze & Guattari) 40
WhatsApp 49, 71
Wiener, Norbert 44, 169
Wikipedia 49, 52, 67, 124
Williams, R. 83
Windows 88, 216
Winner, L. 63
Winograd, T. 56, 59
Wolfenstein 3D (1992) 119
women
    agency 20
    role in computer development 21
Woodcock, J. 145, 199
Woolgar, S. 212, 213
World of Warcraft (2004) 185
world picture 62, 64, 82
World Wide Web 114, 117
writing 53
Writing Space (Bolter) 112
Wuhan, China 127

x86 chip series 213
Xerox 218
Xplora1: Peter Gabriel's Secret World (1993) 113

Yee, N. 224
YouTube 76, 128, 129, 159, 188
You've Got Mail! (1998) 116

Z3 86
Zappavigna, M. 128
zero-sum games 171
Zeus, Konrad 86
Zilog 214
Žižek, S. 72, 76, 77
Zook, M. 125
Zoom 90, 127, 133, 181
Zuboff, S. 53
Zuckerberg, Mark 117